A Policy History of Standards-Based Education in America

Alan R. Sadovnik and Susan F. Semel
General Editors

Vol. 59

The History of Schools and Schooling series
is part of the Peter Lang Education list.
Every volume is peer reviewed and meets
the highest quality standards for content and production.

PETER LANG
New York • Bern • Frankfurt • Berlin
Brussels • Vienna • Oxford • Warsaw

Boyce Brown

A Policy History of Standards-Based Education in America

PETER LANG
New York • Bern • Frankfurt • Berlin
Brussels • Vienna • Oxford • Warsaw

Library of Congress Cataloging-in-Publication Data
Brown, Boyce.
A policy history of standards-based education in America / Boyce Brown.
pages cm. — (History of schools and schooling; vol. 59)
Includes bibliographical references.
1. Education—Standards—United States.
2. Education and state—United States. I. Title.
LB3060.83.B76   379.1580973—dc23   2014048948
ISBN 978-1-4331-2741-0 (hardcover)
ISBN 978-1-4331-2740-3 (paperback)
ISBN 978-1-4539-1530-1 (e-book)
ISSN 1089-0678

Bibliographic information published by **Die Deutsche Nationalbibliothek**.
Die Deutsche Nationalbibliothek lists this publication in the "Deutsche
Nationalbibliografie"; detailed bibliographic data are available
on the Internet at http://dnb.d-nb.de/.

© 2015 Peter Lang Publishing, Inc., New York
29 Broadway, 18th floor, New York, NY 10006
www.peterlang.com

All rights reserved.
Reprint or reproduction, even partially, in all forms such as microfilm,
xerography, microfiche, microcard, and offset strictly prohibited.

CONTENTS

	Acknowledgments	XI
Chapter 1.	Introduction	1
Chapter 2.	The Uneasy Alliance between the Corporate Elite and the Movement Conservatives (1970s)	7
Chapter 3.	A Nation at Risk and a Decade of Reports (1980s–1990s)	33
Chapter 4.	Federal Education Policy Conflicts over Standards-based Education during the Bush and Clinton Years (1988–2000)	59
Chapter 5.	Hawaii, a Case Study (1991–present)	85
Chapter 6.	No Child Left Behind, Race to the Top, and Common Core	109
Chapter 7.	Conclusion	149
	References	173

ACKNOWLEDGMENTS

A portion of chapter 4 is a revised version of what was previously published as Brown, B. (2009a). *Standards-based education reform in the United States since A Nation at Risk*. Honolulu, HI: Curriculum Research and Development Group. Retrieved from http://www.hawaii.edu/hepc/pdf/Reports/FINAL-History_of_Standards-Based_Education_Reform.pdf.

A portion of chapter 5 is a revised version of what was previously published as Brown, B. (2009b). *A policy history of standards-based education reform in Hawaii*. Honolulu, HI: Curriculum Research and Development Group. Retrieved from http://www.hawaii.edu/hepc/pdf/Reports/FINAL-History_of_Standards-Based_Education_in_Hawaii.pdf.

A portion of chapter 7 is a revised version of what was previously published as Brown, B. (2013). The assumptions and possible futures of standards-based education. *Policy Futures in Education, 11*(5), pp. 481–489.

· 1 ·

INTRODUCTION

I would contend that the three main stages of the American economy have created three main different types of educational policy: 1) common schools of the agrarian period (from the colonial period to the late 19th century), 2) compulsory mass schooling and the rise of graduate schools of education during industrialization (from the late 19th century to the late 20th century), and 3) the family of reform models first called "systematic reform" and "school restructuring" in the 1980s and later consolidated under the broad rubric of "accountability" during the post-industrial phase over the last few decades (Emery, 2002).

Standards-based education is a central part of this complex of closely related reform ideas generally referred to as accountability. Building on Apple (2006) these include 1) raising the standards (first in the everyday sense of the term, later as explicit written guidelines in each subject matter and grade or grade spans), 2) testing frequently, and 3) raising the stakes in terms of rewards or sanctions for students, teachers, principals, schools, districts, and states based largely on those test results.

Since the seminal 1983 A *Nation at Risk* study marked the beginning of a major shift in the values debate in educational policy away from equity and equality towards efficiency and excellence, numerous educational reform concepts have come and gone. In this book, I hope to demonstrate that the one that may have had the biggest impact over the longest period since then has been standards-based education. It is also the only reform idea that has survived over the last several decades to become an integral part of local, state, and federal education today.

Many heterogeneous individuals, factions, organizations, governmental agencies, and businesses have contributed to the pervasive presence of standards-based education in American K–12 education today. Apple named the abstract Weberian ideal types of neoliberals, neoconservatives, evangelical Christians, and the professional managerial class as the primary progenitors (2006). Berliner and Biddle tapped the far right, religious right, and neoconservatives (1996). These camps (and a few other important ones, like teacher organizations and teacher training accreditation agencies) have certainly been influential in the propagation and consolidation of this concept, even when the goals and self-interests of their factions and organizations have occasionally been in conflict. These are the people Cuban calls the "policy elites." They are

> a loose network of corporate leaders, public officials, foundation officers, and academics who use both public and private funds to run projects and circulate ideas consistent with their versions of school reforms. They have ready access to the media and the capacity to set a public agenda for discussion. Political party labels do not define them, although there are clearly Republicans and Democratic members who carry their affiliation on their sleeves…These overlapping networks of like-minded individuals share values and tastes. They convene frequently in various forums, speak the same policy talk, and are connected closely to sources of influence in governments, media, businesses, academia, and foundations. They help create a climate of opinion that hovers around no more than a few hundred influentials in policymaking (Cuban, 2004, p. 207).

I hope to explore the notion that, among these many change agents, business may have been the most influential one. They were the most effective in making themselves heard, framing the agenda, sponsoring influential reports, organizing key events, supporting specific pieces of legislation, and generally maintaining the most vigorous, systematic, and sustained policy engagement over several decades.

Ultimately, the greatest impact of business on standards-based education, however, is not merely to be found in a resurgence of human capital theory or the consolidation of the ideology of global competitiveness as a leading outcome desired from American K–12 education. Rather, business' greatest impact may lie in what is not spoken, in what is taken for granted: the desirability of continuing the global economy as it is, in spite of the fact that it may be unsustainable and could be leading us to a wide variety of significant problems in the near-to-medium term future, a question I will address at greater length in the conclusion.

Chapter 2 seeks to understand how the corporate elite began colluding with the movement conservatives in the 1970s. Chapter 3 aspires to be the history of a kind of a "dog pile," with many different elite factions contending, generating reports, and holding influential meetings during the 1980s and 1990s, one that encompassed Democrats as well, making this education reform idea a bipartisan consensus.

After everyone emerged from the dog pile, however, the business-conservative (and nascent "New Democrats") coalition was left still holding the ball. Their reports and representatives gained traction. Their crisis rhetoric, workforce development, and school-to-work policies proved dominant. They became instrumental in how standards-based education became conceptualized in the public policy arena.

The National Governors Association and Business Roundtable each dedicated an annual meeting exclusively to education during the 1980s. This helped consolidate the dominance of a new business-conservatives-presidency-governors-teacher union leadership-new Democrats bloc, decisively displayed at the 1989 Charlottesville National Education Summit with President Bush. This newly emerging bloc was powerful enough to steamroll an attempted preemptive strike by Senate Majority Leader George Mitchell and House Majority Leader Richard Gephardt, who held a press conference right before the summit.

State efforts in California and Minnesota (Berman and Clugston, 1988), city efforts like the Boston Compact, and corporate initiatives like R. J. R. Nabisco's "Next Century Schools" (spearheaded by Lou Gerstner, who would continue to be influential in standards-based education when he became head of IBM shortly thereafter) became models of government-business collaboration. They were the entering spear-point of the ascendant business-conservatives-presidency-governors-teacher union leadership bloc. This bloc, though powerful and rising fast, still wasn't dominant. Even with their help, the signature education reform legislation of President Bush and former governor then Education Secretary Lamar Alexander, *America 2000* (of which standards were a big part), failed to pass a Democratic Congress.

In chapter 4, the competing and cooperating factions really went at it. The coalitions they led often broke up and reconfigured. The "grassroots" started speaking up for themselves, both "left" and "right." Congressional Democrats, especially ones from urban districts, fought a strenuous battle for equity and resources but it was a rear guard one. They were gradually losing control over the policy agenda they held since the mid-1960s.

The social conservatives also started shearing off in significant numbers from their partners in "business." The social conservative grassroots and their leaders (or some might say manipulators) among the self-proclaimed "Republican revolution" conservatives of 1996 were often more interested in school choice, vouchers, culture war issues, and conservative social values than in educational standards, workforce development and "global economic competitiveness" issues. This schism turned into the "standards wars" of the mid-1990s.

By the mid-1990s, it seemed that parents, rank-and-file conservatives, rank-and-file teachers, "Republican revolution" conservatives from the 1994 elections, urban Congressional Democrats—everybody—had a bone to pick with these new standards, albeit often for different reasons. The policy elites were having a hard time keeping those they professed to lead on point.

Urban Congressional Democrats failed to capitalize on these internecine battles. Many of those among the Fortune 500 CEOs did capitalize on them. These were people like IBM's Lou Gertsner, Xerox's David Kearns, and several others. These captains of industry began taking a far more activist, hands-on approach, serving in government and working outside of it, convening national education summits, publishing books, writing influential op-ed pieces, and being profiled in leading magazines, particularly of the business press. As Harvey's noted account of the rise of neoliberalism put it, these CEOs and other "key operators on corporate boards" and their technocratic associates, themselves "leaders in the financial, legal, and technical apparatuses surrounding this inner sanctum of capitalist activity" have become an undeniable "rising class power under neoliberalism," as I discuss in greater detail in chapter 4. (2007, p. 33). Elsewhere, Harvey provided one of the better definitions of neoliberalism when he wrote that:

> The capitalist world stumbled towards neoliberalization as the answer through a series of gyrations and chaotic experiences that really only converged as a new orthodoxy with the articulation of what became known as the 'Washington Consensus' in the 1990s. By then, both Clinton and Blair could easily have reversed Nixon's earlier statement ("We are all liberals now") and simply said 'We are all neoliberals now.' The uneven geographical development of neoliberalism, its frequently partial and lop-sided application from one state and social formation to another, testifies to the

tentativeness of neoliberal solutions and the complex ways in which political forces, historical traditions, and the complex ways in which political forces, historical traditions, and existing institutional arrangements all shaped why and how the process of neoliberalization actually occurred (Harvey, 2007, p. 13).

President Clinton and most of the governors of both parties, in the first blush of the prominence of the Clinton/Al From/corporatist/Democratic Leadership Council/"New Democrats," went right along with them. Obama is only the latest in a long line of Democratic capitulation to corporate interests over that party's traditional support for organized labor.

Amidst this turmoil, the new business-conservatives-presidency-governors-teacher union leadership-Congressional New Democrats bloc managed to pass both *Goals 2000: Educate America Act* (almost a copy of Bush's America 2000) and the *Improving America's Schools Act* (the Elementary and Secondary Education Act reauthorization) in 1994. Now standards were an integral part of federal policy as well as of local and state educational policy, as these jurisdictions chased the slowing increasing share of federal financing of K–12 education. "In 1990–1991, the federal share of total K–12 spending in the United States was just 5.7 percent. By 2005, it had risen to 8.3 percent" (United States Department of Education, 2005, p. 2). *No Child Left Behind* put it all in cement, with full bipartisan support. In fact, without key Democrats like Kennedy in the Senate and Miller in the House, the measure probably wouldn't have passed at all.

Chapter 5 is a microcosm of all of these developments, a case study of similar forces contending in all of their heterogeneity and conflict-cooperation in one state, Hawaii. The story of Hawaii's adoption of standards-based education will be a little different than that of other states, as Hawaii is the only state in the union with a single statewide education district. Long-standing dominance of state governance by the Democratic party will also contribute another unique set of circumstances. Chapter 6 looks at how the recent policy developments that led to the consolidation and quasi-nationalization of standards-based education through No Child Left Behind, Race to the Top and the Common Core State Standards Initiative. Finally, the conclusion, chapter 7, will consider the potential future of standards-based education, as well as the broader implications of standards-based education in society in the near- to medium-term future.

· 2 ·

THE UNEASY ALLIANCE BETWEEN THE CORPORATE ELITE AND THE MOVEMENT CONSERVATIVES (1970s)

This chapter hopes to demonstrate that, during the late 1960s and early 1970s, the corporate elite and movement conservatives began to collaborate closely on the creation of a multi-faceted intellectual, policy, and legal framework of think tanks, academic posts, media outlets, litigation centers, and other related initiatives.

In doing so, many specific historical events such as the rise of the Heritage Foundation and Business Roundtable will be described. These entities in particular exemplify how the groundwork was set for the concerns of business to begin infiltrating the education policy debate during the Reagan-Bush era. The ideas that will be discussed must also be considered in relation to the beginning of major political and economic changes in America that have only accelerated up to the present. Not only the rise of the right, but also with President Carter, we see the beginning of a Democratic political identity that gradually began disavowing a significant role for the federal government in fostering economic and social justice, one that instead negotiates fealty to "free market" economics, corporate dominance of much of American economic and cultural life, and adherence to a particularly robust version of American militarism, a militarism that Bacevich (2010) has recently characterized as the "Washington rules," which Blum (2008) credits with over

50 major military and CIA interventions abroad since World War II. Many of the think tanks and national big business membership organizations that emerged or were rejuvenated during this period would later go on to become influential proponents of standards-based education as the reform model unfolded over the ensuing decades.

In *The Power Elite*, Mills made a distinction between what he called "the 'old guard' of practical conservatives and the 'business liberals,' or sophisticated conservatives" (1956, p. 122).

> What the old guard represents is the outlook of, if not always the intelligent interests, of the more narrow economic concerns. What the business liberals represent is the outlook and the interest of the newer propertied class as a whole. They are 'sophisticated' because they are more flexible in adjusting to such political facts of life as the New Deal and big labor (Mills, 1956, p. 122).

I would disagree with Mills that business liberals or sophisticated conservatives represent the "newer propertied class." For example, Franklin Delano Roosevelt, the impresario of the New Deal himself is a patrician from what, by American standards, is an ancient and privileged dynasty. Also, as the economic and political centers of gravity shifted away from the Northeast towards the Sunbelt and the West after World War II, many of those who made their fortunes in these regions and in newer industries like oil, munitions, chemicals, pharmaceuticals, and aerospace were often the most implacable foes of organized labor and any type of government involvement in the economy. One also has to wonder how "practical" such a thoroughgoing intransigence on the part of so many so-called practical conservatives is. After all, old money doesn't get to be old money without at least some degree of practicality. Still further, as one looks back on the history of 20th century American conservatism, one is apt to think of someone urbane, erudite, and well-spoken as a sophisticated conservative; say, a William F. Buckley, Jr. or a George Will.

Nevertheless, Mills' essential point of two Weberian ideal types—of pragmatic and flexible sophisticated conservatives (willing to work within prevailing political trends) and bellicose practical conservatives (who give no quarter when it comes to being able to externalize the costs while privatizing the profits of their business empires) does seem to be largely borne out by the historical record.

Ever since Roosevelt dramatically enhanced the role of the federal government in the economy and made a significant accommodation with big labor, small activist factions of the corporate elite—practical conservatives—have been fighting back against what they saw as the infiltration of socialism—or worse—into the body politic. As the temper of the times since World War II was resoundingly in favor of business liberals, however, their efforts were largely ineffectual until the progressive aspirations of Johnson's Great Society began collapsing under the weight of stagflation and domestic opposition to the Vietnam War. Though largely marginalized at the time, many initiatives undertaken by practical conservatives since the New Deal did succeed in cumulatively laying the foundation for the union of big business and movement conservatives beginning in the late 1960s and early 1970s.

It could be argued that these began with the initiatives of nationwide business membership groups like the National Association of Manufacturers and Chamber of Commerce. Since they were, in the main, practical conservatives, their efforts were largely futile.

The National Association of Manufacturers is the oldest business association, founded in 1894. Although its policies and membership have fluctuated over the years, it has tended to take anti-union stances and to represent a significant amount of small- to medium-sized businesses. As Levitan and Cooper state, "in 1981, 80 percent [of its member firms] employed fewer than 500 employees" (1984, p. 14). It also typically represents a significant number of Fortune 500 companies as well. They further claim that in 1981, "about two-fifths of the more than 200 National Association of Manufacturers board members were employed by firms on the Fortune 500 list" (Levitan and Cooper, 1984, pp. 13–14). In spite of this apparent clout, they have not always met with much success in the legislative arena (Levitan and Cooper, 1984, pp. 13–14).

The Chamber of Commerce was created in 1912 with the assistance of National Association of Manufacturers. In many ways, it has acquired a stature and influence that dwarfs that of its parent organization. Like National Association of Manufacturers, the Chamber of Commerce too represents a large number of small- to medium-sized businesses (87% of Chamber of Commerce members employ fewer than 50 people), while a strong influence at the board and policy-making levels is still accorded to executives from Fortune 500 companies (Levitan and Cooper, 1984, p. 17–18).

Other organizations were also dedicated to challenging the nascent power of labor unions and expansive state roles in national economies. One prominent one was the Mont Pelerin Society, founded in Switzerland in 1947 by Friedrich von Hayek. Although initially composed primarily of European free market intellectuals and academics, economist Milton Friedman and other Americans were in attendance at the inaugural meeting as well. Over the course of the 1950s, American businessmen, economic policy-makers, journalists, conservative philanthropists, and think tank staffers began joining as well. In September 1958 the society held its first American meeting. The keynote address given by Ludwig von Mises on *Liberty and Property* hinted at themes central to the society's mission—an identification of "human liberty" with "the free market place" (Phillips-Fein, 2009, pp. 45–51).

Yet another important conservative organization was the John Birch Society, founded by a former vice president of the National Association of Manufacturers, Robert Welch, and 11 other industrialists in 1958. They saw Eisenhower's embrace of the salient features of the New Deal and moderate Republicanism as nothing less than communist infiltration, with Ike himself cast an agent of Kremlin influence (Phillips-Fein, 2009, p. 59).

Other centers of practical conservative ideology and policy talk were new think tanks like the American Enterprise Association, founded in 1943 to critique Keynesian trends in moderate Republicanism as much as the prevailing liberal consensus, while still dutifully avoiding accusations of "being a mere pawn of business" (Phillips-Fein, 2009, pp. 60–61).

In spite of this objective, the new organization didn't hesitate to fill its board of trustees with representatives of blue chip companies such as "Coca Cola, Socony Mobil Oil Company, U.S. Steel, and Eli Lilly" (Phillips-Fein, 2009, p. 60). A 1950 Congressional investigation determined that its funding came from similar sources as well: "General Motors ($7,500 in 1949), Ford ($5,000), Chrysler ($3,750), and Con Edison ($3,400)" as well as $5,000 from industrialist Lammot du Pont (cited in Phillips-Fein, 2009, pp. 61–62). The final Congressional report asked the pointed question "Can we assume that the Nation's largest industries would continue to support AEA if it were sponsoring views with which these industries were in basic disagreement?" (cited in Phillips-Fein, 2009, p. 62). In spite of their concerns, Congress did not strip AEA of its tax-exempt status, although the scrutiny did create a brief but significant crisis for the young organization (Phillips-Fein, 2009, p. 62), one compounded by the death of its founder in 1951, the businessman Lewis Brown. For a moment, AEA's very existence seemed to be in jeopardy.

The installation of a new board chairman, General Electric chair A. D. Marshall, and his hiring of William J. Baroody, a "staff economist from the U.S. Chamber of Commerce" as executive vice president, breathed new life into the group (Smith, 1991, pp. 175–176). Among Baroody's responsibilities was to serve as the main fundraiser and research administrator for AEA (Smith, 1991, p. 176). He recognized that a liberal consensus was dominating the conventional wisdom and conservative ideas were relegated to the margins. As Columbia University professor Lionel Trilling observed in 1950:

> In the United States at this time liberalism is not only the dominant but even the sole intellectual tradition. For it is the plain fact that nowadays there are no conservative or reactionary ideas in general circulation…only…irritable mental gestures which seek to resemble ideas (p. ix).

This consensus lasted well into the 1960s, with Kennedy's New Frontier and Johnson's Great Society being widely seen today as high water marks of mainstream liberalism, matched only by the original Progressive era (from the 1890s to the 1920s) and the New Deal of the 1930s. As the economist John Kenneth Galbraith noted in 1964: "with regard to the designation 'liberal,' almost everyone now so describes himself" (cited in Lapham, 2004, para. 3). After initial resistance to the New Deal, collective bargaining and government mandates were by and large tolerated in the boardrooms, if perhaps begrudgingly. Keynesian economics was firmly in the saddle and entities like the Business Advisory Council and the Committee for Economic Development, "which saw government as having a role in tempering the business cycle and in limiting the inequities or addressing the externalities of unregulated capitalism," garnered far more attention and exercised far more clout than did the upstart AEA (Judis, 2000, pp. 109, 119).

Baroody, while perhaps not an original thinker, was nevertheless a very gifted social entrepreneur who saw that the post-war liberal consensus emanated from the power of ideas. Whoever succeeded in marketing their ideas most effectively might eventually succeed in altering that consensus. In this way, both his personal career and the organizational trajectory of AEA provide a crucial foreshadowing of the personalities and processes that would begin in earnest in the early 1970s. As he wrote to a fundraising prospect in 1959:

> I, for one, have been long convinced that the climate of a particular society is, to a substantial degree, the product of ideas emanating from its thought leaders—and ideas are the most powerful of forces. The leftist movement derives a substantial portion of its strength from its virtual monopoly of the so-called intellectual segment of American society through systematic employment of techniques and devices designed to establish what might loosely be referred to as an intellectual reservoir of leftist ideology (cited in Phillips-Fein, 2009, p. 63).

It was Baroody's hope that AEA could emulate these techniques and develop a comparable "intellectual reservoir" of conservative ideas. He threw himself into his work with passion and drive, recognizing that "it will take time, financial resources, and the exercise of good brain power" (cited in Phillips-Fein, 2009, p. 63).

Fortunately, Baroody proved as adroit a fundraiser as he was a visioncaster. "By 1958, AEA was receiving contributions from twenty-six of the fifty largest industrial corporations in the country" as well as "donations of $10,000 or more from companies such as Allen-Bradley, Ford, General Motors, General Electric, Socony Mobil, and U.S. Steel" (Phillips-Fein, 2009, p. 65). By 1960 AEA had grown to 12 employees (Smith, 1991, p. 176) and had an annual budget of $230,000 (Smith, 1991, p. 176) or $900,000 (Micklethwait and Wooldridge, 2004, p. 77), depending on your source. Even if we take the higher figure of $900,000, it was still "less than a fifth of that of the Brookings Institution" (Micklethwait and Wooldridge, 2004, p. 77).

In fact, perhaps due to his success in corporate fundraising (and perhaps due to memories of the 1950 Congressional investigation as well), Baroody understood the need for AEA to downplay their business connections, to help foster the appearance of their organization as a bastion of objective analysis. To that end, AEA changed its name to the American Enterprise Institute for Public Policy Research in 1962 (Phillips-Fein, 2009, p. 66).

This did not end government scrutiny of the American Enterprise Institute (AEI), however. In 1964 Baroody became a senior advisor to the Goldwater campaign, with special responsibility for organizing the writing of Goldwater's "speeches and position papers and consulting on an almost daily basis with Goldwater" (Edwards, 1998, para. 19). Although one historian claims he took "full official leave" from AEI to do this work, his political role as one of the leaders of Goldwater's brain trust did not go unnoticed (Edwards, 1998, para. 19). After the election was over and Goldwater suffered one of the historic drubbings in American presidential politics, the House Subcommittee on Small Business chaired by Representative Wright Patman subpoenaed the tax records of AEI "and the IRS initiated a thorough two-year investigation" (Judis, 2000, p. 123). Alarmed by the scrutiny, AEI's board of trustees considered firing Baroody. Although they wound up retaining him, he dramatically scaled back overtly obvious attempts at influencing the federal legislative process and made a conscious effort to enhance the bipartisan appearance of AEI.

To the true believers in the nascent conservative movement, especially younger ones active in government in Washington at the time, this was apostasy of the highest order. AEI was coming to be seen by some movement conservatives as being too well mannered to have a very decisive impact on policy-making. They thought they needed a more pugnacious force for the insertion of conservative values into the policy debate, a counterweight to what they saw as the powerful influence of the liberal Brookings Institution. This involved swimming upstream against some very powerful intellectual and political currents, however, as the "basic American consensus at the time was firmly liberal in character and feeling, assured of a clear majority in both chambers of Congress as well as a sympathetic audience in the print and broadcast press" (Lapham, 2004, para. 1).

It wasn't just movement conservatives who were starting to feel the need for an enhanced right-wing ideological infrastructure in the late 1960s and early 1970s. It was spreading among corporate leaders and the haute bourgeoisie as well. Patrician eastern establishment writer and long-time editor of *Harper's Magazine* Lewis Lapham captured the mood of these sectors with a description of his experience at the Bohemian Grove in northern California during 1968, a stomping ground of the power elite and perennial bête noire of conspiracy theorists. Here the "misgivings" of the participants "were indistinguishable from panic" (Lapham, 2004, para. 12). These captains of industry and well-placed agenda-setters had a difficult time understanding the riots decimating American cities, a spate of political assassinations, opposition to the Vietnam War at home and the fragging of its officers abroad, the hippie/countercultural movement in general, and escalating antipathy to the free market system. In addition, a champion of their cause and class interests (of sorts), Barry Goldwater, had recently been trounced by Lyndon Johnson during the 1964 presidential election.

Many commentators over the years have noted that the Goldwater campaign resembled not so much a political campaign as a social movement. It may also be considered a symptom of the gradual shift away from the "Nelson Rockefeller" wing of the Republicans towards the rapidly growing power of the Sunbelt and West, and the prelude to a groundswell of reactionary populism within the party.

While the moral, political, and economic ground seemed to be shifting out from under the feet of old money and their technocrats, many of them were at a loss as to how to conceptualize it, even more so as to how to fight back against a seemingly all-powerful enemy. Their "fear was palpable and genuine…although they knew they were in trouble, they didn't know why. Ideas apparently mattered, and words were maybe more important than they had guessed; unfortunately, they didn't have any" (Lapham, 2004, para. 13).

Lapham opined that "Goldwater's autobiography, *The Conscience of a Conservative*, William F. Buckley's editorials in *National Review*, and the novels of Ayn Rand" were about the extent of their stock of ideas at this time (Lapham, 2004, para. 13). To this brief list, we might add books that have since become canonical to the free market intellectual tradition, like von Hayek's *The Road to Serfdom* (1944), Ludwig von Mises' *Planned Chaos* (1947), and Freidman's *Capitalism and Freedom* (1962). We might also include the key works of traditionalists who pined for the eternal verities and clear class positions of a prelapsarian, preindustrial society, like Peter Vierick's *But—I'm a Conservative* (1940), Richard Weaver's *Ideas Have Consequences* (1948), Russell Kirk's *The Conservative Mind* (1953), and Robert Nisbit's *The Quest for Community* (1953). The early "apostate leftists" bear mentioning as well, people like Whittaker Chambers (*Witness*, 1952) and Frank Meyer (*In Defense of Freedom*, 1962). The work of an individual often touted as the godfather of neoconservatism, Leo Strauss, would be another candidate for inclusion on this list, as would Phyllis Schlafly's paean to the Goldwater candidacy *A Choice Not an Echo* (1964), and perhaps a few others.

Nevertheless, Lapham's essential point remains valid. The intellectual infrastructure of the right during the post-World War II period was nowhere near as extensive as that of the liberal consensus (Mattson, 2008). What did exist was outside of the mainstream and had relatively little impact on the conventional wisdom of the day. A mish-mash of libertarian free marketeers, traditionalists, and strident anti-communists/anti-liberals, this group of work also offered little in the way of a consistent ideology.

What movement conservatives and the corporate elite needed were new sources of ideas and a new sense of how to use them to engage with the political process. In the concrete policy realm of Washington, D.C., these needs were felt most acutely by a number of young Congressional staffers and presidential aides, some of whom would later be considered architects of the rise of the modern right.

In 1971 two young Goldwater conservatives, 28-year-old Paul Weyrich, press secretary to Senator Gordon Allott (R-CO) and 30-year-old Edwin Feulner, administrative assistant to Congressman Philip Crane (R-IL) were having one of their frequent lunches together at the Congressional canteen and reviewing a brief issued by AEI on government support for research and development of a supersonic transport airplane, an issue then before Congress. As congressional staffers, they found the information in the report to be fair and concise. The only problem was that the report was released two days after the Senate had already voted 51–46 to halt the project (Edwards, 1998, para. 13–16).

Weyrich called Baroody, head of AEI, and told him "Great report. Why didn't we get it sooner?" (cited in Edwards, 1998, para. 17). Baroody replied "we didn't want to try to affect the outcome of the vote" (cited in Edwards, 1998, para. 18). According to Feulner, "it was at that moment that Paul and I decided that conservatives needed an independent research institute designed to influence the policy debate as it was occurring in Congress—before decisions were made" (cited in Edwards, 1998, para. 21).

Another version of the moment of creation of the Heritage Foundation was when Weyrich surreptitiously sat in on a meeting of a liberal coalition that included

> a dozen congressional aides, a think-tank policy wonk, and a cadre of Democratic interest groups, all coordinating sympathetic op-eds, studies, and demonstrations in an effort to push through a housing bill. Suddenly Weyrich understood not only his enemy but his life calling: to replace the liberal establishment with a conservative one that would guide the movement, at last, out of the wilderness (Grann, 1997, para. 9).

Some consider the Conservative Lunch Club formed by Weyrich, congressional aide Trent Lott, and "Weyrich's coworker in Allott's office," George Will, as a key nucleus of this burgeoning movement (Brock, 2004, p. 43). Others see it in what this club evolved into during 1971–1973, two organizations independent of Congress but nevertheless dedicated to analysis of Congressional policy, the House Republican Study Committee and Senate Steering Committee (Grann, 1997, para. 10; Smith, 1991, p. 199). By 1973 this effort had formalized to such an extent that "conservative congressmen hired an executive director to head their Republican Study Committee" (Smith, 1991, p. 199).

Still others point to the importance of a 1968 meeting between James Lucier, "an assistant to Senator Strom Thurmond," (R-SC), Weyrich, and Victor Fediay "an analyst at the Library of Congress" during which they discussed the need for a conservative counterpart to Brookings that could provide senators with timely information on issues of the day (Edwards, 1998, para. 25). The trio spent the rest of the year trying to interest corporate representatives in the idea, to no avail (Edwards, 1998, para. 25). In 1969 the trio, joined by William Roberts, "a professor of law at the Catholic University of America" flew to Wisconsin to confer with Frederic (Fritz) Rench, "a long time friend and mentor" of Weyrich (Edwards, 1998, para. 26). After meeting with the delegation, Rench agreed to write a business plan and budget for the proposed organization and spent the summer of 1969 doing so in the office of Senator Strom Thurmond (Edwards, 1998, para. 26–33). The entity was to be called the Analysis and Research Association (ARA) and to be funded initially at $80,000 per year (Edwards, 1998, para. 33).

For the rest of 1969 and early 1970, the participants tried to pique the interest of corporate America with their proposal, with no success (Edwards, 1998, para. 34). In the midst of these efforts, during the summer of 1970, Weyrich was given a letter from Jack Wilson, the newly appointed "assistant for political affairs" of Joseph Coors, the Denver brewing magnate (Edwards, 1998, para. 35). Coors had directed Wilson "to conduct a nationwide search for the right 'investment' in the conservative movement" in the course of which Wilson "sent letters to a long list of prominent political figures, including Colorado's senior U.S. Senator Gordon Allott, asking for suggestions" (Edwards, 1998, para. 36).

According to the authorized history of the Heritage Foundation, Weyrich's hands started to tremble as he read the letter. He immediately called Wilson and said, "We need to talk—I have an opportunity in mind for Mr. Coors" (Edwards, 1998, para. 37).

Wilson came out to Washington to confer with Weyrich, Lucier, and others. Coors followed. Weyrich arranged meetings for Coors with Senators Cliff Hansen (R-WY) and Strom Thurmond (R-SC), Congressmen Henry Schadeberg (R-WI) and Ed Foreman (R-NM), "and Walter Mote, an aide to Vice President Agnew" (Edwards, 1998, para. 38). Although Coors was receptive, he was also considering donating money to AEI. Eager to keep their dreams for a new think tank alive, Weyrich arranged for himself, Feulner, Coors, and Wilson to meet with Lyn Nofziger, "a deputy assistant to President Nixon for congressional relations" in Nofzinger's office (Edwards, 1998, para. 39).

Coors asked Nofziger for his opinion of AEI. Nofziger walked to a bookshelf, "blew some dust off of an AEI study" and said "that's what they're good for—collecting dust" (Edwards, 1998, para. 41). Coors got on board. He donated $250,000 for 1971–1972 (Edwards, 1998, para. 42), Lucier became president and Wilson treasurer, and ARA set up shop near the Supreme Court (Edwards, 1998, para. 44) with Weyrich as its director.

ARA was beset by operational problems from the start. Coors has said "they were dedicated but not unified" (Edwards, 1998, para. 47). Before long, Wilson told Weyrich that they would have to try again as a different entity

(Edwards, 1998, para. 47). They commandeered "a dormant tax-exempt organization," the Robert M. Schuchman Memorial Foundation (Edwards, 1998, para. 48) and installed Weyrich, Coors, Wilson, and Feulner on the board.

Coors was to become a charter member in a small "cadre of ultraconservative and self-mythologizing millionaires bent on rescuing the country from the hideous grasp of Satanic liberalism" (Lapham, 2004, para. 8). Besides Coors, these included "Richard Mellon Scaife in Pittsburgh, Lynde and Harry Bradley in Milwaukee, John Olin in New York City, the Smith Richardson family in North Carolina, and David and Charles Koch of Wichita" (Lapham, 2004, para. 16).

Richard Mellon Scaife of Pittsburgh was an heir to the Mellon oil and banking fortune, who had won control of the family foundations after feuding with his sister over funding priorities. Lynde and Harry Bradley were two brothers who developed a prosperous electronics company, Allen-Bradley. Harry was a dedicated member of the John Birch Society. When Allen-Bradley was sold to Rockwell International in 1985, it significantly improved the financial position of the foundation, which often gave to academics and intellectuals (Micklethwait and Wooldridge, 2004, p. 79). John Olin earned his money in chemicals and munitions (Institute for Policy Studies Right Web, 2009, para. 2). The Smith Richardsons were heirs to the Vicks line of medicines and balms (Smith Richardson Foundation). Fred Koch, the father of David and Charles Koch, had made the family fortune in oil and gas and his sons developed a penchant for donating to libertarian causes (Micklethwait and Wooldridge, 2004, p. 78).

These "ultraconservative and self-mythologizing millionaires" directed the foundations under their control to fund programs with the conscious intent of "reshaping the public policy agenda and constructing a network of conservative institutions and scholars" (Smith, 1991, p. 181). The Philanthropy Roundtable provided many of these individuals and foundation staffers with the opportunity to network, calibrate rhetoric, and coordinate funding priorities (Hazen, 2005, para. 15).

This incarnation of the prototype of the Heritage Foundation as the Robert M. Schuchman Memorial Foundation quickly encountered problems as well, caused by a rift between "members of the old board [who] preferred a more traditional approach to public policy, relying on conferences and the publication of papers" and "new members, led by Weyrich and Feulner, who wanted to affect the legislative process promptly and directly" (Edwards, 1998, para. 50). Coors told Weyrich and Feulner to try again with a third entity. On February 16, 1973, the Heritage Foundation was incorporated in the District of Columbia (Edwards, 1998, para. 53). During the Thanksgiving holiday of 1973, they received their Internal Revenue Service letter certifying their tax-exempt status, effective November 27 (Edwards, 1998, para. 56). The next business day, the Heritage Foundation began operation, retaining Schuchman's small staff of 10 (Edwards, 1998, para. 57–58).

Richard Mellon Scaife of Pittsburgh joined Coors as a financial backer with an initial contribution of $900,000 (Edwards, 1998, para. 49; Smith, 1991, p. 200; Micklethwait and Wooldrige; Judis, 2000, p. 126). Early financial backers besides Coors and Mellon Scaife included the Nobel Foundation of Oklahoma and the John M. Olin Foundation (Smith, 1991, p. 200).

Weyrich has variously been called the Lenin of the right (Micklethwait and Wooldridge, 2004, p. 81) and the Robespierre of the right (Grann, 1997), probably because of his ambitious vision, extraordinary gift for organization, obsessive concern for ideological purity (even among the faithful on the right), and often violent rhetoric. As an example of his rhetoric, in 1973 Weyrich said: "We are different from previous generations of conservatives. We are no longer working to preserve the status quo. We are radicals, working to overturn the present power structure of the country" (cited in Grann, 1997, para. 10). Shortly thereafter, Weyrich also said "It may not be with bullets but it is a war nevertheless. It is a war of ideology, it's a war of ideas. It's a war about our way of life" (cited in Grann, 1997, 11). According to Weyrich himself, his own views were neither those of Lenin nor Robespierre but rather those of a different authoritarian. "My view is Maoist. I believe you have to control the countryside and then the capital will eventually fall" (Grann, 1997, para. 30).

Nevertheless, the skills of a firebrand and doctrinal enforcer are not always those of an operational manager. His brief tenure of less than a year as founding director of the Heritage Foundation appears to have been rather tumultuous. The authorized history of the Heritage Foundation describes his March 1974 departure charitably, with Weyrich "guided as usual by his activist impulses" to stave off disaster for the Republican party in the Fall elections through the creation of the Committee for the Survival of a Free Congress (Edwards, 1998, para. 61), a political action committee, and its counterpart, the Free Congress Foundation (Grann, 1997, para. 11).

Other accounts are less charitable. The magazine *New Republic* characterized him as "a case study of the conservative mind—a metaphor for the right's deep-seated inability to accept the compromising nature of power" (Grann, 1997, para. 5). In the Grann piece, *Robespierre of the Right*, Weyrich is portrayed as the conservative nerd from hell, "given to storming around the office, his normally pale skin blood-red, his pants pulled high above his belly, lecturing those around him on how to be good conservatives" (Grann, 1997, para. 11). It seems Weyrich was more comfortable as an insurgent, a rebellious outsider, than as the operational manager of a functional ongoing concern that was rapidly becoming a part of the very establishment he so despised. He lasted barely a year as director.

After the new president, Jerry James, left within a few months, he was succeeded by a more effective leader, Governor Ronald Reagan's "former secretary of business and transportation," Frank Walton, who began work on June 9, 1975 (Edwards, 1998, para. 65). Walton was able to more than double Heritage's annual budget, from $413,497 for 1974 just before he came aboard to slightly above $1 million in 1976 (Edwards, 1998, para. 65). $420,000 of that million came from a single funder, Richard Mellon Scaife, who would go on to contribute "at least $3.8 million" "over the next eight years" beginning with 1973 (Micklethwait and Wooldridge, 2004, p. 78). James also actively used direct mail fundraising (Edwards, 1998, para. 67). "Individual donations, many of them in the $25 to $50 range, have accounted for as much as 40 percent of its annual budget, in marked contrast with the more traditional policy research organizations" (Smith, 1991, p. 200). Heritage grew at a blistering pace in the 1970s.

One of Heritage Foundation's founders, Ed Feulner, resigned as executive director of the House Republican Study Committee to assume the presidency of the foundation in 1977 (Smith, 1991, p. 200), a tenure that would last until the present day. In the first year and a half of his presidency, Feulner succeeded in raising its annual budget from $1 million to $2.8 million (Judis, 2000, p. 126). Feulner was not only able to lure foundations like Smith Richardson and Olin, but also Fortune 500 corporations like General Motors, Chase Manhattan, Pfizer, Mobil, and Sears, and major foundations like Nobel (Judis, 2000, p. 126).

AEI had undergone a major resuscitation during the 1970s and remained larger than Heritage. As the decade drew to a close, AEI had 45 full-time researchers (Micklethwait and Wooldridge, 2004, p. 77). By 1980 its annual income was $9.7 million, "$500,000 more than Brookings" (Micklethwait and Wooldridge, 2004, p. 77). The counterestablishment had arrived.

After leaving the Heritage Foundation, Weyrich's Committee for the Survival of a Free Congress succeeded in bringing a number of radical right-wingers into Congress in 1978, including the future Speaker of the House and a major architect of the right's rise to power, Newt Gingrich. Weyrich's remarkable organizational successes kept coming throughout the 1970s. In 1979 he told Jerry Falwell "Out there is what one might call a moral majority." Falwell replied "That's it. That's the name of the organization" (Grann, 1997, para. 14).

Thus the Moral Majority was created, uniting movement conservatives and elements of the corporate elite with evangelical Christians, felling "the greatest track of virgin timber on the political landscape" (Grann, 1997, 14) and also contributing to the decline of mainstream American Christianity's traditional affiliation with the "social gospel" exemplified by such people as Dorothy Day, Daniel Berrigan, William Sloane Coffin, and Dr. Martin Luther King, Jr.

In 1971 past president of the American Bar Association, conservative Democrat Lewis Powell, a 64 year old Richmond, Virginia corporate lawyer who sat on 11 corporate boards drafted a 6,000 word confidential memo for the U.S. Chamber of Commerce that argued passionately against *The Attack on the Free Enterprise System*. It was written at the request of his friend, neighbor, Chamber of Commerce education committee chairman, and "head of the Southern Department Stores chain," Eugene B. Sydnor, Jr. (Anderson, 1972a, p. F7).

Powell used alarmist language to outline the threat faced by business from many sectors of society in the early 1970s, to lambaste the apathy of business for not fighting back, and to offer a comprehensive and systematic plan on how to regain its stature, possibly under the guidance of a central nationwide coordinating body like the Chamber of Commerce. This initiative would monitor and infiltrate schools and the academy, evaluate textbooks, and develop a staff of highly-respected pro-business scholars and speakers, encouraging them and allied intellectuals to publish and lecture often. Media outlets such as television, radio, the press, academic journals, books, paperbacks, and pamphlets should be monitored and used to disseminate pro-business messages. Business should even develop their own media, emulate the political achievements of labor, and systematically build support in the judiciary and other key political arenas as well.

The stridency and thoroughness of Powell's proposal was due to what he perceived as the extreme gravity of the situation. Nothing less than the very "survival of what we call the free enterprise system" was at stake and, with it, any hope for "the strength and prosperity of America and the freedom of our people" (Powell, 2004, para. 38). Indeed, "no thoughtful person can question that the American economic system is under broad attack" (Powell, 2004, para. 10).

Powell granted that "there always have been critics of the system" but that this criticism was "wholesome and constructive" so long as it took a reformist bent and didn't question any of the bedrock assumptions of American capitalism (Powell, 2004, para. 11). To Powell's mind, however, the criticism of the late 1960s and early 1970s sought to "subvert or destroy" the system (Powell, 2004, para. 11). What is worse, this subversion was no longer "sporadic or isolated" from a "few extremists"; instead it was "broadly based," "consistently pursued" and came "from perfectly respectable elements of society: from the college campus, the pulpit, the media, the intellectual and literary journals, the arts and sciences, and from politicians" (Powell, 2004, para. 12, 14). Television was particularly to blame for giving these voices a platform (Powell, 2004, para. 15). Such "respectable elements" were even more likely to "fatally weaken or destroy the system" than the handful of celebrity activists of the New Left mentioned by name in the brief (Powell, 2004, para. 21). While the left's critique may stem from "political demagoguery or economic illiteracy," that can only be considered "of slight comfort" because its potential damage to the free market system remained so grave (Powell, 2004, para. 29).

Powell then chided the business elite, "the boards of directors and the top executives of corporations great and small and business organizations at all levels" for what he perceived as their "appeasement, ineptitude and ignoring the problem" (Powell, 2004, para. 31). Their defense must be along the lines of "guerrilla warfare with those who propagandize against the system," against those who try "insidiously and constantly to sabotage it" (Powell, 2004, para. 32).

But to truly be effective this warfare had to be fought collectively and in close coordination, which required "organization," "careful long-range planning and implementation," and "consistency of action over an indefinite period of years, in the scale of financing available only through joint effort, and in the political power available only through united action and national organizations" (Powell, 2004, para. 41). Powell suggested the Chamber of Commerce might be the ideal body to provide that coordinating function, perhaps in conjunction with "other national organizations (especially those of various industrial and commercial groups)" (Powell, 2004, para. 43).

Powell was especially sensitive to the political function of education and blamed the academy's long experience with liberalism for that ideology's pernicious and powerful influence on society. He also noted that the gradualism of its onset over decades mitigated against notice of it by the business elite (Powell, 2004, para. 45–46). He suggested that ideological "balance" was lacking in the academy, with few conservatives or moderates to speak for their side, which allowed the incessant creation of anti-business cadres among graduates, who would then march out into those sectors of society that are particularly influential in the ongoing battle of ideas: "the news media, especially television," "government," "politics," arts and letters, and education at various levels (Powell, 2004, para. 47, 49). Especially pernicious is when "these 'intellectuals' end up in regulatory agencies or governmental departments with large authority over the business system they do not believe in" (Powell, 2004, para. 50).

While Powell admitted that the principle of academic freedom is "sanctified" and that "it would be fatal to attack this as a principle," he nevertheless saw appeals to rectify the alleged lack of ideological balance as "a great opportunity for constructive action" (Powell, 2004, para. 51). He suggested the Chamber of Commerce might also want to consider bypassing the university system to create its own "staff of highly qualified scholars in the social sciences who do believe in the system," much like conservative think tanks would do during the 1970s and beyond (Powell, 2004, para. 53). A "speakers bureau" composed of the "ablest and most effective advocates from the top echelons of American business" might be an effective strategy as well, much like the Business Roundtable, Achieve, Inc., and individual business leaders would do in the 1980s and beyond (Powell, 2004, para. 54).

The ideological infrastructure should not only tout the values of American corporatist democracy, but also point out "its basic relationship to individual rights and freedoms" in a way that improves on "existing textbooks," which are typically "superficial, biased and unfair" (Powell, 2004, para. 57). The overall action program for creating a stronger conservative presence in education would be

> a long road and not one for the fainthearted. But if pursued with integrity and conviction it could lead to a strengthening of both academic freedom on the campus and of the values which have made America the most productive of all societies (Powell, 2004, para. 66).

This sense of being in it for the long haul permeated similar injunctions from the other major architects of the right's dream of creating a counter-establishment, the perception that they were engaged in a multi-decade task of working through the universities, the schools, the media, and independently created intellectual venues.

Powell opined in 1971 that "business has been the favorite whipping-boy of many politicians for many years" (Powell, 2004, para. 81) and that business has less influence on government than almost any other sector in American society, particularly when it comes to lobbying before Congress (Powell, 2004, para. 83). To counteract this, business has to learn the lessons of methodical collective action already used by "labor and other self-interest groups…that political power is necessary," "must be assiduously cultivated," "used aggressively and with determination—without embarrassment and without the reluctance which has been so characteristic of American business—to penalize politically those who oppose it" (Powell, 2004, para. 87, 94).

As a part of this holistic program, Powell opined that the Supreme Court and judiciary "may be the most important instrument for social, economic and political change" (Powell, 2004, para. 89). Shareholders, which he estimated to number around 20 million, may be another source of strength as well, those who have provided "the capital which fuels the economic system which has produced the highest standard of living in all history" (Powell, 2004, para. 10).

He closed his action plan on an ominous note: "business and the enterprise system are in deep trouble, and the hour is late" (Powell, 2004, para. 114). After delivering the memo dated August 31, 1971 to his friend Eugene Sydnor, Powell and Sydnor traveled together to Washington to brief COC executive vice president Arch Booth on the issues contained in the memo (Phillips-Fein, 2009, p. 161; Landay, 2002, para. 16). The Chamber of Commerce published it in its periodical, *Washington Report* (Brock, 2004, p. 39).

Powell was nominated to the Supreme Court by President Nixon on December 9, 1971 and confirmed on January 7, 1972 (Supreme Court Historical Society, para. 1). Sydnor thanked his friend with a note saying it was an "excellent presentation of the vitally important cause for American Business to go on the offensive after such a long period of inaction and indecision in telling the American people the facts of life as they unhappily exist today" (Phillips-Fein, 2009, pp. 160–161).

The document circulated among the legal departments of such corporations as General Motors, where Powell's "law school friend, Ross L. Malone" served as general counsel (Landay, 2002, para. 15) and DuPont, the executive suites of other leading American corporations (Phillips-Fein, 2009, p. 161–162), and among prominent movement conservatives and free market intellectuals.

Although the Chamber of Commerce ultimately decided to pass on Powell's ambitious and potentially costly call to action, others were less hesitant (Landay, 2002, para. 31). It "influenced or inspired the creation of the Heritage Foundation, the Manhattan Institute, the Cato Institute, Citizens for a Sound Economy, Accuracy in Academe, and other powerful organizations" (Powell, 2004, para. 3).

This was in part because major conservative funders fell under its thrall as well. Joseph Coors is on record as saying that his reaction to the Powell memo was a major impetus for him to involve himself deeply in conservative politics; it "'stirred' him up and convinced him American business was 'ignoring' a crisis" (Edwards, 1998, para. 45–46). John Olin wrote to AEI's president William Baroody that "the Powell memorandum gives us a reason for a well organized effort to re-establish the validity and importance of the American free enterprise system" (cited in Phillips-Fein, 2009, p. 162). One of the early pro-business litigation centers, the Pacific Legal Foundation, formed in 1973 (Grossman, 1993, para. 6), "quoted the Powell memorandum at length in its prospectus" (Phillips-Fein, 2009, p. 162). In 1975 an overarching National Legal Center for the Public Interest was created "to assist in the establishment of independent regional litigation foundations dedicated to a balanced view of the role of law in achieving economic and social progress" (cited in Grossman, 1993, para. 6). This organization would go on to help create six comparable organizations scattered throughout the country, funded by "the Olin, Scaife, Bradley, and Smith Richardson Foundations" (Grossman, 1993, para. 7).

Washington Post investigative reporter Jack Anderson made the Powell memo public in two stories on September 28 and 29, 1972. In the first column, he called it "a militant political action program" that was "now being circulated among top executives by the U.S. Chamber of Commerce" (Anderson, 1972a, p. F7). Anderson quoted from it extensively and noted that "the FBI failed to turn up [the memo] during its field investigation of Powell," which prevented Senators during the confirmation process from asking him "whether he might use his position on the Supreme Court to put his ideas into practice and to influence the court in behalf of business interests" (Anderson, 1972a, p. F7). This was especially important as the use of the judiciary to counteract the legal ramifications of anti-business sentiment was given such a prominent role in the memo. Powell, who had also served on the Virginia Board of Education and as a trustee of Washington and Lee University, was equally keen that business "mold pro-business attitudes at the high school and college level" (Anderson, 1972a, p. F7).

The *New York Times* story the next day followed Anderson's general pattern of a combination of synopsis and quotation (Graham, 1972, p. 31). Like Anderson, the *New York Times* piece noted that Powell was not questioned closely during the Senate confirmation hearings on his views towards business. Anderson's second piece mused aloud that Powell's "views were so militant that it raises a question about his fitness to decide any case involving business interests" (Anderson, 1972b, p. C27). He also characterized it as "a blueprint for an assault by big business on its critics" (Anderson, 1972b, p. C27).

Ironically, the publicity generated by the Anderson columns gave the memorandum widespread publicity and increased support for its ideas (Landay, 2002, para. 54). For many in the business community, the memo seemed to capture their zeitgeist perfectly, their sense of being under siege, while also serving as a stirring call to arms and savvy plan for comprehensive action. The Chamber of Commerce was soon "besieged" by businessmen requesting copies (Landay, 2002, para. 54).

The most effective business lobbying effort of the decade, however, didn't come from such established organizations as the Chamber of Commerce or National Association of Manufacturers but rather from a new entity, the Business Roundtable. The origins of the Business Roundtable can be found in three precursor business groups, the Labor Law Study Group, Construction Users Anti-Inflation Roundtable, and March Group. The Labor Law Study Group was founded "in 1965 by executives of General Electric and American Smelting and Refining to combat organized labor's attempt to repeal section 14(b) of the Taft-Hartley Act" (Bowman, 1996, p. 354). The Construction Users Anti-Inflation Roundtable was a group of "one hundred steel and construction companies" formed in 1969 at the behest of U.S. Steel president Roger Blough "to pressure unions to hold down their wage demands" (Judis, 2000, p. 120). The March Group was a select group of executives concerned about what they took to be the declining influence of business on federal government policies. They were assembled over the course of late 1971 and early 1972 by John Harper, chairman of the Aluminum Company of America (ALCOA), and Fred Borch, the chairman of General Electric, (Judis, 2000, p. 121).

The movement towards the unification of these three groups was facilitated by a high-powered meeting in 1972 in Washington between Borch, Harper, "Secretary of the Treasury John Connally, Deputy Treasury Secretary Charls Walker, and Federal Reserve Board Chairman Arthur Burns" (Judis, 2000, p. 120–121). During the meeting, they discussed "the growing hostility towards business" in society at large in which the government officials urged the corporate "executives to found a new organization that would lobby Congress and the White House directly" (Judis, 2000, p. 121).

In 1972 the Labor Law Study Group and Construction Users Anti-Inflation Roundtable two organizations united to form the Business Roundtable. In 1973 the March Group agreed to join as well.

Very early in the life of the new organization, a consultant's report "gave a prominent place to the Powell memorandum," chided the founders for not "taking Powell's comments seriously enough," and called on them to engage in a "total attack program" to defend the prerogatives and stature of big business (Phillips-Fein, 2009, p. 193). The Powell memo was attached as an appendix.

The Business Roundtable grew rapidly, even though it restricted its membership to CEOs of Fortune 500 companies. After its first five years of existence, it already had "192 member companies, including 113 of the top Fortune 200" (Judis, 2000, p. 121). Cumulatively, they accounted for "nearly half of the country's GDP" (Judis, 2000, p. 121). Its first presidents were such captains of industry as Harper, "Thomas Murphy of General Motors, Irving Shapiro of Dupont, and Borch's successor at GE, Reginald Jones" (Judis, 2000, p. 121).

The Business Roundtable differed from such prominent groups as the Committee on Economic Development in that it was not a research organization that sought to alter policy through publications but rather through direct lobbying of government officials. Their "discreet lobbying helped to defeat the liberal legislative agenda for the decade" (Phillips-Fein, 2009, p. 198). Among their most successful efforts during that period were opposition to "a consumer protection agency, labor law reform, and new antitrust legislation" and support for "corporate tax cuts and natural-gas price deregulation" (Himmelstein, 1989, p. 140).

The Business Roundtable also differed from business membership organizations like the Chamber of Commerce and National Association of Manufacturers in a number of salient ways. While the Business Roundtable limited its membership to the CEOs of Fortune 500 companies, the other two organizations have traditionally represented a significant number of small- and medium-sized businesses, in addition to serving corporations at the commanding heights of the economy. Secondly, Business Roundtable lobbying was conducted by the CEOs and chairmen themselves, rather than staff members or professional lobbyists. Finally, the Business Roundtable's approach to lobbying tended to be more flexible and pragmatic than that of the "practical conservatives" at Chamber of Commerce and National Association of Manufacturers, and often found its greatest successes with Democrats, beginning with the Carter administration.

This began a decades-long withdrawal by the Democratic party away from the equity and social justice concerns of progressives. For example, in his January 19, 1978 State of the Union address, Carter said that

> we really need to realize that there is a limit to the role and the function of government. Government cannot solve our problems, it can't set our goals, it cannot define our vision. Government cannot eliminate poverty or provide a bountiful economy or reduce inflation or save our cities or cure illiteracy or provide energy. And government cannot mandate goodness (Carter, 1978, para. 19).

According to a brief introduction to the Powell memo on the Reclaimdemocracy.org website, in 1978 Powell penned "the majority opinion in Bank of Boston v. Belloti, a...decision that asserted a First Amendment 'right' for corporations to influence ballot questions," a decision that played a significant role in moving the Democrats to the right by increasing the importance of fundraising in Congressional and Presidential politics (cited in Powell, 2004, para. 6).

In recent decades, the Powell memo has come to occupy an almost canonical status in histories on the rise of the right in America. Some, in particular former Senator Bill Bradley aide Schmitt (2005), have sought to downplay its influence, in part because it is not mentioned in many of the most definitive volumes on the recent rise of the right: "Lee Edwards' *The Conservative Revolution*, James A. Smith's *The Idea Brokers*, Sidney Blumenthal's *The Rise of the Counterestablishment*, Godfrey Hodgson's *A World Turned Right-Side Up*, or George Nash's authoritative *The Conservative Intellectual Movement in America Since 1945*" (Schmitt, 2005, para. 7). Schmitt goes on to suggest a genealogy of the rise of the importance of the Powell memo, offering the Alliance for Justice's 1993 report of the right's infiltration of the legal system, *Justice for Sale*, as the leading candidate for rediscovery of the Powell memo after decades of neglect (Schmitt, 2005, para. 8; Grossman, 1993). This article gave particular attention to Powell's call for the active use of the courts by business and conservatives and how this injunction eventually led to the creation of a variety of pro-business litigation centers across the nation. Schmitt suggests this trend was furthered by Judis' *The Paradox of American Democracy* (2000), which credited "Powell with convincing businessmen that they should be more politically active" (Schmitt, 2005, para. 9). Schmitt goes on to mention a reference to the Powell memo in Micklethwait and Wooldridge (2004) based on an account in the authorized history of the Heritage Foundation (Edwards, 1998). Schmitt suggests that "the most breathlessly detailed account of the Powell memo," however, is to be found in Landay (2002), an essay he nominates as "probably the source of most of the recent interest in the memo" (Schmitt, 2005, para. 10).

The memo was also called a "major feature in a PowerPoint presentation on the Conservative Message Machine" (Schmitt, 2005, para. 4). Although Schmitt doesn't mention him by name, the author and impresario of this presentation was Rob Stein, a former Clinton deputy director of the Department of Commerce and former "senior advisor to the chairman of the Democratic National Committee" (Lapham, 2004, para. 8). After leaving political life, Stein became a hedge fund manager and began showing his PowerPoint presentation to elite big-money donors in the Democratic party during this last decade, in an attempt to replicate the messaging achievements of the right by creating a new organization, the Democracy Alliance (DeParle, 2005, para. 7). Stein's presentation also seems to have been a major impetus goading Lapham into penning his essay *Tentacles of Rage, The Republican Propaganda Mill, A Brief History* (2004). Stein noted that fifty funding organizations had pumped "roughly $3 billion over a period of thirty years" to anti-liberal causes (cited in Lapham, 2004, para. 9).

In the rest of his account, however, Schmitt is less persuasive. True, many of the leading figures of the rise of the modern right and its union with the corporate elite did not explicitly use the Powell memo as their plan of action. True, the memo focuses on the Chamber of Commerce, who ultimately did not play the leadership role Powell had hoped. Less true, perhaps, is Schmitt's assertion that the memo seems to be "much more of a call for the mainstream establishment to defend itself against critics from the further left" (Schmitt, 2005, para. 13). As I have argued above, the "mainstream establishment" at the time was largely "liberal." It is probably true, however, that the audience Powell hoped to address would probably identify themselves as moderate conservatives.

In spite of Schmitt's cautionary note, the importance of the memo seems hard to overstate, especially because of its influence on key figures, funders, and organizations central to the rise of the modern right and the fact that its blueprint for the rise of the modern right was largely followed. While the prime movers may not have always been acting specifically under the direct influence of the memo itself, many important ones often were. In spite of it all, the memo provides a succinct and comprehensive outline of how the modern right came to power. It also played a significant role in the formation of the Heritage Foundation, BR, and organizations, many of which would go on to become major exponents of standards-based education. Even Schmitt himself admits, "some of Powell's recommendations do bear an uncanny resemblance to the institutions of the modern right" (Schmitt, 2005, para. 11).

To be sure, Powell's was not the only important memo of the era for the right. In 1970 (Grann, 1997, para. 11), Pat Buchanan, an aide to Nixon aide H. R. Haldeman, had made "himself the White House expert on how the liberal beast operated" through close study of "Brookings and other tax-exempt institutions" (Smith, 1991, p. 197). In 1971 Buchanan drafted a blueprint to combat liberalism that was remarkably similar to the Powell memo (Edwards, 1998, para. 22). It was presented to Nixon within days of his reelection, and reflected a strategy "to make permanent the New Majority" (cited in Edwards, 1998, para. 22). This missive called for a "conservative counterpart to Brookings" (Grann, 1997, para. 11), a think tank that could act as a

> 'repository of its political beliefs'...a 'talent bank' for Republicans when in office, a 'tax-exempt refuge' for them when out of office, and a 'communications center' for Republican thinkers across the nation. 'The AEI is not the answer' (cited in Smith, 1991, p. 197).

Schmitt sees the Buchanan memo as having "foreseen the political and institutional structures of the right" (2005, para. 14). As the Powell memo was not the only important memo to contain the types of thoughts and recommendations it did, so too were Feulner and Weyrich not the only ones to suggest and implement the organizational strategies needed to carry out those ideas. While they may have been among leading lights of the new right, they had other counterparts in the corporate and political worlds as well. Judis (2000) singles out three prominent lobbyists and politicos in particular. These are "Bryce Harlow, Proctor and Gamble's chief representative in Washington and an eminence grise among Washington lobbyists," "Nixon's Secretary of Defense Melvin Laird," a Goldwater Republican and influential figure in the conservative takeover of the Republican party, and "Deputy Secretary of the Treasury Charls Walker," who later would go on to "become Washington's most powerful tax lobbyist" (Judis, 2000, p. 119).

As Feulner and Weyrich were not the only ones to suggest and implement new organizational strategies, so too was Powell not the only impresario of ideas along these lines. Here, we should add Irving Kristol and William Simon as well, although their influence would arguably not peak until the latter part of the 1970s.

Kristol was "a former leftist and Trotskyist who had become a columnist for the *Wall Street Journal*, the editor of a new journal, *The Public Interest*, and a professor of public policy at New York University" (Judis, 2000, p. 116). He saw restraint of corporate power by such things as consumer and environmental protection laws as leading America implacably towards "state capitalism," which he saw as a "huge potential threat to the individual liberties Americans have traditionally enjoyed" (Kristol, 1978, p. 22). His many writings created so much of the intellectual framework of the neoconservative movement, that he is often described as one of its "godfathers." While Kristol may not have been a very original thinker, he was a gifted proselytizer who understood the power of ideas and, according to Lapham (2004), also possessed of a significant amount of personal charm. Indeed, as Kristol has written, "what rules the world is ideas, because ideas define the way reality is perceived" (Kristol, 1978, p. 140).

Simon served as Treasury Secretary under President Ford and then went on to succeed John Olin as the head of the Olin Foundation in 1977. His influential 1978 book *A Time for Truth* reiterated many of the themes that animated Powell, Buchanan, Weyrich, Feulner, Harlow, Laird, Walker, and Kristol. In an oft-repeated passage, he wrote of the pressing need for

> funds generated by business [to] rush by multimillions to the aid of liberty, in the many places where it is beleaguered. Foundations imbued with the philosophy of freedom...must take pains to funnel desperately needed funds to scholars, social scientists, writers and journalists who understand the relationship between political and economic liberty" (Simon, 1978, p. 230).

Simon's message of extreme urgency and his passionate identification of capitalism with individual freedom was remarkably similar to that of Powell's. Elsewhere in his book, Simon called for

> a massive and unprecedented mobilization of the moral, intellectual and financial resources which reside in those who still have faith in the human individual, who believe in his right to maximum responsible liberty and who are concerned that our traditional free enterprise system, which offers the greatest scope for the exercise of our freedom, is in dire and perhaps ultimate peril (1978, p. 229).

Kristol made a similar point in his essay *On Corporate Philanthropy* (1978). "When you give away your stockholders' money, your philanthropy must serve the longer-term interests of the corporation. Corporate philanthropy should not be, and cannot be, disinterested" (Kristol, 1978, p. 144).

The COC and another national business organization of long standing, NAM, had both become moribund by the close of the 1960s. Beginning with the 1970s, however, both entities were enjoying a renaissance and had even began to collaborate on a number of measures, very much in the spirit of collective action urged by the Powell memo (Judis, 2000, p. 120).

During the 1970s, with the newly created Heritage Foundation on its right flank, the AEI was able to reposition itself as the bastion of mainstream conservatism and engineer a significant increase of revenue and the proliferation of prestigious contacts and fellowships throughout the decade. The young upstart, Heritage, also saw its revenue increase rapidly throughout the decade as well. Both organizations would send dozens of staffers to the incoming Reagan administration and the Heritage Foundation's magisterial *Mandate for Leadership* (1981) would serve as a detailed policy guide for the incoming president's team (Greenberg, 1998, para. 5; Judis, 2000, p. 125).

The powerhouse of American business lobbying during the 1970s, the BR, was also influenced by the message of the Powell memo, with one of its earliest consultants appending it to a report that urged the new organization to go on a "total attack program." After a decade of legislative accomplishments, by 1980 their membership included "the 10 largest corporations in the…Fortune 500 list—Exxon, General Motors, Mobil, Ford, Texaco, Standard Oil of California, Gulf, IBM, General Electric, and Standard Oil (Indiana)" as well as "21 of the top 25; 40 of the top 50…70 of the top 100…113 of the top 200; and 131 of the top 500" as well as the top public utilities, commercial banks, life insurance companies, retailers, and transportation companies (McQuaid, 1981, p. 115).

The cumulative effective of all of this targeted funding, intellectual labor, and policy engagement was to "set a counter-movement in motion to replace the institutions and expunge the ideas of American liberalism" (Landay, 2002, para. 6). This was accomplished by creating "an institutional infrastructure and ideological apparatus to produce its own intellectuals, disseminate ideas, and eventually control most of the commanding heights and institutions in which knowledge is produced, circulated and legitimated" (Giroux, 2009, para. 2). Often times, however, these appeals were as much to emotion, to "people's deeper feelings and values," as to reason, in part by "using messaging" created on the assembly lines of "marketing, public relations, and corporate image-management" (Johnson, D., 2003, para. 18).

This chapter demonstrated, during the late 1960s and early 1970s, the corporate elite and movement conservatives collaborated closely on the creation of a multi-faceted intellectual, policy, and legal framework of think tanks, academic posts, media outlets, litigation centers, and other related initiatives. By the time of Reagan's inauguration in 1981, these "assembly lines were working at full capacity" (Lapham, 2004, para. 19). Indeed, they helped to generate the numerous reports during the Reagan-Bush years that framed the terms of the educational policy debate, often in ways conducive to the ongoing evolution of standards-based education. This is because the major change agents of this period were so successful in framing the terms of the national debate (Callahan, 1999, para. 3). Or, as Schattschneider put it more succinctly, "whoever decides what the game is about also decides who gets into the game" (cited in Callahan, 1999, para. 2). This chapter helped explain who got into the game.

· 3 ·

A NATION AT RISK AND A DECADE OF REPORTS (1980s–1990s)

Milton Friedman has a famous quote on the relationship between crisis, ideology, and change, and the role of the intellectual class in mediating among the three.

> Only a crisis—actual or perceived—produces real change. When that crisis occurs, the actions that are taken depend on the ideas that are lying around. That, I believe, is our basic function: to develop alternatives to existing policies, to keep them alive and available until the politically impossible becomes politically inevitable (1982, p. ix).

This chapter is in large part the story of a concerted effort by think tanks, governmental agencies, and blue-ribbon commissions to establish a voluminous rhetorical infrastructure that both kept the seed ideas of standards-based education "alive and available" and fomented the sense of crisis that led to their eventual "inevitability."

This chapter hopes to gauge the impact of A Nation at Risk and a plethora of other influential reports circulating in the educational policy debate of the 1980s and early 1990s, to examine how they prepared the way for standards-based education to emerge as one of the most influential American K–12 education reform ideas in following decades. Briefs from national business organizations like the U.S. Chamber of Commerce, National Association of

Manufacturers, Committee for Economic Development, and—especially—the Business Roundtable set the parameters of the policy agenda and delineated many of its key terms. Dynamic figures from the national corporate elite also helped to propagate this rhetoric in the mainstream media. The efforts of the Minnesota, California, and Hawai'i state Business Roundtables were extremely important precursors in the political adoption of many of these ideas at the state level. In addition to their work, a select group of energetic governors also helped shape the policy talk of the era.

The National Governors Association and Business Roundtable each held different annual meetings dedicated exclusively to education during the 1980s, in 1985 (Alexander, 1986) and 1989 (Emery, 2002) respectively. Both conferences helped consolidate the ideas that would later coalesce into standards-based education. The first national educational summit, held in Charlottesville in 1989, promulgated a number of national educational goals. This could be considered the first tentative iteration of the standards-based education reform idea, codified a few months after in Bush's 1990 State of the Union address, which will be discussed later in this chapter. Subsequent reports, like the famous *Secretary's Commission on Achieving Necessary Skills* (SCANS) report (United States Department of Labor, 1991), would soon become influential in the actual concrete drafting of initial state standards, another historical episode I will investigate at greater length later in this chapter.

These developments need to be seen in their economic and political contexts as well. With the appointment of Paul Volcker to head the Federal Reserve in August 1979 and the election of Ronald Reagan to the presidency in November 1980, the liberal consensus that had dominated American politics and economic policy since the Great Depression began to disintegrate. The ideological infrastructure cultivated by a loose coalition of New Right movement conservatives, corporate elites, evangelical Christians, and nascent New Democrats started to bear fruit. After a decade of assiduous labor, the counter-establishment was poised to become the establishment. The supply-side economics of the Chicago School enjoyed a new vogue. Government spending on social welfare programs was reduced. The wealthy enjoyed tax cuts. Military spending was enhanced. The influence of organized labor declined. As a cardinal example of this, one need look no further than Reagan's decertification of the Professional Air Traffic Controllers Organization union after their 1981 strike, "one of the most important events in late twentieth century U.S. labor history" (Arnesen, 2007, pp. 1123–1126). Many formerly public functions also began to be privatized. Economic policy shifted away from the governmental spending and "pump priming" favored by acolytes of John Maynard Keynes towards the all-pervasive faith in the markets professed by Milton Friedman and economists of the Chicago School.

Reagan campaigned hard on one of the conservative articles of faith, famously pledging to "get government off the backs of the American people." One specific way he promised to do so was by eliminating the federal Department of Education, which had just been created by the Carter administration. After assuming the presidency, however, Reagan didn't attempt to dissolve the agency. Instead, he appointed Terrel Bell to lead it. In August 1981 Bell appointed David Gardner, president of the University of California, to chair an 18 member blue ribbon panel representing "the geographic, racial, and ethnic diversity of the country" to look into the state of American education (Bell, 1993, p. 593). Agreeing to serve were two other university presidents, "a Nobel Prize winner, a distinguished corporate executive, two local school board presidents (including the president of the National School Boards Association), and a variety of other prominent educators" (Bell, 1993, p. 593).

The report was released on April 26, 1983 during a ceremony held at the White House. President Reagan thanked the commissioners for a report that endorsed campaign trail staples like school prayer, vouchers, and the elimination of the federal Department of Education "when in fact it did none of these things" (Ansary, 2007, para. 13). As one commissioner, Gerald Holton, put it: "The one important reader of the report has apparently not read it at all" (Ansary, 2007, para. 13).

Small matter. The report turned out to be a bombshell nonetheless, gaining a level of media notoriety accorded to few federal reports before or since. Its emotional and highly wrought language clearly struck a chord with the media and the public. While there had been previous studies linking educational achievement with a healthy economy (U.S. Chamber of Commerce, 1982) none had the impact of *A Nation at Risk*, arguably the single most influential education policy document of all time.

Part of its appeal may perhaps be found in the sensational claims it made. The foundations of our society were being eroded by "a rising tide of mediocrity that threatens our very future as a Nation and a people" (National Commission on Excellence in Education, 1983, para. 2).

The damage being done to America's global economic competitiveness by this "rising tide of mediocrity" was one of the central recurring themes of the report. In fact, one of the first sentences of the report read: "Our Nation is at risk. Our once unchallenged preeminence in commerce, industry, science, and technological innovation is being overtaken by competitors throughout the world" (National Commission on Excellence in Education, 1983, para. 2).

Recognition of the rapidly changing nature of the international economy was implicit in statements of this sort, changes which have come to be known as globalization, neoliberalism, the Washington Rules/Washington consensus, Bretton Woods II, or any number of other labels one can give these developments. This new phase of global capitalism was made possible by advances in high technology (particularly computers and telecommunications), and characterized by the proliferation of transnational corporations, increasingly integrated international trade, direct foreign investment, the accelerating movement of capital across national borders, supply chains that stretched around the globe, and the proliferation of labor outsourced abroad.

Even though globalization was just starting to emerge when *A Nation at Risk* came out, the brief could already say with accuracy that "the world is indeed one global village," in which America retained only a "slim competitive edge" in the markets of an increasingly interdependent world economy (National Commission on Excellence in Education, 1983, para. 8). It was losing preeminence in such key manufacturing sectors as automobiles (to Japan), steel (to the South Korea), and machine tools (to Germany) (National Commission on Excellence in Education, 1983, para. 9). These powerful new competitors were "determined, well-educated, and strongly motivated" and well suited to take advantage of a "steady 15-year decline in industrial productivity, as one great American industry after another [fell] to world competition" (National Commission on Excellence in Education, 1983, para. 8, 40).

The report is clear on the central place of knowledge in this new phase of global capitalism. "Learning is the indispensable investment required for success in the information age we are entering...Education is one of the chief engines of a society's material well-being" (National Commission on Excellence in Education, 1983, para. 8, 39).

Much of the report's rhetorical power came from alarmist language linking educational achievement with global economic competitiveness. Another source was how it placed its call for education reform securely within the framework of national security. In an oft-quoted passage from the second paragraph, the report noted that

> If an unfriendly foreign power had attempted to impose on America the mediocre educational performance that exists today, we might well have viewed it as an act of war…

We have, in effect, been committing an act of unthinking, unilateral educational disarmament (National Commission on Excellence in Education, 1983, para. 2).

The report also offered prescriptive measures to address the issues it raised. In them, we can begin to see the elements that would later coalesce into standards-based education. In the findings section, this was even more explicit. There, the report strongly criticized secondary school coursework as "homogenized, diluted, and diffused to the point that they no longer have a central purpose," creating a "cafeteria style curriculum in which the appetizers and desserts can easily be mistaken for main courses" (National Commission on Excellence in Education, 1983, pp. 16–17). This could be considered as a nascent plea for what would later come to be known as content standards. In the same section, expectations are defined as "the level of knowledge, abilities, and skills school and college graduates should possess" which allow students to "demonstrate their mastery of subject matter" and "tell students which subjects are most important" (National Commission on Excellence in Education, 1983, p. 17). This could be seen as a nascent plea for what would later come to be known as performance standards. Indeed, the report mentioned the word "standards" on numerous occasions. "We should expect schools to have genuinely high standards rather than minimum ones" (National Commission on Excellence in Education, 1983, para. 26). Or, later in the report:

> In contrast to the ideal of the Learning Society, however, we find that for too many people education means doing the minimum work necessary for the moment, then coasting through life on what may have been learned in its first quarter. But this should not surprise us because we tend to express our educational standards and expectations largely in terms of "minimum requirements." And where there should be a coherent continuum of learning, we have none, but instead an often incoherent, outdated patchwork quilt (National Commission on Excellence in Education, 1983, para. 29).

Although the word "standards" is used here in the everyday sense as "high expectations," as the decade wore on, it gradually began to take on the technical sense familiar to educational professionals today.

Throughout the 1980s the majority of business involvement in education was limited to relatively small-scale, community-based, ad hoc initiatives like "adopt a school" and CEO "principal for a day" type arrangements. By that time, schools were also beginning to experiment with management techniques imported from business, such as performance-based contracting, zero based budgeting, management by objectives, program planning based budgeting, and total quality management. These techniques were all predicated on the establishment of standards or goals beforehand and evaluating performance based upon these, usually through the use of quantitative data. These are some of the salient characteristics that would soon become central to standards-based education.

More important than specific management techniques imported from business, or identification of elements of standards-based education in embryo in A Nation at Risk, was the role the report played as a clarion call. It reconceptualized education's purpose as one primarily of halting America's declining international economic competitiveness. It also changed the nature of the participation of business in schools. Instead of the one-off projects mentioned above or the adaptation of specific business management techniques, business began a concerted, conscious, often collective effort to frame the debate by issuing a flurry of reports centered around crisis rhetoric, emanating from an interwoven group of corporate leaders, academics, and think tank analysts (Barnhardt, 2000). These individuals were

> overwhelmingly white, male and very often exceedingly affluent and well connected. Many are directors and chairs of large multinational corporations—Ford, AT&T, Chase Manhattan, Mellon Bank, Digital Computers, to name a few. A number also sit on the boards of organizations like the Council for Economic Development, Council on Foreign Relations, Trilateral Commission, and the Conference Board (Slaughter, 1985, p. 218).

In a phrase: the power elite. Many early reports focusing on comparing and contrasting America's educational system with those of competitors abroad, typically found America wanting. An early warning from the National Science Board in 1983 came in the form of a report called *Educating Americans for the 21st Century* (National Science Board, 1983). Alarmed by declining enrollment in science and math classes and declining test scores in these subjects, the report urged that "by 1995, the Nation must provide, for all its youth, a level of mathematics, science and technology education that is the finest in the world, without sacrificing the American birthright of personal choice, equity and opportunity" (National Science Board, 1983, p. v).

Many other key reports from this period came from a select group of individuals who shuttled easily between government, academia, think tanks, foundations, and elsewhere; a bi-partisan issue from the start. In fact, top leadership at the Business Roundtable noted that they tended to do better on specific issues with Democratic administrations than Republican ones. This trend was accelerated with Al From's creation of the Democratic Leadership Council in 1985 and the rise of the New Democrats. Left and right were united by the ideology of human capital and global economic competitiveness.

After the National Commission on Excellence in Education issued its report, it solicited feedback in a number of different "National Forums on Excellence in Education" held across the country. Two important reports were entered into the public record at the National Forum on Excellence in Education in held in Indianapolis on December 6–8, 1983. One was that of Jim Campbell (1983), "chairman of the United States Chamber of Commerce's Education, Employment and Training Committee." Another was that of Paul Peterson (1983) for the Twentieth Century Fund's Task Force on Federal Elementary and Secondary Education Policy, *Making the Grade*.

The U.S. Chamber of Commerce's 1982 report *American Education: An Economic Issue* marked one of the first times the business community had come together in a collaborative effort concerning schools. The study said Japanese industry was more productive because their education system was better.

Campbell's talk on December 8, 1983 reiterated much of the previous report. It mentioned that the Chamber of Commerce had an active education policy committee since the 1960s and that its members had long been involved in educational matters in a variety of ways. He claimed the chamber's interest in education stemmed from the fact that the United States was "facing severe shortages of skilled workers" and "unprecedented international competition" (Campbell, 1983, pp. 3–4). In the same section where Campbell decried the coming skills shortage he also admitted that many new jobs will be "service-oriented" and won't "require traditional four-year college degrees but rather...the kind of education, training, and retraining available through the vocational and career education programs of the public school system" (Campbell, 1983, p. 3).

The Twentieth Century Fund "is an independent research foundation that undertakes economic, political, and social policy studies" (Brookings Institution, 2011, para. 9). Their Task Force on Federal Elementary and Secondary Education Policy included "prominent leaders in higher education and public school administration" (Presseisen, 1985, p. 44). Like many other reports of the period, *Making the Grade* claimed to be motivated by "an unusual sense of urgency" and urged the creation of an adequate pool of "skilled and capable individuals without whom we cannot sustain a complex and competitive economy" (Peterson, 1983, p. 3). Although the report didn't utilize the nomenclature of standards per se, it did urge the development of literacy in spoken and written English, as well as higher order skills like "reasoning, critical analysis" and facility with "complex ideas," all of which can be said to impose an implicit set of standards (Peterson, 1983, p. 11). *Making the Grade* saw an enhanced federal role to carry this out, one as important as "national leadership in health, agriculture, the physical sciences, and weaponry" (Peterson, 1983, p. 18).

Shortly after *A Nation at Risk* and the United States Chamber of Commerce and Twentieth Century Fund reports, the floodgates opened. Much of the literature that followed continued in the same vein, although dissenters arose early. For example, Albrecht noted that "the fascination of the public and the media with *A Nation at Risk* has created another problem: it has blunted and obscured the carefully researched, thoughtful, and imaginative reports of Ernest Boyer, John Goodlad, and Theodore Sizer" (1984, p. 684). Furthermore, "the nationalistic rhetoric of the report makes deliberate and thoughtful consideration of its recommendations seem somehow unpatriotic" (Albrecht, 1984, p. 684). It also urged a cautionary note regarding the incessant call to action present in *A Nation at Risk*.

> "History is not kind to idlers," the commissioners tell us. Yet it seems to me that a more accurate reading of history clearly suggests that history is not kind to the impetuous, the irresponsible, and the unthinking. But action is what we're getting, though much of it, particularly from political bodies, is unquestionably harmful (Albrecht, 1984, p. 684)

Aronowitz and Giroux published *Education Under Siege* in 1985. In their revised edition of 1993, they opined that

> In the current debate around the crisis of education and the role that federal policy should play in resolving it, U.S. society may be facing a dilemma that calls into question its very foundation as a democratic nation. There are hints of the magnitude of the crisis in the language of recent reports on public education and in the current assault on public education that has been waged by the Reagan/Bush administrations (Aronowitz and Giroux, 1993, p. 213).

In spite of these cautionary notes, the many reports issued from 1983 onward reiterated remarkably consistent themes. To some extent, this homogeneity was encouraged and cultivated by President Reagan. He called 1983–1984 the "National Year of Partnerships in Education" between "business, government agencies and communities" which would be coordinated, tellingly, by his "special assistant for private sector initiatives," not the Department of Education (McKenzie and Cromer, 1984, p. 133). Other early documents included those from the Business-Higher Education Forum, the Education Commission of the States' Task Force on Education for Economic Growth, and the College Board. More would follow throughout the decade.

The Business-Higher Education Forum was "a group representing corporate and university chief executives" (Rich and Devitis, 1992, pp. 60). At the behest of President Reagan (Slaughter, 1985, p. 219), they charged themselves in 1982 with exploring "ways in which our national competitive position could be further strengthened through increased innovation and productivity" (Anderson and Saxon, 1983, p. vii). The report they generated, *America's Competitive Challenge*, was funded in part by the Andrew W. Mellon and National Science Foundations (Slaughter, 1985, p. 219). It urged the formulation of a coordinated national strategy to improve education, ongoing technical innovation, the wise use of capital, and enhanced cooperation between business and the academy as the cornerstones of renewed American economic competitiveness (Passow, 1984, p. 679). Signatories to the report including such leading lights of business and academia as

> John F. Burlingame of General Electric, Philip Caldwell of Ford, Robert Anderson of Rockwell International, James E. Olson of AT&T...Derek Bok of Harvard, David Saxon of the University of California, Richard Cyert of Carnegie-Mellon, and Matina Horner of Radcliffe (Slaughter, 1985, p. 220).

As might be expected from an organization led by captains of industry, they adopted rhetoric comparable to the Powell memo. They demanded fealty to the economy above all other sectors of society, as well as ongoing perception management to cultivate this disposition among the general population.

> As a nation, we must develop a consensus that industrial competitiveness is crucial to our social and economic well being. Such a consensus will require a shift in public attitudes about national priorities, as well as changes in public perceptions about the nature of our economic malaise (Anderson and Saxon, 1983, p. 2).

They even went further than most reports of the period in their defense of the free enterprise system. They argued strongly against "protectionism, national economic planning, income redistribution and plant closing restrictions" as "counterproductive and un-American" (Slaughter, 1985, p. 221). Certainly, plant closings due to management decisions to outsource labor on the part of big business were precisely those actions that contributed to a withering of the

American manufacturing base. These corporate decisions gave the lie to the supposed imperative of these reports, that of fostering high skill jobs for the high tech economy.

The Education Commission of the States was an entity created by state governments to help them engage in educational policy advocacy at the national level. Their Task Force on Education for Economic Growth was composed of a "range of leaders: governors, legislators, corporate chief executives, state and local school board members, educators, leaders of labor, the scientific community, and many others" (Hunt, 1983a, p. 14). Under the leadership of North Carolina Governor James Hunt, the task force drafted *Action for Excellence*.

After an opening paean to America's supposed infatuation with "newness" and "progress," the report raised the usual specters of economic competition from abroad, particularly Japan and West Germany, who may soon "outstrip us in inventiveness and productivity," a development that "is suddenly troubling Americans" because of its ominous implications for "economic competition in a global arena" which "will be even more intense tomorrow" (Hunt, 1983b, pp. 14–15).

Hunt's task force urged the Education Commission of the States to help foster the creation of similar task forces at the state and local levels to conduct needs assessments, facilitate school improvement, and encourage "close partnerships between education, business, and government" (Rich and Devitis, 1992, pp. 60). "A real emergency is upon us; a conviction that we must act now, individually and together, and a passionate optimistic conviction that action, soon enough and in the right direction, can succeed" (Hunt, 1983b, p. 14).

Elsewhere, the rhetoric was similarly urgent: "There are few national efforts that can legitimately be called crucial to our national survival. Improving education in America—improving it sufficiently and improving it now—is such an effort" (Hunt, 1984, p. 11). Hunt underscored the imperative for concrete action: "We have had an abundance of research, a plentiful supply of analysis and an impressive piling up of reports. Public concern is rising. What we need now is action: action for excellence" (Hunt, 1984, p. 11).

Hunt's task force was funded "by 15 leading corporations and foundations, including Aetna Life & Casualty Insurance Foundation, AT&T, Control Data, Dow Chemical, Xerox, Texas Instruments, RCA, Ford Motor Company, and IBM" (Spring, 1998, p. 151). With such backing, it may not be surprising that the report urged business to take a more active role in "setting goals for education in America. If the business community gets more involved in both the design and delivery of education, we are going to become more competitive as an economy" (Hunt, 1983b, p. 18).

The College Board is a membership organization which then consisted "of more than 2,500 colleges, schools, school systems and educational organizations" and was "concerned about the vast number of high school graduates inadequately prepared for college" (College Board, 1983, p. 1). As a result of this concern, they drafted a report entitled *Academic Preparation for College: What Students Need to Know and Be Able to Do* which, among other things, "provided a framework for curricula that outlines, and provides justification for, the knowledge and skills students need to get the most out of college education" (College Board, 1983, p. 1). This type of terminology and these types of objectives foreshadowed standards-based education. It also referred to the need for balance between quality and equality, demonstrating a lingering attachment to the traditional value of equity so prevalent during the 1960s and 1970s, slowly being supplanted by a heightened emphasis on quality (College Board, 1983, p. 2).

The report also recommended "Basic Academic Competencies" in the "Basic Academic Subjects" of "English, Arts, Mathematics, Science, Social Studies, and Foreign Language" (College Board, 1983, p. 3). These competencies for the college-ready student were formatted as a list of approximately 5–10 skills. Objectives listed under "basic academic subjects" resemble what would later come to be known as "content" standards; what a student should know. For example, the mathematic recommendations were as follows.

The Basic Academic Subjects
Mathematics

- The ability to apply mathematical techniques in the solution of real-life problems and to recognize when to apply those techniques.
- Familiarity with the language, notation, and deductive nature of mathematics and the ability to express quantitative ideas with precision.
- The ability to use computers and calculators.
- Familiarity with the basic concepts of statistics and statistical reasoning.
- Knowledge in considerable depth and detail of algebra, geometry, and functions.
- More specifically, college entrants will need the following preparation in mathematics.

Similarly, the objectives listed under "Basic Academic Competencies" resemble what would later come to be known as "performance" standards; what demonstrates adequate mastery. Again, for mathematics, these are:
Basic Mathematics-Related Academic Competencies
Mathematics

- The ability to perform, with reasonable accuracy, the computations of addition, subtraction, multiplication, and division using natural numbers, fractions, decimals, and integers.
- The ability to make and use measurements in both traditional and metric units.
- The ability to use effectively the mathematics of: integers, fractions, and decimals; ratios, proportions, and percentages; roots and powers; algebra; geometry.
- The ability to make estimates and approximations, and to judge the reasonableness of a result.
- The ability to formulate and solve a problem in mathematical terms.
- The ability to select and use appropriate approaches and tools in solving problems (mental computation, trial and error, paper-and-pencil techniques, calculator, and computer).
- The ability to use elementary concepts of probability and statistics (College Board, 1983, pp. 3–4).

Other business groups released comparable reports in the years that followed, in which one can see the contours of standards-based education emerging. The Committee for Economic Development, that beacon of the Keynesian accommodation between big business, government, and organized labor in the postwar era, that entity that overshadowed the American Enterprise Association for decades, issued *Investing in Our Children: Business and the Public School* in 1985. It was the result of "an investment of hundreds of thousands of dollars" and two years of effort by "the nation's most prominent business leaders and university presidents" (Doyle and Levine, 1985, p. 114). These included

> Owen Butler, chairman of Procter & Gamble…Ralph Lazarus, head of Federated Department Stores; Ronald Davenport, head of Sheridan Broadcasting; James W. McKee, Jr., head of CPC International Corporation; and Donna Shalala, president of Hunter College. The presidents of Johns Hopkins University, Spelman College, the Florida State University System, and the New York University System all served on the subcommittee. Corporate involvement was no less distinguished; IBM, Lucky Stores,

CBS, ARA Services, 3M, Whitney Communications, Phillips Petroleum, Bankers Trust, and R. J. Reynolds were all represented (Doyle and Levine, 1985, p. 114).

Similarly, it was funded by

> the Ford Foundation, the Edna McConnell Clark Foundation, the Exxon Education Foundation, the Procter & Gamble Fund, Metropolitan Life, the William and Flora Hewlett Foundation, R. J. Reynolds Industries, Inc., the John M. Olin Foundation, Inc., the Atlantic Richfield Foundation, Northrop Corporation, the Pfizer Foundation, Inc., Standard Oil Company (Ohio), the Phillips Petroleum Foundation, Inc., and the Hospital Corporation of America (Doyle and Levine, 1985, p. 118).

The finished product was by and large the work of David Doyle (director of educational policy studies at the American Enterprise Institute) and Marsha Levine (a consultant there), who had "co-directed the Committee for Economic Development's study of business and the schools" for two years (Doyle and Levine, 1983, p. 113). The study was publicized by "widespread media reports and an aggressive dissemination program" that made it "known to most U.S. educators" (Doyle and Levine, 1983, p. 113). The report asserted that "economic productivity and the quality of education cannot be separated" (Doyle and Levine, 1983, p. 114). It also asserted that "education has a direct impact on employment, productivity, and growth, and on the nation's ability to compete in the world economy. Therefore, we cannot fail to respond" (Public Broadcasting Frontline, 2002, para. 4).

Four of the reports issued during the 1980s focused on teacher training, certification, and professionalization. Three of these were from Carnegie foundations: *A Nation Prepared: Teachers for the 21st Century* (Carnegie Forum on Education and the Economy, 1986), *A National Board for Teaching? In Search of a Bold Standard* (Shulman and Sykes, 1986), and *The Condition of Teaching: A State Analysis* (Carnegie Foundation for the Advancement of Teaching, 1988). The other major teacher training policy brief of the period was *Tomorrow's Teachers: A Report of the Holmes Group* (1986). Much of the findings of these four reports were predicated on notions similar to standards: creating hierarchical structures better able to utilize the technocratic tweaks of experts, even as they claimed to be flattening out hierarchies in the middle and lower levels of management (Popkewitz, 1991, p. 146). They largely promoted an ideology of guild craft modeled after law and medicine.

These reports were peppered with the same gloomy assessments that had become the norm. *A Nation Prepared* said that graduates couldn't do the "increasingly complex work required of them" (Carnegie Forum on Education and the Economy, 1986, p. 15). A *Nation Prepared* also reiterated a theme common to many of the reports of the 1980s, coping with the enhanced use of technology in the workplace.

> A heavily technology-based economy will be unable to invest vast sums to maintain people who cannot contribute to the nation's productivity. American businesses already spend billions of dollars a year retraining people who arrive at the workplace with inadequate education (Carnegie Forum on Education and the Economy, 1986, p. 20).

Throughout much of the 19th century, men were well represented in the teaching profession. With the rise of academic schools of education and the differentiation of school administration as an occupation distinct from teaching around the turn of the 20th century the teaching corps soon became primarily female. By the 1960s and 1970s, academically well-prepared women, the pool from which teachers had traditionally been drawn from for much of the 20th century, were beginning to enter more remunerative professions like business, law, and medicine in ever greater numbers. This left academically less prepared women to fill teaching positions, making teaching during much of the 1970s and 1980s what some have called "the profession of last resort." This made it vulnerable to calls for "professionalization," especially when these initiatives also had the support of both major teacher unions, the American Federation of Teachers and National Education Association.

The Carnegie Foundation for Education and the Economy even went so far as to establish a National Board for Professional Teaching Standards in 1988. It was composed of "63 members including teachers (the majority), school administrators, local board members, governors (past and present), teacher educators, children's advocates, and business leaders," with the foundation committed to funding it to the tune of $5 million over five years (National Governors' Association, 1988a, p. 1; National Governors' Association, 1988b). Standards were beginning to be applied to the teaching profession as well as to academic subjects. The National Board for Professional Teaching Standards continues to exist, offering a rigorous and well-respected national certification for excellence in teaching practice. Many states have programs that subsidize teachers' participation in this program. Hawai'i, a state whose experience with standards-based education will be examined closely as a case study in a later chapter, is one such state.

Most of the studies in the 1980s that revolved around reform of the teaching corps used the professions of law and medicine as their templates, especially around the concepts of guild certification and guild control. Many of these studies also urged greater autonomy for teachers, albeit to reach educational goals set by technocrats outside of and above the classroom. This is the essence of an industrial management technique that might be termed "control from a distance," a notion that would later become central to standards-based education, an "industrial metaphor" that "has several associated beliefs:"

> that people are lazy by nature and need specific direction, close management, and material incentives to work most efficiently; that teachers are just like other workers; that schools are just like any other plant or work place that need to be organized for maximum efficiency; that school administration should be hierarchical and patriarchic; that administrators should be separate from, and superior in authority to, teachers; and that the outcomes of school can be measured, and the measures could be used to compare schools and teachers. The achievement products could thus be related in straightforward ways to costs, and therefore to efficiency (Smith, Miller-Kahn, Heinecke, & Jarvis, 2004, p. 195).

Business associations and business-oriented think tanks closed out the decade with a large number of reports. These included the Hudson Institute's *Workforce 2000: Work and Workers for the Twenty-First Century* (1987), National Center on Education and the Economy's *America's Choice, High Skills or Low Wages* (1990), Educational Testing Service's *From School to Work, Policy Information Report* (Barton, 1990), National Alliance of Business' *A Blueprint for Business on Restructuring Education* (1989) and *Education: The Next Battleground for Corporate Survival, An Urgent Message from Twenty-One Harvard Business School Students* (1990), Business Roundtable's *The Role of Business in Education Reform: Blueprint for Action; Report of the Business Roundtable Ad Hoc Committee on Education* (1988), *Essential Components of a Successful Education System: The Business Roundtable Education Public Policy Agenda* (1989a), *Business Means Business About Education. A Synopsis of the Business Roundtable Companies' Education Partnerships* (1989b), and *The Business Role in State Education Reform* (Fosler, 1990) a National Alliance of Business-Business Roundtable collaboration, *The Business Roundtable Participation Guide* (1991), Heritage Foundation's *A Businessman's Guide to the Education Reform Debate* (1990), and Conference Board's *Business Leadership: The Third Wave of Education Reform* (1989) and *Corporate Support of National Education Goals, Report No. 978.* (Berenbeim, 1991).

Many of these reports can be characterized as "how to" manuals to help top corporate executives engage with the educational policy reform process, typically at the state and local levels, both logistically and in arming them with the appropriate rhetoric. Or, in the case of an entire special edition of *Fortune* dedicated to corporate involvement in education reform, mass media mythologizations of this engagement in process (Fortune, 1990; Morrison, 1990).

Although these reports covered a variety of topics, methods, and rhetoric, almost all mentioned curriculum reform at some point, an injunction that would soon morph into standards-based education. After the National Alliance of Business released their reports mentioned above, from then on they let the Business Roundtable take the lead as the main source of formal, collective business engagement in education reform during this crucial period when the contours of standards-based education began to emerge.

"In 1987, Hudson's landmark study *Workforce 2000* accurately forecasted the changes the American workforce would encounter with the new millennium" (*Hudson Institute*, 2010, para. 4) and became a significant influence on the many "school-to-work" and "workforce development" initiatives that soon began to proliferate at local, state, and federal levels in the years to come.

America's Choice, High Skills or Low Wages contained the usual doom-and-gloom rhetoric that had become commonplace. "America is headed toward an economic cliff" because so much of the economic growth in America during the 1970s and 1980s was generated by a larger percentage of American adults who were working, most notably the large amounts of women who had recently entered the workforce (National Center on Education and the Economy, 1990, p. 21). The authors of the report felt that this percentage had probably peaked. Therefore, future economic growth and global economic competitiveness would largely be dependent upon enhanced productivity. "The key to maintaining, to say nothing of improving, our standard of living is productivity—more products and services from every member of the workforce" (National Center on Education and the Economy, 1990, p. 14).

To generate this enhanced productivity, the report recommended improving what may be called the "worst school-to-work transition system of any advanced industrial country" by embracing "the third industrial revolution now taking place in the world," one based on "the advent of the computer, high speed communication and universal education," by creating a "national system capable of setting high academic standards" and assessment centered around the attainment of a "Certificate of Initial Mastery" by "age 16, or shortly thereafter" (National Center on Education and the Economy, 1990, pp. 14–15, 17–18). Attainment of this certificate would then track students towards college, work, or further technical or professional training (National Center on Education and the Economy, 1990, p. 18). Ideally, this new system would facilitate the creation of "high performance work organizations," supposedly a key feature of the third industrial revolution.

The Educational Testing Service's report *From School to Work, Policy Information Report* (Barton, 1990), like many released during this period under the auspices of big business, was less concerned with standards per se than with enhancing linkages between what was taught in schools and the job performance employers allegedly required from their employees. They also focused on prognostications regarding "shortages of skilled workers," diverging "quality of life, income, and life prospects," among various subgroups within America, and an increasingly "culturally diverse work force" (Atwater et al, 1991, p. 1). In suggesting what schools should teach, however, they foreshadowed language similar to what we would later find in content standards.

A Businessman's Guide to the Education Reform Debate was one of the Heritage Foundation "backgrounders" their media- and politically-savvy president Edwin Feulner was so fond of, policy briefs that passed what he called the "briefcase test," reports short and simple enough for a busy executive to be able to throw into his or her briefcase and read later (Rogalsky, 2007, para. 19). *A Businessman's Guide to the Education Reform Debate* phrased its arguments in the "no nonsense" rhetoric so beloved by corporate executives.

> American business understands well that the nation's public schools are like a money-losing industrial giant that cannot produce a product that satisfies its customers. Leaders of America's major companies understand too that the nation's schools must improve if the United States is to remain competitive in world markets (Allen and McLaughlin, 1990, p. 2).

The Conference Board "is a global, independent business membership and research association working in the public interest" (*About Us*, 2010, para. 1). Their report *Business Leadership: The Third Wave of Education* summarized the proceedings of their 1989 meeting, a conclave featuring "talks by 16 leaders in business and education" and focused on "(1) the effect of institutionalization of educational policy and corporate organization on involvement in educational reform; and (2) the effect of business leadership in selected cities on education coalitions" (Ashwell and Caropreso, 1989, p. 1).

In addition to sponsoring the creation of influential reports, the engagement of business with education prospered at the local level as well. This can be seen in a number of collaborative, comprehensive, multi-party school-to-work initiatives, with the Boston Compact (announced during September 1982) being perhaps the most prominent (Ferrar and Cippollone, 1988).

Business influence was also growing at the federal level as well. Prominent federal government reports on education were strongly wedded to human capital theory, global competitiveness ideology, and crisis rhetoric (United States Department of Education, 1986, 1987; United States Department of Labor, 1989). Particularly influential was the report of the Secretary of Labor's Commission on Achieving Necessary Skills, the so-called SCANS report (United States Department of Labor, 1991), which many of the states used as their initial template in developing the first iterations of actual standards beginning in the 1990s.

The Commission said they wrote "as concerned representatives of the nation's schools, businesses, unions, and government" (United States Department of Labor, 1991, p. i). The number of executives from top American corporations, however, was striking. The global competitiveness ideology is established front and center, in the preface, the "letter to parents, employers, and educators."

> For most of this century, as this nation took its goods and know-how to the world, America did not have to worry about competition from abroad...Today, the demands on business and workers are different. Firms must meet world class standards and so must workers (United States Department of Labor, 1991, p. i).

They also made some major assumptions about the nature of "a productive, full and satisfying life." Basically, in the judgment of the commission, this comes from salaried employment in a rapidly globalizing economy. "All American high school students must develop a new set of competencies and foundation skills if they are to enjoy a productive, full, and satisfying life" (United States Department of Labor, 1991, p. i). These "competencies and foundation skills" were what became so influential in subsequent years for the technical development of actual state standards documents, especially the focus on the "basic skills" of "reading, writing, arithmetic/mathematics, listening, and speaking," and in how closely they already aligned with traditional academic subject matters (United States Department of Labor, 1991, p. xi). This is not to imply a kind of classical Greek "seven arts" approach to learning, however. No. These and many other criteria were proposed to facilitate the adaptation of the student to the changing economy, a point the SCANS report was very consistent about. In fact, its general orientation was so closely oriented toward salaried work that its impact is as powerful in the history of the "school-to-work" model (arguably culminating in the School-to-Work Opportunities Act of 1994) as it is in the "standards-based education" model.

Numerous states used the SCANS report as a model document from which to develop their own state standards. Some states mentioned their debt to the SCANS report explicitly. Others may not have mentioned the report by name, but reiterated how they used the "basic skills" and other organizing concepts found in the SCANS report. A Heritage Foundation backgrounder on the report identified a number of the states that found the report helpful: Florida, Texas, Michigan, New Hampshire, New Jersey, and Alaska (Miller, 2001, para. 15–19).

Another example of business influence at the federal level was the privileged access to the White House's Task Force on Regulatory Relief enjoyed by the Business Roundtable. This task force was one of the first entities created by President Reagan upon taking office. It was chaired by Bush since its inception in 1981. In one 1987 communication, the roundtable sent Bush a report suggesting the "EPA back off on restrictions to the disposal of nuclear waste, OSHA cease asking for regulations compelling construction firms to notify workers of exposure to hazardous substances, and Congress repeal fuel economy standards for cars," all in the name of eliminating "major obstacles to international competitiveness" (Borman, Castanell, and Gallagher, 1994, p. 73).

At first glance these requests may not seem to apply to education. Upon further reflection, however, their focus on "competitiveness" dovetails with the most important theme resounding throughout all of the many educational policy reform reports issued during the Reagan-Bush years. They also exemplify how "the corporation is an externalizing machine, in the same way that a shark is a killing machine" (Achbar and Abbott, 2004). The legal roots of this imperative can be seen in the landmark Michigan Supreme Court case *Dodge v. Ford Motor Company* (1919):

> A business corporation is organized and carried on primarily for the profit of the stockholders. The powers of the directors are to be employed for that end. The discretion of directors is to be exercised in the choice of means to attain that end, and does not extend to a change in the end itself, to the reduction of profits, or to the nondistribution of profits among stockholders in order to devote them to other purposes (1919, p. 8).

By the 1980s this was a settled and central part of American corporate law. Any account of corporate involvement in education reform must be considered in this light, not merely as a means of externalizing their training costs, but as part of a larger agenda of externalizing as many different costs as possible.

In addition to work at the local and federal levels, the business community became proactive at the state level as well, most notably in Minnesota, California, and Hawai'i. In all of these states, efforts were led by the state incarnations of the Business Roundtable and a remarkably successful consulting firm, Berman Weiler Associates, which drafted all of the major reports in these states. A collaboration between "Roundtable CEOs" and "the reform movement" secured passage of a "major education bill, SB-813" in California in 1983 (Berman, 1988a, p. i). "Since then, student test scores have shown some improvement, standards have been raised, and morale in the schools appears to be stronger" (Berman, 1988a, p. i).

Building on these accomplishments, the California Business Roundtable rehired the same consulting firm they worked with on the legislative effort, Berman Weiler Associates (Berman, 1983). This time, the consultants were tasked with conducting a "gap analysis" of California educational needs, interviewing "a diverse array of stakeholder groups," visiting schools, and distilling this data into a 296-page report entitled *Restructuring California Education: A Design for Public Education in the Twenty-First Century*. It was intended to "stimulate discussion and serve as one basis for Californians to agree on an agenda for change" and included all of the requisite references to "shifts to the information age and global competition" in "the passage to the 21st century," which will be "challenging, a time of both opportunities and difficulties" and require significant adaptation by the K–12 public education system (Berman, 1988a, p. i). In one of their key findings, they recommended reforms that contained salient aspects of standards-based education.

> Rather than prescribing the educational process, the state should set performance goals for the system, measure how well schools are meeting those goals, [and] institute ways to hold schools accountable for performance (Berman, 1988a, p. ix).

In 1989 President Bush, who had campaigned wanting to be the "education president," challenged the Business Roundtable to develop a coherent agenda for public education. Accepting this charge, the roundtable devoted their entire 1989 annual meeting to the topic. Building on the California and Minnesota reports from Berman Weiler Associates (sponsored by the California and Minnesota Business Roundtables), the national organization developed the first iteration of what would come to be known in many of their subsequent reports as the "essential components of a successful education system" (Business Roundtable, 1989a; Emery and Ohanian, 2004, pp. 141, 148).

They centered around outcome-based accountability systems, a hallmark of standards-based education. They also codified the national Business Roundtable's approach of urging state branches to use local contractors to study education reform and develop proposals for state government. This was later distilled into a pamphlet entitled *The Role of Business in Education Reform: Blueprint for Action* (Business Roundtable, 1988). At the 1989 meeting of the Business Roundtable, they agreed to a sustained, ten-year engagement with education reform (Emery and Ohanian, 2004, p. 35).

In their accommodation with America's long tradition of local control of education, the Business Roundtable made common cause with a powerful ally: the National Governors Association. Like the Business Roundtable, the National Governors Association had recently held an annual meeting dedicated exclusively to education, in 1986 at Hilton Head, South Carolina. There, they arrived at positions that foreshadowed the Business Roundtable's essential components of a successful education system (Borman, Castanell, and Gallagher, 1994, p. 73).

South Carolina Governor Richard Riley played a central role in the deliberations of the National Governors Association (Riley, 1986). Later, as chairman of the "Commission for Educational Quality of the Southern Regional Education Board" he worked "to develop a set of 12 education goals" that predated the national education goals announced at the Charlottesville summit "by several months" (Lewis, 1993, p. 428). The National Governors Association also appointed Governors Bill Clinton and Carroll Campbell of Arkansas and South Carolina to co-chair a committee on education goals at this time.

The Business Roundtable and the National Governors Association also shared something else in common: ready access to President George H. W. Bush, who charged both to develop a coherent educational policy. The efforts of both organizations came to fruition with the famous Charlottesville summit. Perhaps sensing an opportune political climate, leading business organizations like

> the Business Roundtable, the U.S. Chamber of Commerce, and the National Association of Manufacturers, established the Business Coalition for Education Reform to lobby for national achievement standards, improvements in the teaching profession, fairness in educational funding and other reforms (Borman, Castanell, and Gallagher, 1994, p. 78).

In addition to this partnership, the Business Roundtable also continued along their efforts, which proved to be more enduring and influential than those of the Business Coalition for Education Reform.

President Bush asked the National Governors Association to join him for an education summit at the University of Virginia in Charlottesville on September 27–28, 1989. The federal role in education, usually relatively minor owing to a centuries-long tradition of local control, had been growing since the National Defense Education Act of 1958 and the other federal laws that followed. With the summit, the federal role was poised to grow much larger.

The summit was the first meeting called by a president with the governors for any purpose and was decidedly bipartisan. The National Governors Association's education task force co-chairs came from both major parties, as did the summit's working group, co-chaired by Republican and Democratic governors. The Democrats in Congress, however, were reluctant to cede their traditional leadership on the issue to the Republicans, the executive branch, and the governors. Their leadership may have also been miffed at being excluded from the summit. Days before the Charlottesville summit, Senate majority leader George Mitchell (D-ME) and House majority leader Richard Gephardt (D-MO) announced their own set of national education goals (Miller, 1989, para. 4). Among the proposed goals was

> improving the performance of American students in mathematics, science, and foreign languages until it exceeds that of students from other industrialized nations, a clear commitment to subject matters usually considered crucial to global economic competitiveness (Miller, 1989, para. 15).

They also called for a broad-based conference to follow up on the work of the summit. Even for the Democratic Congressional leadership, business leaders would be among the key stakeholders at the conference (Miller, 1989, para. 11). By the end of the event, President George H. W. Bush and the nation's governors had agreed to set six national educational goals and create a bipartisan body to monitor progress in attaining them, the National Educational Goals Panel. "Astonishingly, no teachers, professional educators, cognitive scientists, or learning experts" were invited to help develop them (Ansary, 2007, para. 27).

As chair of the Education Commission of the States, co-chair of the National Governors Association education committee, and as governor in his own state of Arkansas, Bill Clinton played a leading role in the development of these policies (Ravitch, 2000, p. 432).

President George H. W. Bush and the governors issued a joint statement, *A Jeffersonian Compact*, on September 28, 1989. It called for national educational goals as a prerequisite for continued international economic competitiveness (Bush and the National Governors Association, 1989). Jefferson was such an avowed proponent of decentralized political power that he wondered:

> what country can preserve its liberties, if its rulers are not warned from time to time, that this people preserve the spirit of resistance? Let them take arms. The remedy is to set them right as to the facts, pardon and pacify them. What signify a few lives lost in a century or two? The tree of liberty must be refreshed from time to time, with the blood of patriots and tyrants. It is its natural manure (Jefferson, 1787, pp. 268–269).

Judging by such sentiments, he might not have appreciated an attempt to increase federal power in his name. *A Jeffersonian Compact* stated that

> The President and the nation's Governors agree that a better educated citizenry is the key to the continued growth and prosperity of the United States...And as a Nation we must have an educated workforce, second to none, in order to succeed in an increasingly competitive world economy...We believe that the time has come, for the first time in U.S. history, to establish clear, national goals, goals that will make us internationally competitive (Bush and National Governors Association, 1989, para. 2–3).

"Successful restructuring efforts" would require "active, sustained parental, business, and community involvement" (Bush and National Governors Association, 1989, para. 27). The document also repeatedly mentioned the need for "accountability" as well. A few months later, President Bush announced these goals during his 1990 State of the Union address.

> By the year 2000, every child must start ready to learn. The United States must increase the high school graduation rate to no less than 90 percent. And we are going to make sure our schools' diplomas mean something. In critical subjects, at fourth, eighth, and 12th grades, we must assess our students' performance. By the year 2000, U.S. students must be the first in the world in math and science achievement. Every adult must be a skilled, literate worker, and citizen. Every school must offer the kind of disciplined environment that makes it possible for our kids to learn. And every school in America must be drug free (Bush, 1990, para. 23–28).

The Conference Board, "an organization formed in 1916 to improve the business enterprise system and to enhance the contribution of business to society," surveyed 1,600 American businesses regarding their attitudes towards education reform, particularly their opinion of the six educational goals promulgated by the National Governors Association in 1990 (Walker, 1990) and what kind of commitments they might be willing to make to see them through (Borman, Castanell, and Gallagher, 1994, p. 79). The 176 respondents were strongly in favor of workforce skills development and global economic competitiveness, with the latter being more important to larger firms with more than 50,000 employees (Borman, Castanell, and Gallagher, 1994, p. 79).

A Nation at Risk referenced many of the social benefits routinely ascribed to American education. It allows people to "participate fully in our national life," which is "essential to a free, democratic society," and fosters "a common culture" (National Commission on Excellence in Education, 1983, para. 9). In fact, the authors say that the concern of the commission "goes well beyond matters such as industry and commerce. It also includes the intellectual, moral, and spiritual strengths of our people" (National Commission on Excellence in Education, 1983, para. 9). To address these concerns requires finding the right balance between "the twin goals of equity and high quality schooling" (National Commission on Excellence in Education, 1983, para. 26).

In spite of these allusions, a content analysis of the main body of the report (excluding the introduction, findings, and recommendations) can help the reader infer which goals the commission valued the most. For example, variations on the word "competition" (in the economic sense) are repeated five times. Comparably, "excellence" (not counting its usage in the proper name of the commission) is mentioned nine times. "Equity" and "equitable" are only mentioned one time each.

In the long-standing values debate between equity and quality, *A Nation at Risk* comes down firmly on the side of quality. It further alleges that "quality" education (mentioned three times) has been undermined by the

> often conflicting demands we have placed on our Nation's schools and colleges. They are routinely called upon to provide solutions to personal, social, and political problems that the home and other institutions either will not or cannot resolve (National Commission on Excellence in Education, 1983, p. 8).

Considering the provenance of the report, with a conservative Republican administration that campaigned heavily on a limited role for the federal government, such a statement suggests the commissioners might be using the pursuit of "quality" as a means of dissolving the civil rights and social justice agenda that had become an embedded component of the "equity" and "equality" arguments. These assumptions had largely defined the debate since the 1954 Supreme Court decision of *Brown v. Board of Education of Topeka*.

The high public profile of the report and its preponderance of references to competition, excellence, and quality provided a lever that business was ready, willing, and able to take hold of to use to shift the policy debate towards their interests, defining quality in terms advantageous to their fiscal bottom lines. The central purpose of this shift was allegedly to maintain America's global economic competitiveness in a rapidly changing world economy, an imperative which dominated the many reports that followed. Nevertheless, macro-structural economic changes solidified under the Reagan-Bush regime belie this claim and suggest other motivations might have been at work.

For example, much of the talk of global economic competitiveness centered around calls to renew America's global industrial competitiveness specifically. To be sure, throughout much of the post-war era, it had been possible for a single wage-earner in the manufacturing sector (often without a college degree) to provide his or her family with a middle-class lifestyle. On the other hand, manufacturing as a percentage of GDP peaked shortly after World War II and the service sector had come to dominate the economy since then.

Another key component of global economic competitiveness ideology involved workforce development for the "high skill, high wage" jobs of the "new economy" in the information age. Examined empirically, these jobs were never abundant and certainly never enough to base a national economy the size of America's on. The few such jobs that existed were decidedly scarcer after the technology bubble, which began in 1995 and crashed in 2000. Furthermore, many of these jobs were outsourced abroad (particularly to India) soon after they were created.

Throughout the Reagan-Bush years, the major national business organizations, the governors, and the executive branch collaborated on a reform agenda that was starting to resemble standards-based education as we know it today. The key agenda setters concurred: big business should set the agenda and frame the debate, according to their needs and based on the crisis rhetoric found in a decade of reports they themselves largely commissioned.

These reports often played upon middle class fears, ambitions, and norms: competition, individualism, acquisition, and "standards of living." In return for honoring these types of goals, the children of the middle class were told they would be among those selected for greater rewards in the vast sort and select mechanism that is American K–12 education (Spring, 1988). The travails of those unable or unwilling to subscribe to these standards was not considered, as this might question the legitimacy of the economic and educational systems (Slaughter, 1985, p. 222). This was to be avoided at all costs.

This chapter assessed the impact of *A Nation at Risk* and other influential reports issued during the 1980s and early 1990s by national business organizations such the U.S. Chamber of Commerce, National Association of Manufacturers, Business Roundtable, and others. It also looked into how the rhetoric and actions of key governors and dynamic members of the national corporate elite helped pave the way for standards-based education to emerge as one of the leading K–12 education reform ideas in America.

· 4 ·

FEDERAL EDUCATION POLICY CONFLICTS OVER STANDARDS-BASED EDUCATION DURING THE BUSH AND CLINTON YEARS (1988–2000)

How did standards-based education as we recognize it today come to be such an accepted and integral part of federal education policy, and what obstacles had to be overcome for this to occur? In this chapter, I will look at the role specific corporate leaders, governors, teacher union leaders, and others played in shepherding bills like *America 2000* (Bush, 1990, 1991; Chira, 1992; Kolb, 1998; Miller, 1991a,b,c,d; Miller, 1992a, b, c, d; National Council on Education Standards and Testing, 1993; Stedman, 1991; Stedman and Riddle, 1992; Tirozzi, 1991; United States Congress, 1991a; United States Department of Education 1991; Winfield and Woodward, 1992) and *Goals 2000* (A Goals 2000; Berlak, 1995; Clinton, 1993; Purpel, 1995; United States Congress, 1994a,b; United States Department of Education, 2005) through the legislative process, as well as the social and political contexts of this effort (Diegenmueller, 1995; Firestone, 1997; Jennings, 1998; Kosar, 2005; Resnick and Nolan, 1995; Standards: Struggling, 1995; Starr, 1998; Stoskopf, 2000; Thompson, 1999; Vinovskis, 1999a, b). In this chapter, I will also examine the "standards wars." These controversies erupted after the initial promulgation of voluntary model national standards, especially in history (Cheney, 1994; Johnson and Diegenmueller, 1995; Morrison, 1996), language arts (International Reading Association, 1999; National Committee for Teaching English and International Reading Association, 1996), and mathematics. Paradoxically, at its moment of seeming triumph, the model was also at its most vulnerable, under heavy threat from parents, rank and file teachers, conservatives, and the religious right. Finally, I will investigate how proponents weathered this resistance so that by the time Clinton secured reauthorization of the Elementary and Secondary Education Act in 1996 (the *Improving America's Schools Act*), standards had become an integral part of federal educational policy, with significant practical ramifications at the state and local levels.

The overall education reform policy talk of this period was often highly partisan. The "right" (Bennett, 1994; Doyle, 1991, 1993; Finn, 1993; Hirsch, 1996; Ravitch, 1995a, b) was wedded to this crisis rhetoric (Barnhardt, 2000; Wilson, 2005) in American education. Their design specifications for improvement were typically based on the assumptions of the bipartisan human capital literature of the period (Dertouzos, 1990; Lafer, 2002; Marshall and Tucker, 1992; Reich, 1991; Thurow, 1992). Some on the so-called left might not embrace such partisan labels. They might instead assert they are merely correcting the misleading use of data by the "right." The "left" camp argued that the crisis was largely manufactured. They also yearned for education to get back to its progressive roots by serving a diverse set of intellectual, affective, and social goals (Dewey, 1966; Berliner and Biddle, 1996; Bracey, 2000, 2004, 2007a, b; Schrag, 1997). As an example of the tension between these two camps, the "right" even referred to the "left" as "revisionists" (Stedman, 1994).

The case of the 1991 Sandia report, which saw no major crisis in American education, in many ways exemplifies this "left revisionist" perspective (Ansary, 2007; Bracey, 2007a, b; Huelskamp, 1993a, b; Miller, 1991e, 1992e; Project Censored, 1994; Ravitch, 2007; Schneider and Houston, 1993; United States Congress, 1991b). I will discuss this intriguing counterfactual at greater length later in the chapter.

The numerous national education summits led by specific corporate leaders (IBM's Louis Gerstner in particular) often brought together the president and governors again. It has its own literature as well, often highlighting the efforts of particular top corporate executives (Archer and Walsh, 1996; Business Roundtable, 1992a, b, 1993, 1995, 1996, 1998, 1999, 2000a, b, c, 2001; Gerstner, 1994; Gerstner, Semerad and Doyle, 1995; Hammonds, 1999; Hill and Warner, 1994; Jossey-Bass, 2001; Mickelson, 1999, 2000; Otterbourg, 1997; Public Broadcasting Service Frontline; Text of policy statement, 1996).

Collectively, these efforts were instrumental in getting the wobbly reform model back on a firm footing.

When the National Governors Association convened on February 25, 1990 shortly after Bush's State of Union address, they adopted a modified version of the six national education goals mentioned in his speech. They also called for 21 additional new objectives. Many of these dealt with the resources needed to achieve the original six goals, what were often called "opportunity-to-learn" standards. The modified version, later codified in law by *Goals 2000* stated that

1. All children in America will start school ready to learn.
2. The high school graduation rate will increase to at least 90 percent.
3. American students will leave grades four, eight, and twelve having demonstrated competency in challenging subject matter, including English, mathematics, science, history, and geography; and every school in America will ensure that all students learn to use their minds well, so they may be prepared for responsible citizenship, further learning, and productive employment in our modern economy.
4. U.S. students will be the first in the world in science and mathematics achievement.
5. Every adult American will be literate and will possess knowledge and skills necessary to compete in a global economy and exercise the rights and responsibilities of citizenship.
6. Every school in America will be free of drugs and violence and will offer a disciplined environment conducive to learning (Harnischfeger, 1995, p. 107).

In July 1990 the President and the National Governors Association established the National Education Goals Panel to create annual report cards on progress made towards the achievement of these goals, chaired by Governor Roy Romer of Colorado (National Education Goals Panel, 1993, 1996, 1997, 1998, 1999a, 1999b, 1999c). When speaking to the panel in 1991, President Bush said. "There are only a few moments in our lives when we are called upon to join a crusade, and I honestly believe this is one of them. We have a crisis in American education, and we've simply got to do something about it" (Bush, 1991, para. 4). Although national standards and assessments had not yet been established, they were anticipated by grades 4, 8, and 12 assessments of "critical subjects" President Bush called for and endorsed by the National

Governors Association, particularly goal three with its call for "demonstrated competency" in "challenging subject matter, including English, mathematics, science, history and geography" (Bush, 1990. Para. 23–28; Harnischfeger, 1995, p. 107).

The work done at the Charlottesville education summit of 1989 and the National Governors Association meeting of 1990 laid the groundwork for an ambitious education improvement plan drafted by Bush's secretary of education Lamar Alexander and the deputy secretary of education and former CEO of Xerox, David Kearns. The prominent right-wing education reform advocate, Chester Finn Jr., was also involved (Miller, 1991b, para. 3; Kolb, 1998, p. 142; Finn, 1993, pp. 247–256, 263–266). This legislation was announced by President Bush on April 18, 1991 (United States Department of Education, 1991, p. 49). Called *America 2000*, it consisted of four main components:

[1] reform of existing schools through such initiatives as expanded school choice, voluntary national examinations, report cards on educational performance at all levels, and development of new standards for student performance;
[2] development with business sector support of New American Schools, which would be model schools created without concern for the current constraints that affect the structure and content of schooling;
[3] establishment of skill standards for the workforce and administration of diagnostic assessments to enhance workers' current skills; and
[4] designation of at least 535 communities as America 2000 Communities, selected because they embrace the education strategy and commit themselves to supporting a New American School (Stedman, 1991, p. 4).

America 2000 called for the president and governors, in conjunction with the National Education Goals Panel, to set "New World Standards to be achieved in five core subject areas," and assess, report on, and incentivize progress towards these standards (Stedman, 1991, pp. 7, 14). Under this plan, standards would be voluntary and drawn up by some entity other than the federal government. States and school districts could then utilize them as model documents to craft their own. Although it was unclear as to who would draft the initial standards, in announcing the new initiative President Bush suggested the governors would have a prominent role (United States Department of Education, 1991, p. 51).

Implementation of this ambitious plan—which President Bush called "a revolution more than a program"—quickly ran into political trouble. The right was more interested in school choice, and the left was still frustrated by conservative Republican moves that killed their preferred education reform bill in October 1990, the *Equity and Excellence in Education Implementation Act* (Kosar, 2005, p. 94). After *America 2000* was announced, Democrats offered a new education bill, *S 2*, which incorporated many of the elements of the previous *Equity and Excellence in Education Implementation Act*. What *America 2000* and *S 2* shared was a codification of the six national education goals. *S 2* and its counterpart in the House of Representatives, *HR 3320* both failed to include education standards or incorporate much of *America 2000*. House hearings repeated the mainstream Democratic position that educational achievement was primarily a matter of the socio-economic status of students' families and the amount of resources available to schools, the long shadow of the Coleman Report being cast still (1966). This reiterated the old tension between equity and excellence that dominated much of the reform debate in the 1980s. For the Democrats, enhancing student achievement was primarily a matter of getting more money to schools.

Sensing an unfavorable political climate in Congress, the Bush administration tried to implement *America 2000* without legislation. They worked closely with the business community, who were asked to invest $200 million in a "New American Schools Development Corporation." This attempt to circumvent Congress set up a turf battle between Congress and the executive branch. House Education and Labor committee members testified to an appropriations committee that congressional approval would be needed to enact *America 2000* (Miller, 1991a, para. 1). Several months later, Congress put language in an education bill prohibiting the administration from using any funding to enact *America 2000's* proposals. As Secretary Alexander contended, "To be blunt about it, some members of Congress are afraid of a national exam" (Miller, 1991c, para. 11). The struggle for power continued in a different form with dueling proposals for the creation of a national education advisory group. Secretary Alexander had been attempting to establish such a group under the auspices of the National Education Goals Panel, one that would focus on national standards and assessments. House Democrats responded with legislation that would create a similar entity, albeit one with a higher proportion of Democratic representation and considerably less sympathetic to standards and testing.

The two branches of government were able to come to an understanding. On June 27, 1991, the Education Council Act was passed, creating the National Council on Education Standards and Testing, although Congressional Democrats remained suspicious of the very concept of standards. The act asked the council to examine "the desirability and feasibility of establishing national standards and testing in education," with a report due on December 31, 1991 (United States Congress, 1991a, pp. 2–3).

This compromise did not resolve the partisan debate. House hearings continued to document Democratic distaste for the substance of *America 2000*, in spite of support for the initiative from traditional Democratic allies like teacher unions heads Albert Shanker of the American Federation of Teachers and Keith Geiger of the National Education Association.

Since *A Nation at Risk* was released in 1983, there had been a clamor from government and business creating a sense of crisis in keeping with the crisis-response-solution dialectic. This succeeded in motivating a number of school reforms. Many states set up commissions similar to the National Commission on Excellence in Education, often with a strong business influence, such as the one set up in Texas in 1984 led by Ross Perot. Numerous governors made education a top gubernatorial priority, such as Bill Clinton of Arkansas, Lamar Alexander of Tennessee, Richard Riley of South Carolina, and Roy Rohmer of Colorado. Several state judiciaries penned rulings calling for more equitable local funding (notably Texas, New Jersey, and Kentucky). Site-based decision-making became fashionable as well, in Hawai'i among other places (Bell, 1993, pp. 593, 595).

The crisis rhetoric sold well politically to be sure. Reagan Education Secretary Terrel Bell said it helped Reagan steal "the election issue from Walter Mondale" during the 1984 campaign "and it cost us nothing" (Ansary, 2007, para. 16). Ironically, Reagan, who campaigned on abolishing the Department of Education, wound up fostering a dramatically enhanced federal interest in education. This is a big part of what enabled George H. W. Bush to campaign as wanting to be the "education president."

Part of the political appeal was that fostering a sense of crisis had repercussions beyond education. Hammering on this theme, Bush Sr. and prominent Reagan era conservatives like Bill Bennett, Chester Finn, and Lamar Alexander aided by

> business leaders like IBM chairman Lou Gerstner…gradually managed to convert not only the issue of economic equity but a whole range of liberally oriented children's

issues—healthcare, welfare, nutrition, preschools, daycare, decent housing, recreational opportunities, inner-city youth and job programs—into a debate focused almost exclusively on tougher education standards and an emphasis on outcomes over resources (Schrag, 2000a, para. 5).

With Bush displaying a lackluster record in education when the election year of 1992 rolled around, having failed to pass *America 2000*, it allowed Clinton to campaign as a potentially more effective education president (Bell, 1993, p. 595).

To demonstrate how this crisis rhetoric was decisive in the consolidation of standards-based education, I would like to make a brief aside to focus on a little known report from the Sandia Laboratory in New Mexico. This is a compelling drama that even made Project Censored's number 3 slot in 1994 in their annual review of the top 25 items of "news that didn't make the news" in 1994 (Project Censored, 1994). Bush's Secretary of Energy, Admiral James Watkins, urged the federal scientific research laboratories "to become more involved in education" (Huelskamp, 1993a, p. 718). Long concerned with science, technology, engineering, and mathematics education, researchers at the Sandia laboratory took up Admiral Watkins' challenge after the 1989 Charlottesville summit and attempted "to provide an objective, outsider's look at U.S. education" (Huelskamp, 1993b, p. 4).

"The New Initiatives Department of Sandia's Strategic Studies Center [was] asked to conduct a wide-ranging analysis of local, state, and national education systems to determine where Sandia could make its most effective contribution" (Huelskamp, 1993a, p. 719). To their "surprise, on nearly every measure, [they] found steady or slightly improving trends," albeit with important caveats.

> First, it is not clear that all measures analyzed are appropriate barometers of performance for the education system; some may be irrelevant. Second, even if a measure is appropriate, steady or slightly improving performance may not be adequate to meet future societal requirements. Finally, on some appropriate measures, performance of the U.S. education system is clearly deficient (Huelskamp, 1993a, p. 719).

Their main findings were as follows: high school graduation rates had "remained steady for 20 years, hovering somewhere between 75% and 80%" (Huelskamp, 1993a, p. 719). When dropouts reentering the system and completing high school were accounted for, the rate for young adults rose to "85%," a rate "still improving and among the world's best," although minority and urban youth non-completion rates remained high (Huelskamp, 1993a,

p. 719). National Assessment of Educational Progress scores held steady or even improved. While average Scholastic Aptitude Test scores had "dropped since the 1960s," this was due a massive influx of minority test takers, not "decreasing student performance" (Huelskamp, 1993a, p. 719). Still, "nearly 60% of today's young people pursue postsecondary studies at accredited institutions" and 25% of young people persist to a bachelor's degree, the highest rate in the world (Huelskamp, 1993a, p. 719). Per pupil K–12 education spending had risen by 30% over the last 15 years, although here "special education and fixed costs such as insurance and retirement funds" were the primary drivers (Huelskamp, 1993a, p. 719). Per pupil spending rates were "about average" compared to the rest of the world (Huelskamp, 1993a, p. 719). The number of students earning natural science and engineering bachelors had reached approximately 200,000 per year, up drastically from 20 years ago and holding at approximately 4–5% of all bachelors earned. Foreign-born students were earning a substantial percentage of technical doctorates to be sure (50% in engineering and 25% in science) (Huelskamp, 1993a, p. 719). A little over half of them chose to remain in America. They "found little credible data" that supported negative international comparisons in student performance and degree attainment (Huelskamp, 1993a, p. 719). The United States led the world in the number of technical and non-technical degrees attained by women and minorities. "The overall technical degree attainment by the workforce is unparalleled in the world" (Huelskamp, 1993a, pp. 719–720).

- Between 1975 and 1988, average SAT scores went up or held steady for every student subgroup.
- Between 1977 and 1988, math proficiency among seventeen-year-olds improved slightly for whites, notably for minorities.
- Between 1971 and 1988, reading skills among all student subgroups held steady or improved.
- Between 1977 and 1988, in science, the number of seventeen-year-olds at or above basic competency levels stayed the same or improved slightly.
- Between 1970 and 1988, the number of twenty-two-year-old Americans with bachelor degrees increased every year; the United States led all developed nations in 1988 (Ansary, 2007, para. 47).

The Sandia report also contradicted the alleged "skills gap," a major component in the general theme of declining international competitiveness.

> Of late, much debate in education has focused on the system's inability to produce students with adequate "skills" for the work force. According to many, this deficiency is a primary cause for a decline in U.S. international economic competitiveness. However, our review of the limited research on the education and training practices of business found that very few companies offer training that is intended to compensate for inadequate academic preparation of new employees. Rather, the training focuses on such social "skills" as punctuality and personal appearance (Huelskamp, 1993a, p. 720).

As damning as these empirical findings were to the elite perception management program of the national business community and the national bipartisan political consensus that took its cues from them, even more so were the straightforward conclusions the researchers drew. Implementation of a wide variety of initiatives

> without proper coordination or a clear understanding of desired outcomes could result in little or no gain. American society has not clearly articulated the changes required to meet its future goals. In fact, we assert that forming a consensus on required changes may be the greatest challenge facing education today. However, national consensus is itself debatable. The U.S. education system was built on a combination of local control, state influence, and federal interest. The existence of over 15,000 independent school districts nationwide attests to this (Huelskamp, 1993a, p. 720).

The *Education Week* account drew a similar conclusion from the report. "Unfortunately, much of the current reform agenda, though well intentioned, is misguided...Based on a 'crisis' mentality, many proposed reforms do not properly focus on actual problems" (Miller, 1991e, para. 3).

This was not what the Bush administration wanted to hear, especially in the midst of a contentious battle with Congress over the passage of *America 2000* and under strong pressure from the far right to pass some sort of national school voucher program. What happened next is open to debate and makes a fascinating case study of what can happen when so-called expertise-driven, pure, unbiased, and empirical research meets the politicized realm of actual policy-making.

The lead researcher of the Sandia report claimed that they put their preliminary findings out to peer review in early 1991 with "the U.S. Department of Education, the National Science Foundation, and other researchers (most notably Gerald Bracey)" (Huelskamp, 1993a, p. 719). Within weeks, they found themselves "swept up in the national debate on the status of education" (Huelskamp, 1993a, p. 719). Congressional Democrats knew the draft report was circulating on Capital Hill. Rumors of its suppression were rampant. The Democrats arranged for Huelskamp to testify before the Subcommittee on Elementary, Secondary, and Vocational Education of the Committee on Education and Labor of the House of Representatives on July 18, 1991 (Huelskamp, 1993a, p. 718). "We knew it was only a matter of time before their chain was jerked," one Democratic committee aide said, "so we wanted to get them on record while we could" (Miller, 1991e, para. 26).

Diane Ravitch, then a key member of the conservative educational establishment and a long time proponent of standards-based education, had been appointed Assistant Secretary of Research for the U.S. Department of Education about six weeks before she first heard of the report. In spite of the dissatisfaction with it, the Department of Energy submitted it to the Department of Education. While she claims she had "no role in the evaluation," her department's "top professional research staff" found "the use of the data inadequate and unprofessional" (Ravitch, 2007, para. 5). After it became clear the Department of Energy had no intention of publishing the report, its authors spoke to a senator from their state of New Mexico, Republican Pete Dominici.

Dominici called for a meeting on September 24, 1991 (Miller, 1991e, para. 27) "and invited half a dozen other senior Republican senators" (Ravitch, 2007, para. 6). Ravitch attended with "Deputy Secretary David Kearns, the former CEO of the Xerox Corporation, [who] had joined the U.S. Department of Education a few months earlier" (Ravitch, 2007, para. 6). Peggy Dufour, "the chief education adviser to Secretary of Energy James T. Watkins" was also in attendance (Miller, 1991e, para. 6, 27).

In a 2007 back-and-forth in the *Huffington Post*, Bracey and Ravitch offered dueling accounts of what transpired at that meeting. Bracey said Kearns told Huelskamp "You bury this or I'll bury you" (Bracey, 2007a, para. 5). Ravitch denied it, saying Kearns was "probably the most civil person I have ever met" who never threatened anyone (Ravitch, 2007, para. 10). *Education Week* said "administration officials, particularly Mr. Kearns, reacted angrily at the meeting" (Miller, 1991e, para. 28).

On September 24, 1991, the *Albuquerque Journal* became the first daily newspaper organ to break the story in journalism. In a September 31 op-ed piece, Secretary of Energy Watkins excoriated the report (Miller, 1992d, para. 34). As more media attention was directed towards the saga, Ravitch took an increasingly active role in the media denouncing the report (Miller, 1992d, para. 35).

Peggy Dufour was outspoken in her criticism as well. She told *Education Week* in October 1991 that professional governmental reviews by the National Science Foundation and National Center for Education Statistics supported the Department of Energy's position. In a particularly scathing assessment, National Science Foundation director of Policy Research and Analysis Peter W. House wrote that "the report rests on a partial and flawed analysis, which does not reflect a full understanding of relevant reported research; that the narrative does not constitute a cohesive analysis, and that the conclusions presented are not adequately supported" (Miller, 1991e, para. 21).

When asked to discuss it before a New Mexico legislative committee, Huelskamp declined. He wrote them to say that "due to recent events, my management has decided that my continued involvement in the educational arena is not in Sandia's best interest" (Miller, 1992d, para. 37).

Nevertheless, scholars continued to use the Sandia data. Both lead author Huelskamp and "Lee Bray, the Sandia vice president who had overseen the analysis" shared their material with Bracey (Bracey, 2007a, para. 3). Impressed, Bracey suggested to Huelskamp that they should publish the Sandia report and Bracey's comparable research together in a single volume. Huelskamp said "We can't. We've got internal political problems" (Bracey, 2007a, para. 4). According to *Education Week*, "sources said the researchers had told them that they feared losing their federal funding if they spoke with reporters" (Miller, 1991e, para. 4). Other sources said the researchers "were told it would never see the light of day, that they had better be quiet. I fear for their careers" (Miller, 1991e, para. 9).

But academics continued to use it again and again. David Berliner cited it in a paper, *Educational Reform in an Era of Disinformation*, which "he presented at a meeting of the American Association of Colleges for Teacher Education in February, 1992" (Miller, 1992d, para. 29). Robert R. Rath, the executive director of the Northwest Regional Education Laboratory "used the report quite widely" in the area served by his organization, although he acknowledged "it's clear that the political leadership in Washington doesn't like this report and has tried to discredit it" (Miller, 1992d, para. 39). Joe Schneider, executive director of the Southwest Regional Research Laboratory, and Paul D. Houston, the superintendent of schools in Riverside, California, claimed the Sandia report "inspired them to write a book making similar arguments" (Miller, 1992d, para. 33). Schneider "had presented the report at a Southwest Regional Research Laboratory board meeting and Houston had "invited him to present it at a back-to-school meeting for administrators and parent leaders" (Bracey, 2007b, para. 7).

Almost immediately after the invitations to this meeting were received, Dufour got on the phone to Houston to nix it with Schneider, implying his organization might jeopardize their federal funding if the meeting went forward (Bracey, 2007b, para. 8). The book, *Exploding the Myths: Another Round in the Education Debate* was published in February 1993 (Schneider and Houston, 1993). It included the Sandia report as an appendix.

The controversy had yet to subside by 1992. In July the National Center for Education Statistics issued a statement referring to the Sandia report. "There continues to be a tendency to state conclusions or speculate about underlying patterns that are not supported by the data, or at least the data presented" (Miller, 1992d, para. 18–19). By September 1992, the administration began taking the offensive. Dufour admitted frankly that the Sandia researchers had "chosen to play this out in a political arena, and when you do that, the gloves come off" (Miller, 1992d, para. 35).

Bray later told Bracey after Bray's retirement that the report "was definitely suppressed" (Bracey, 2007a, para. 8). It was only published two years later in 1993 in a "small journal" for academic specialists, the *Journal of Educational Research* (Bracey, 2007a, para. 9).

Ravitch countered that "David Kearns knew, as did all the senators in that room, that there is no way that a report, an opinion, an essay, or any other expression of one's views can be suppressed," that the decision not to publish it through governmental channels "was based on evaluations of its quality by professional staff at the Departments of Energy and Education" (Ravitch, 2007, para. 10). Bracey replied that publication of the *Journal of Educational Research* "received zero media attention," far less than what important government reports often receive (Bracey, 2007b, para. 6).

Although Huelskamp stated "the draft report has been the subject of congressional testimony, editorials in the media, [and] an audit by the General Accounting Office" (Huelskamp, 1993a, p. 718), by the time Project Censored was on the case, it seemed he just wanted to move on. He told Project Censored "Sandia was not interested in replying to [their] questionnaire and that all further inquiries should be directed to a public information official" (Project Censored, 1994, para. 10). When Project Censored was finally able to get in touch with a second public information official willing to talk, the official said that "the study now has been published in the Kappan and that finished it" (Project Censored, 1994, para. 15).

The one academic critique of any substance agreed with all of the major findings of the Sandia report (Stedman, 1994, p. 145). Stedman further agreed with the report's finding of stable achievement levels. However, he argued while "performance generally has been stable, it remains at low levels" (Stedman, 1994, p. 145). Huelskamp preempted this line of criticism when he acknowledged early in the *Phi Delta Kappan* piece that "steady or slightly improving performance may not be adequate to meet future societal requirements" (Huelskamp, 1993a, p. 719). Stedman further opined that "few students achieve proficiency in the major academic areas; most have major gaps in their knowledge and skills" without describing what he meant by "knowledge and skills" and where he got the data to support his claims (Stedman, 1994, p. 145).

Although it is difficult to sift through all of the back-and-forth "he said, she said" accusations of this saga, an educated guess of what transpired can be made. A group of thorough, systematic, and intelligent researchers at Sandia Laboratory took seriously their department head's call to engage more with education. They completed a major longitudinal study on the state of American education, benchmarked against international standards. Unfortunately, they arrived at empirical conclusions out of step with the political needs of the executive branch and the business sector.

This episode is a fascinating case study in the relationship between educational policy research and educational policy making. Because the Sandia report arrived at a conclusion at odds with the crisis rhetoric fueling *America 2000* and the march towards standards-based education, it also raises the notion that perhaps *America 2000* and standards-based education were not based on empirical data but ideologically motivated. As such, I am led to consider it in light of Smith, Miller-Kahn, Heinecke, and Jarvis' (2004) typology of educational policies.

According to their scheme, there are four ideal types: instrumental ones, which "have effects consonant with the original intentions and ideals behind them"; symbolic ones, which "may have no effect at all because [they function] primarily as a symbol, without any substantive instrument that logically could be expected to further policy goals"; a third category is beyond scrutiny because, lacking "basic information, the public cannot possibly know the effects of a policy or participate intelligently in the debate over its values"; and a fourth category of policies whose "effects may be unintentionally deleterious" with the policy producing "unanticipated effects or costs, or effects contrary to the policy goals" (Smith, Miller-Kahn, Heinecke and Jarvis, 2004, pp. 8–10). Standards-based education seems to exhibit characteristics of all four typologies.

The tensions between equity and excellence, between federal and local control over education, simmered throughout 1991. At a June 1991 meeting of the National Education Goals Panel chaired by Governor Romer, members agreed on the need for higher standards but were divided as to who should develop and evaluate them. During this period, the traditional Democratic emphasis on equity emerged in discussion of opportunity-to-learn standards, which were benchmarks for resources (Kosar, 2005, p. 100). Issues of school choice, favored by the Bush administration as a sop to right-wing allies, proved divisive and interfered with efforts to arrive at a compromise bill (Miller, 1992a, para. 1). That year, the National Education Goals Panel released its first report. Although it advocated strongly for national standards, it failed to prod Congress to further action, in spite of the panel and the administration's efforts to broker a compromise (Stedman and Riddle, 1992, p. 4).

Meanwhile, the newly formed National Council on Education Standards and Testing was proceeding with its work as well. During a September 1991 meeting of that entity, their standards task force chair, Marshall Smith, presented a paper proposing the establishment of content, performance, and delivery standards. The terminology and definitions of standards-based education were beginning to take shape.

Shortly after Smith's briefing, the National Council on Education Standards and Testing issued a highly anticipated report in support of national standards in January 1992. *Raising Standards for American Education* stated that

> The council initially discussed standards and assessments as a way to help measure progress towards the National Education Goals but came to see the movement toward high standards as a means to help achieve the Goals. While mindful of the technical and political challenges, the Council concludes that national standards and a system of assessments are desirable and feasible mechanisms for raising expectations, revitalizing instruction, and rejuvenating educational reform efforts for all American schools and students. Thus, the National Council on Education Standards and Testing endorses the adoption of high national standards and the development of a system of assessments to measure attainment of those standards (National Council on Education Standards and Testing, 1993, p. 14).

According to the report, echoing *A Nation at Risk*, in the "absence of well-defined and demanding standards, education in the United States has gravitated toward de facto national minimum expectations" (National Council on

Education Standards and Testing, 1993, p. 8). Therefore, the national standards proposed in the report were

> critical to the nation in three primary ways: to promote educational equity, to preserve democracy and enhance the civic culture, and to improve economic competitiveness. Further, national education standards would help to provide an increasingly diverse and mobile population with shared values and knowledge (National Council on Education Standards and Testing, 1993, p. 9).

To allay stubborn fears that standards might enhance federal control over education policy, the report stressed that the proposed national standards should be voluntary. It also proposed that a National Education Standards and Assessment Council be created to validate the work of states on standards and assessments. In keeping with the National Council on Education Standards and Testing's sense of itself as advisory, they did not want to engage in the controversial issue of who should draft the standards. They painted with a broad brush, merely saying: "a wide array of developers" should do the work (National Council on Education Standards and Testing, 1993, p. 11). Their report also noted a "fundamental shift of perspective among educators, policymakers, and the public from examining inputs and elements of the educational process to examining outcomes and results" (National Council on Education Standards and Testing, 1993, p. 14). Although the report recommended delivery standards (another phrase for opportunity-to-learn standards) to assess resources and track equity, it was mute as to where this funding would come from.

The national testing component called for in the report came under immediate fire as a threat to equity and local control. 50 "prominent educators and testing experts" issued a statement the same day the council's report was released favoring such a national test (Chira, 1992, para. 1). Some feared national testing would reproduce "the caste-like status of non-European groups in American society," in effect "blaming the victims" (Winfield and Woodard, 1992, para. 5). These attitudes carried forward into the Congressional debate in March 1992.

In its deliberations on the National Council on Education Standards and Testing report, the House Subcommittee on Elementary, Secondary, and Vocational Education focused their critique on the idea of national testing, the lack of emphasis on delivery standards, and leaving their formulation to the states most unable to provide adequate resources to schools. Some committee members cited a report from the Office of Technology Assessment that noted that "high-stakes tests caused negative, unintended consequences in the past" (Miller, 1992b, para. 17). For all the fanfare with which the report was released and in spite of significant initial support, it wound up doing little to forward the stalled agenda of *America 2000*. Furthermore, with a presidential election year looming, Democrats in Congress were ill inclined to negotiate further with the executive branch, especially when these efforts continued to be embroiled in school choice and voucher issues (Miller, 1992a, para. 1, 3).

Absent cooperation from Congress and with *America 2000* and the *Raising Standards for American Education* report seemingly dead in the water, President Bush threatened to veto any education legislation that reached his desk. Only a Republican Senate filibuster saved him from the potential political embarrassment of having to reject an education bill on the eve of an election. Few mourned its passing. As an aide for the House Education and Labor committee put it, "it's no secret that nobody's really enthusiastic about this bill" (Miller, 1992e, para. 13).

Towards the end of his administration, President Bush bypassed a recalcitrant Congress by awarding grants through the Department of Education, National Endowment for the Humanities, National Science Foundation, and various groups for the development of "voluntary national standards in seven school subjects (science, history, geography, the arts, civics, foreign languages, and English)" (Ravitch, 2000, p. 432). These would "describe what children should be expected to learn in every major academic subject. These standards were intended to create a coherent framework of academic expectations that could be used by teacher educators, textbook publishers, and test developers" (Ravitch, 2000, p. 432).

Incoming president (and former chair of the National Governors Association when it played a leading role in conceptualizing national educational goals) Bill Clinton tried to re-energize standards-based education reform with three new initiatives. These plans, *Goals 2000*, the *Improving America's Schools Act*, and voluntary national tests, bore many similarities to *America 2000* (Kosar, 2005, p. 105).

Five weeks after Clinton took office, Congress began to move on his education agenda. The Senate Committee on Labor and Human Resources held a hearing on "the need to improve national education standards and job training opportunities," inviting testimony exclusively from the Secretaries of Education and Labor, Richard Riley and Robert Reich (United States

Congress, Senate, Committee on Labor and Human Resources, 1993, p. 2). The secretaries spoke of the need to adapt American education to a globalizing economy ever more dependent on technology and information, and in favor of occupational and educational standards. This was yet another milestone on the way to an ever-increasingly intertwined relationship between standards-based education, business, global economic competitiveness ideology, workforce development, and school-to-work. Riley also discussed a proposal from Clinton for a voluntary program that would fund states to create their own standards. These would in turn be certified by a new federal council. Clinton's proposal would have also created an "Opportunity-to-Learn Commission." This commission would be charged with the development of

> voluntary standards to address such issues as: the capability of teachers to provide quality instruction to their areas; the extent to which teachers and administrators have continuing and ready access to the best knowledge about teaching and learning and how to make needed school changes, and the quality and availability of challenging curricula geared to meet world class standards (United States Congress, Senate, Committee on Labor and Human Resources, 1993, p. 14).

As Clinton and his officials began protracted negotiations with Congress, the traditional battle lines of equity versus quality remained in place. Congress argued for equity and resources through opportunity-to-learn standards and the administration argued in favor of voluntary content and performance standards. After months of back and forth, President Clinton transmitted the *Goals 2000: Educate America Act* to Congress on April 21, 1993 (Clinton, 1993, para. 1). In summary, the bill was to do the following:

[1] Set into law the six National Education Goals and establish a bipartisan National Education Goals Panel to report on progress toward achieving the goals;
[2] Develop voluntary academic standards and assessments that are meaningful, challenging, and appropriate for all students through the National Education Standards and Improvement Council;
[3] Identify the conditions of learning and teaching necessary to ensure that all students have the opportunity to meet high standards;
[4] Establish a National Skill Standards Board to promote the development and adoption of occupational standards to ensure that American workers are among the best trained in the world;

[5] Help States and local communities involve public officials, teachers, parents, students, and business leaders in designing and reforming schools; and
[6] Increase flexibility for States and school districts by waiving regulations and other requirements that might impede reforms (Clinton, 1993, para. 5–10).

By May 1993 both chambers had begun hearings on the measure, although they focused more on the job training component than on standards. Reauthorization of Title I of the *Elementary and Secondary Education Act* was a bigger priority than standards to Representative William Ford, chair of the House Subcommittee on Elementary, Secondary, and Vocational Education. After Clinton called for "tough world-class academic and occupational standards for all our children" in his *1994 State of the Union address* (1994, para. 23), Congress finally sent a bill to conference committee in March 1994.

The most contentious issues were opportunity-to-learn standards and abiding fears that the measure might enhance federal control over education. In spite of these concerns, *Goals 2000* was signed into law on March 31, 1994 (United States Department of Education, 2005, para. 11). In the process of reconciling so many disparate and conflicting viewpoints, "a very confused piece of legislation" was created (Kosar, 2005, p. 132). Many of its most significant provisions were left voluntary to the states.

Among the eight goals it articulated were a number that reiterated global economic competitiveness ideology, particularly goals 3, 5, and 6.

(3) By the year 2000, all students will leave grades 4, 8, and 12 having demonstrated competency over challenging subject matter including English, mathematics, science, foreign languages, civics and government, economics, arts, history, and geography, and every school in America will ensure that all students learn to use their minds well, so they may be prepared for responsible citizenship, further learning, and productive employment in our Nation's modern economy.
(5) By the year 2000, United States students will be first in the world in mathematics and science achievement.
(6) By the year 2000, every adult American will be literate and will possess the knowledge and skills necessary to compete in a global economy and exercise the rights and responsibilities of citizenship (United States Congress, 1994b, para. 3, 5–6).

By the mid-1990s the standards-based education reform model seemed to be gaining momentum. It was entering state and federal law. National disciplinary organizations had completed or were in the process of drafting voluntary national standards. Some states had drafted their own individual standards. The concept seemed to have the support of influential education leaders as well as a bipartisan group of policymakers and key aides. Paradoxically, however, at this moment when critical mass seemed to be in sight, the movement also began to falter (Diegmueller, 1995; Firestone 1997).

The "Republican Revolution" of 1994, when control over Congress shifted from the Democrats to the Republicans, made the always politically contentious debates between "equity," "equality," "quality," and "accountability" even more so. Some of the voluntary national standards drafted by the national disciplinary organizations had controversial receptions. The state standards were inconsistent in terms of quality and design. Debates over the proper balance between the local/state and federal roles in education seemed intractable. The entire reform idea looked like it was about to disintegrate.

Even though *America 2000* passed into law on March 31, 1994, business leaders continued sounding the alarm about global economic competitiveness. A month after a *New York Times* headline exclaimed *The American Economy: Back on Top*, Gerstner published in op-ed in the same newspaper entitled *Our Schools Are Failing: Do We Care?* (1994). In it he repeated the familiar litany. "It is a deeply dangerous situation. We cannot transform business and the economy without a labor force that is prepared to solve problems and compete on the global level" (Gerstner, 1994, p. A11).

Gerstner's piece went on to claim that American business was spending $30 billion on worker training and losing $25–30 billion "each year as a result of poor literacy among workers. We can't squander $60 billion and remain competitive" (Gerstner, 1994, p. A11). "The future is even bleaker," he said, going on to cite a National Association of Manufacturers survey that claimed "30% of companies cannot reorganize work activities because employers can't learn new jobs, and 25% can't upgrade their products because their employees can't learn the necessary skills" (Gerstner, 1994, p. A11). Among the remedies offered were what would eventually become the essential aspects of standards-based education: "a greater emphasis on outcomes, the specific tasks that graduates are prepared to do" (Gerstner, 1994, p. A11).

A year later, Gerstner went on to publish a book elaborating on his call for outcomes-based education, enhanced by the business management technique of total quality management (Gerstner, Semerad, and Doyle, 1995).

It was also during the mid-1990s that business began switching gears, from merely sounding the alarm to trying to shape the contours of standards-based education. The Business Roundtable took the lead (Business Roundtable, 1992a,b, 1993, 1995, 1996, 1998, 1999, 2000a,b,c, 2001).

Given the laxity in quality control in *Goals 2000* regarding standards, it is not surprising that by mid-1995, 47 states applied for funding under the measure and none were refused, even though "few developed adequate standards and assessments" (Kosar, 2005, p. 133). In a concession designed to placate those who feared the National Education Standards and Improvement Council might become a mechanism of control by the federal government, the pre-existing National Education Goals Panel was given considerable authority over the council. The panel would also nominate members to the council, and evaluate, approve, and disapprove "criteria for the certification of State content standards, State student performance standards, State assessments, and State opportunity-to-learn standards," as well as the "voluntary national content standards, voluntary national student performance standards, and voluntary national opportunity-to-learn standards" (United States Congress, 1994a, para. 1). Since 12 of the panel's 16 members were state officials (8 governors and 4 state legislators), they had little incentive to make certification standards so difficult they might be setting up their states to fail (Kosar, 2005, p. 134). In this way, practical politics further diluted the "standards of standards."

The new law prohibited use of the National Education Standards and Improvement Council certification for high-stakes testing, such as "graduation, grade promotion, or retention of students for a period of four years from the date of the Act," although they would be free to do so after that (United States Congress, 1994a). The status of opportunity-to-learn standards in the Act was contradictory, in an effort to appease opposing liberal and anti-statist factions in Congress, which led to an ongoing confusion and ambiguity about the status of these standards as well. The curious compromise in the implementation of the act was that every participating state wound up submitting "plans clarifying how they would raise standards and fashion opportunity-to-learn standards, but never to seek NESIC approval for those standards" (Kosar, 2005, p. 135).

In the autumn of 1994, two events further exposed the dramatic challenges facing the emerging standards-based reform idea. The first was the October 20, 1994 op-ed piece Lynne Cheney in the *Wall Street Journal* entitled "The End of History" (Cheney, 1994, p. A22). Her article precipitated a major controversy. Significant media attention was given to the history standards that had just been released by the National Center for History in the

Schools at the University of California at Los Angeles, one of the many disciplinary organizations the Department of Education and others had contracted with to draft standards in core curricular areas in the waning months of the Bush administration. The history standards reflected a position similar to the multicultural movement. They highlighted previously neglected women and people of color instead of continuing to valorize the traditional roster of pale dead males. They also gave prominence to what many perceive as shortcomings in the mainstream conventional wisdom about how American history is portrayed in school materials and the mainstream media. This perspective often gives short shrift to such matters as genocide, land theft, slavery, misogyny, and imperialism. These topics are rarely discussed in school civics, social studies, and history classes.

The Senate even joined in the debate, voting 99 to 1 to condemn the history standards (Johnston and Diegmueller, 1995, para. 1).

This "negative" view of America was an attractive target for the politicians who came to power during the "Republican Revolution" of November 1994. Many of them campaigned on "culture war" issues. Cheney's article gave emboldened Republican hard-liners additional justification to attack the history standards and the rest of Clinton's overall education initiative. The Republican critique centered largely on the perceived over-involvement of the federal government in local and state education.

Despite persistent threats to abolish the Department of Education, by the time Congress passed its next round of education measures in the Appropriations Act of 1996 in April, the department was funded at the same level as the previous year (United States Congress, 1996, pp. 230–238). The legislation also modified *Goals 2000* by deleting opportunity-to-learn standards and abolishing the NESIC before any members had even been appointed.

Opportunity-to-learn standards, system delivery standards, and other similarly named standards were an important part of the policy debate in the early years of this concept. They basically involved making explicit the amount of financial resources that would be necessary to implement the other types of standards. After only a few years, these types of standards fell to the wayside, never to be heard from again.

Republican antipathy to a perceived over-involvement of the federal government in education can also be seen in their two year delay of a vote on the appointment of Marshall Smith, the former chair of the standards task force of the National Council on Education Standards and Testing, to Deputy Secretary of the Department of Education. This was likely in part because of his association with standards. For their conservative base, standards remained a Trojan horse, a ploy for the federalization of education. So abiding was their distrust that one right-wing policy analyst called it "an Orwellian exercise in government-approved truth" (Morrison, 1996, para. 8).

Since the NESIC was abolished, "there was no organization to evaluate the drafts prepared by the groups that had been funded to write voluntary national standards, nor was there any other formal public review process" (Ravitch, 2000, p. 432). Any sense of a rigorous national standard for evaluation of standards collapsed.

The first set of voluntary national standards to emerge were the math standards, created by the National Council of Teachers of Mathematics without any federal resources. These standards grew out of the 1983 report by the Commission on Precollege Education in Mathematics, Science and Technology. Subsequent discussion of the matter at various conferences led the council to convene a Commission on Standards for School Mathematics in 1986 to begin drafting standards. These were released in March 1989 as *Curriculum and Evaluation Standards for School Mathematics* (National Council of Teachers of Mathematics, 1989).

They were well received initially, especially as a welcome and definitive break from the discredited "new math." Upon further scrutiny and with an accumulation of experience as to how they played out in the classroom, many, especially parents, began to chafe. Their de-emphasis on correct answers, basic computational skills, and perceived over-reliance on calculators seemed to many an assault on basic numeracy. Frustrated parents in California "led by mathematicians and engineers" organized themselves under the name Mathematically Correct, using "the Internet to find like-minded mathematicians, teachers, and parents" beginning in 1995 (Ravitch, 2000, p. 440).

Other curricular areas did benefit from federal funding. These included the following (and their date of release and who drafted them): the arts (March 1994; Consortium of National Arts Education Associations), civics and government (November 1994; Center for Civic Education), science (November 1995; National Research Council of the National Academy of Sciences, National Academy of Engineering, and Institute of Medicine), foreign languages (January 1996; consortium of the American Council on the Teaching of Foreign Languages and disciplinary associations), and English language arts (March 1996; National Council of Teachers of English and International Reading Association).

Curricular areas that issued standards without the aid of federal resources included health (May 1995; Joint Committee on National Health Education Standards), physical education (June 1995; National Association for Sport and Physical Education), and economics (January 1997; consortium of the National Council on Economic Education and disciplinary associations) (Watt, 2000, pp. 7–11). Among these, however, few received nearly as much publicity as the history, mathematics, and English language arts standards.

The English language arts standards have been called "an unmitigated disaster" lacking rigor, substance, "content and actual standards" (Ravitch, 2000, p. 437). In 1994 the Department of Education ceased funding the project. In spite of the loss of federal funding, the National Council of Teachers of English and International Reading Association continued their work on language arts standards (in conjunction with the Council of Chief State School Officers). They were released in March 1996 (Watt, 2000, p. 7). One primary complaint that emerged against the standards was made against their call for students to "develop an understanding of and respect for diversity in language use, patterns, and dialects" (National Council of Teachers of English and International Reading Association, 1996, para. 11). In Ravitch's own words, the standards "essentially says we should not hold students to any standards!" (Watt, 2000, p. 438). Others considered them more of a pedagogy than standards per se (Watt, 2000, p. 441).

Another major piece of education legislation passed during the Clinton administration was the *Improving America's School Act*, signed into law during October 1994. It "required each state to develop state content and performance standards for mathematics and reading by the 1997–1998 school year and assessments by the 2000–2001 school year appropriate for all students, including the disadvantaged" (Watt, 2000, p. 13).

This stage in the development of standards-based education was marked by some curious contradictions. On the one hand, it was the culmination of a process that began as far back as 1983 with the release of *A Nation at Risk*. The federal government's Department of Education had invested over $24 million in "the development of curriculum frameworks and content standards in 30 states" (Olson, 1995, para. 9). Standards enjoyed the support of Democratic and Republican presidential administrations, a bipartisan group of governors, and key elements of the federal bureaucracy (Standards, 1995, para. 4).

Furthermore, a wide variety of disciplinary organizations had either completed or were hard at work drafting subject matter standards, as were the states themselves. As Olson says, "forty-six states have applied for federal grants under the *Goals 2000: Educate America Act*...to develop content standards and a related system of assessments" (Olson, 1995, para. 7). In spite of this support, questions were beginning to emerge as well.

> Who should set standards and who has the right to say whether they are good enough? Are the proposed standards really for all children, from the gifted and talented to those with special needs? Will all students have access to the instruction and resources needed to achieve the standards? Will the standards dictate a national curriculum in a country that has a strong tradition of local control in education? What role, if any, should the federal government have played in developing standards? And are the emerging documents both politically balanced and academically rigorous? (Standards, 1995, para. 6).

Perhaps some drafters underestimated the difficulties inherent in crafting documents as complex as standards. It was also unclear as yet how the educational systems could utilize them. The voluntary national standards drafted by the national disciplinary organizations themselves were under political attack from the right and left. States and districts chafed at what they saw as attempts to undermine long traditions of local control. The link between standards and "better assessments, teacher training, new textbooks, and other resources to help students achieve the standards" was often absent or weak (Standards, 1995, para. 2). The definition of "standards," nomenclature for comparable activities, and links (or lack thereof) "to statewide tests, professional development, and graduation requirements" varied widely among the states (Olson, 1995, para. 18).

The challenges facing this burgeoning reform notion were so pervasive that *Education Week* saw fit to devote its April 12, 1995 issue to the subject. In spite of these challenges, the movement pressed forward, aided by a number of events. These events included the second National Education Summit convened in March 1996, the re-election of President Clinton in November 1996, the State of the Union address in February 1997, the third National Education Summit held in September 1999 and the fourth National Education Summit called in October 2001 (Watt, 2000, p. 12).

The second National Education Summit was held at IBM's Palisade, New York conference center and hosted by Louis Gerstner, CEO of IBM. CEOs of blue chip American companies, the National Governors Association, and leading conservative education thinkers were all involved (Horn, 2004, p. 23). Emerging from the summit was a preference for state- and locally-generated standards and enhanced consideration of workforce development issues in drafting them. CEOs represented by the Business Roundtable kept up the pressure for workplace readiness.

Another impetus for the survival of standards-based education came with the multi-pronged efforts of Mid-continent Research for Education and Learning (McREL) to calibrate, reconcile, and consolidate widely varying state and local standards. As a part of this initiative, they examined "4,100 benchmarks distributed among 256 standards" to create an online database (Kendall and Marzano, 1996, para. 41; Mid-continent Research for Education and Learning, 2009). Next, they engaged in a study designed to boil down the subject matter content standards to key essentials. As a follow-up, they also "convened a National Dialogue on Standards-Based Education in April 2001 to give stakeholders a mechanism for meeting face-to-face and online to continue refining the dialogue regarding standards" (Watt, 2000, p. 12).

Other organizations contributed to the ongoing refinement. The Council for Basic Education published "a book presenting condensed, edited and commonly-formatted versions of the national standards" (Watt, 2000, p. 21). Business and the governors continued their long-standing support for standards by collaborating to establish another database of standards, as well as a methodology for their evaluation, through the Achieve Resource Center on Standards, Assessment, Accountability and Technology. Achieve, Inc. assumed much of the traditional role played by the Business Roundtable in educational policy reform efforts.

There were other initiatives as well. For example, the Coalition for Goals 2000 tasked itself with "developing a set of self-guiding tools which school districts can use to develop their own academic standards based on national and state benchmarks" (Starr, 1998, para. 24), and "collaborated with the Education Leaders Council to create a results card for analyzing the impact of state standards" (Watt, 2000, p. 12).

The Department of Education conducted a review in 2000 to evaluate "the alignment of each state's assessment system with its content and performance standards to ensure they met requirements for funding Title 1 programs" (Watt, 2000, p. 13). After passage of Bush's hallmark education legislation *No Child Left Behind* in 2002, his education secretary Rod Paige convened a committee to revamp standards and assessments and receive public feedback. At the conclusion of this process, his department promulgated new regulations on the matter.

Among the most ambitious standards and assessment initiatives of the 1980s and 1990s was the New Standards Project. This national coalition teamed up "approximately 17 states and seven urban school districts, co-directed by Lauren Resnick of the Learning, Research, and Development Center of the University of Pittsburgh and Marc Tucker of the National Center on Education and the Economy in Washington, D.C." (Spalding, 2000, p. 2) It strove to create a unified system of standards and performance assessment. Their initial portfolio-based assessment initiative proved too difficult to grade on a mass, standardized basis, although it had the unintended and positive impact of enhancing teacher professionalism in the process.

This chapter explored how President Bush, his Secretary of Education Lamar Alexander, and others worked to pass Bush's signature piece of education legislation, *America 2000*. Because it ran into political difficulties from the right on matters of school choice and the left on matters of equity, ultimately, it failed to pass. Sensing he didn't have the congressional support to pass *America 2000*, Bush enacted portions of it by executive authority, primarily by underwriting the drafting of model national standards that state and local jurisdictions could look to as guides. This chapter also examined the impact of these voluntary national standards in fomenting the standards wars during the tenure of the next president, Clinton, who had been instrumental earlier, at the Charlottesville summit and other venues, in crafting education policy during this period. When Clinton assumed the presidency, he reintroduced *America 2000* to Congress as *Goals 2000* substantially unchanged and, this time, it passed. This success was not unqualified. President Clinton and a variety of other business leaders, researchers, and governors fought back against resistance to standards-based education from a wide variety of quarters. Their successful defense helped make the concept a settled part of state and federal education policy with the *Improving America's Schools Act* of 1996. As the 1990s drew to a close, every state except Iowa had drafted standards.

· 5 ·
HAWAII, A CASE STUDY
(1991–PRESENT)

In this chapter I will sketch the political context that made Hawaii one of the early adopters of this model, a context that also guided successive iterations of standards by Hawaii in the years that followed. Finally, I will summarize the literature evaluating Hawaii's standards by external experts and the recent status accorded it as a triumphant underdog in Race to the Top.

Although Hawaii is typically recognized as the "50th state" in the United States of America, the sovereignty of the Kingdom of Hawaii was never extinguished, legally, politically, or morally. "King Kamehameha III established Hawaii's public school system in 1840" (Hawaii Department of Education, March 31, 2014, para. 13). It "is the ninth-largest U.S. school district and the only statewide educational district in the country" (Duncan and Abercrombie, 2014, para. 3). Hawaii is the only school district in the nation that is simultaneously (in statutory language) the "statewide education agency" and "local education agency" (United States Department of Education, 2012, p. 3). It is also the only state that provides almost all of the state and local share of its education financing from general revenue provided by state income taxes. It is "comprised of 255 schools and 33 charter schools, and serves more than 185,000 students" (Hawaii Department of Education, 2014, para. 13).

Hawaii engaged with the standards-based education reform model earlier than most states. To sketch the political and educational context for Hawaii's early adoption of standards-based education, we must examine a number of local initiatives undertaken during the late 1980s and early 1990s. These include 1) the *Hawaii Report* drafted by Berman Weiler Associates (Berman, 1988b), 2) Act 366, Session Laws of Hawaii, 1989, which created school-community based management (Hawaii State Legislature, 1989), 3) the Department of Education's Project Ke Au Ho during Charles Toguchi's tenure as Superintendent (1991 onward), 4) a task force on educational governance headed by then Lt. Governor Ben Cayetano (early 1990s), 5) Act 334 that created the Hawaii Commission on Performance Standards (Hawaii State Legislature, 1991), 6) the Hawaii Department of Education, University of Hawaii College of Education, and Kamehameha Schools collaboration on assessment and accountability (1992–1993), and 7) the establishment of the Hawaii Performance Standards Review Commission and subsequent committees in 1994 in Hawaii Revised Statutes 302A-201 (Hawaii State Legislature, 1994), subsequently repealed in 2009.

After having already drafted two influential policy reports for Minnesota and California, the Hawaii Business Roundtable commissioned Berman Weiler Associates to draft a similar brief on educational policy reform in Hawaii. This was released in 1988. While it did not advocate for standards-based education per se—understandably, as the idea had not yet fully emerged—it did use global competitiveness ideology as one of the ideological drivers for the reforms it suggested. For example, while Hawaii public education strives to close the present gap, other states will be taking steps to prepare their citizens for a challenging future in an increasingly competitive and rapidly changing world (Berman, 1988b, p. 6).

Comparably, the report also stated that

> Hawaii public schools must enable all students, without exception, to learn to their potential and to master the knowledge, skills and values needed for social and economic success in the 21st century" (Berman, 1988b, p. 6).

While the *Hawaii Report* may not have advocated for standards-based education per se, it did use rhetoric that anticipated it in a number of ways. For example, it called for the Board of Education to "establish core competencies and mastery examinations at grade six and ten that schools would gradually revise and focus the curriculum to enable all students to master core competencies" (Berman, 1988b, p. 26). It also used the word "standards" in the everyday sense of "high expectations," although it was precisely during this period of the late 1980s and early 1990s that we witnessed a collective shift of the use of the word in policy talk from this everyday sense towards the more technical sense of the word that we are familiar with today. "High standards expected for all students. All students would be expected to master the same core competencies to prepare them for the transition to education and/or work" (Berman, 1988b, p. 39). Or, similarly, "there can be no more important change in schooling than raising the expectations for each and every young person. Although teachers are ultimately most responsible for setting high expectations" (Berman, 1988b, p. 40).

Ultimately, however, the most influential impact of the report on public K–12 education in Hawaii was to be found in its call for decentralization. The report noted "the BOE mandated School Community Councils in 1978. However, these councils have little authority. Consequently, most are either ineffectual or defunct" (Berman, 1988b, p. 20). Nevertheless, the report recommended giving the idea another try, modeled on the burgeoning reform idea of school/community-based management (SCBM). As mentioned above, Hawaii has the only state-wide education district in the United States. Antibureaucratic sentiment was pervasive during this time, so the call for decentralization resonated among policy makers.

"In December 1988, one month after the release of the Hawaii Plan, DOE Superintendent Charles Toguchi and DOE staff conducted a site visit to the Dade County Florida schools" to see the SCBM idea in action (Berman, 1988b, p. 23). Perhaps in response to Toguchi's findings during this trip, "then-Governor John Waihee urged the Legislature to pass legislation allowing SCBM schools" during the Legislature's opening day in 1989 (Erbes, 2003, p. 22). The Legislature responded by passing Senate Bill 1870 in April 1989, which the Governor signed into law during June of that year. Passage had been made possible in part by "the support of business and community leaders" (Erbes, 2003, p. 22). Other key stakeholders quickly followed suit as well. In July 1989

> the Hawaii State Teachers Association signed a "Memorandum of Understanding" with the BOE supporting SCBM. In November 1989 the BOE adopted SCBM policy and implementation guidelines, and in January 1990 Waialae Elementary submitted a "Letter of Intent" to become the first SCBM (Erbes, 2003, p. 22).

Waialae Elementary later went on to become one of the first charter schools in the state as well, shortly after enabling legislation passed in 2000.

To support this decentralization initiative, the Superintendent of Education Charles Toguchi "launched Project Ke Au Hou ('A New Era') to 'enhance greater school-level decisionmaking' and 'reconceptualize and transform the state and district offices to become primarily support-providers to schools' (Hawaii Department of Education, 1991a, p. 1).

The vision of Project Ke Au Hou was developed with "widespread input from school, district, and state levels within the Department of Education (DOE), as well as input from community organizations and others" and

> shifting authority and positions from district and state levels to the school level to ensure that decisions affecting students and the learning environment are directly responsive to individual classroom and pupil needs (Hawaii Department of Education, 1991b, p. 1).

As Toguchi initiated this project in early 1991, this mandate for "shifting authority" and "responsiveness" reverberated with consistent calls throughout the *Hawaii Report* for "accountability."

Another impetus for decentralization was a task force on educational governance led by then Lt. Governor Ben Cayetano during the early 1990s. In 1991 the Hawaii State Legislature passed Act 334 (Hawaii State Legislature, 1991). This created an 11-member Hawaii Commission on Performance Standards, which was approved by Governor John Waihee on July 8, 1991. The findings section of Act 334 noted "one of the unresolved issues in Hawaii's educational system is accountability" (Hawaii State Legislature, 1991, p. 1045). Absent such accountability, it would be "difficult to determine the success or failure of the system in meeting the central goals of education as stated in the Hawaii Goals for Education dated September 29, 1990" (Hawaii State Commission on Performance Standards, 1994, p. 5).

The Act further asserted that standards could "insure that students in Hawaii's public school system are able to master basic skills and essential competencies necessary to succeed in life" (Hawaii State Legislature, 1991, p. 1045). The charge to the newly created commission was to "set the performance standards of achievement expected of students in public schools and the means to assess educational achievement." The session law mandated an interim report by June 30, 1992, and a final report due shortly before the 1993 regular session (Hawaii State Legislature, 1991, p. 1045).

As the Hawaii Commission on Performance Standards and Project Ke Au Hou began their work on standards and decentralization, a group of professors from the University of Hawaii College of Education's Department of Curriculum and Instruction launched a critique on a related subject, the shortfalls of the Department of Education's exclusive reliance on standardized Stanford Achievement Tests, preferring instead what was then referred to as "authentic assessments."

When David Ericson was chair of the Department of Curriculum and Instruction in the fall of 1992, he and a number of colleagues from the department penned a letter on the matter. It was supposed to be sent to Superintendent Toguchi first and then to the two major local daily newspapers later but the department secretary accidentally reversed the order and sent it to the newspapers first and Toguchi second. This sparked a front page headline in one of the papers saying something to the effect that "University of Hawaii Professors Blast Department of Education." While Toguchi was not pleased with this adverse publicity, he convened a collaborative effort between the University of Hawaii, Department of Education, and Kamehameha Schools to address the issue of authentic assessments. He also urged to the committee to focus on the additional topic of accountability as well. Approximately 80 people from these three entities worked for about a year to develop a *Hawaii State Framework for Student Assessment and Accountability* (Ericson, 2011).

In its findings, we see a Hawaiian example of the linkages between standards, curriculum, instruction, and assessment that were becoming commonplace on the mainland United States as this model evolved.

> The state framework for student assessment and accountability is an interactive system. In this system, state standards are primary and provide the focal point and foundation for a student assessment and accountability system. These standards include content domain standards, performance standards and system delivery standards which can be linked with similar standards developed at the national level. The model illustrates that curriculum, instruction and assessment are based on educational standards, standards that represent what is valued and what is considered important for our students to know and be able to do (Hawaii School University Partnership, 1994, p. 3).

What was unique about the interpretation of standards in the *Hawaii State Framework for Student Assessment and Accountability*, however, was that "curricular and instructional efforts should be driven by standards of excellence embedded in the various content domains for understanding experience" in order to "inform our vision of a fully educated person" (Hawaii School University Partnership, 1994, p. 4). This notion of anchoring standards-based education in a "vision of a fully educated person" was never typical of the model. Certainly, today, it has fallen to the wayside in favor of a more instrumental approach that focuses more narrowly on what students should supposedly know in each subject matter during each grade.

The Hawaii State Commission on Performance Standards started out on its work by reviewing the local and national literature, with particular attention paid to the work done by Colorado, Kentucky, Idaho, and California, by the national professional organizations, and by the influential Secretary of Labor's *Secretary's Commission on Achieving Necessary Skills Report*. Then, over 100 local subject matter experts were consulted for their input on "what students should know, be able to do and care about by the time they leave 12th grade" (Hawaii State Commission on Performance Standards, 1994, p. 4). This feedback was distilled into a draft document then taken to the people of Hawaii for their comments in "ten public forums... held on six different islands" (Hawaii State Commission on Performance Standards, 1994, p. 4). This feedback was incorporated into a revision of the draft document, in conjunction with model standards documents, under the general guidance of Pacific Resources for Education and Learning (PREL) staff.

Finally, PREL convened meetings of the commission to solicit their feedback and eventual approval of the draft standards. At this time, the commission also "decided to establish content standards" as a "prerequisite to performance standards" (Hawaii State Commission on Performance Standards, 1994, p. 6). Although they clearly specified that they did not want to link the draft standards with "any specific assessment procedure," they did discuss key criteria that should guide the state's assessment efforts and they recommended participation in both the development of the Center for Research on Evaluation, Standards, and Student Testing's (CRESST) history assessment instrument and the New Standards Project (Hawaii State Commission on Performance Standards, 1993, p. 137). The bulk of the December 1993 *Preliminary Final Report* of the commission was composed of their draft standards (Hawaii State Commission on Performance Standards, 1993).

The commission's June 1994 *Final Report* was far more voluminous and divided the more thoroughly elaborated "content and performance standards" into two sections: "by content area (i.e. in all grade levels in language arts, math, science, etc.) [and] by grade level sections (i.e. all content areas sectioned K–3, 4–6, 7–8, 9–12)" (Hawaii State Commission on Performance Standards, 1994, p. v). Another salient difference between the preliminary report and the final report was the latter's more intensive focus on the establishment of an assessment system coordinated with the standards, guided by six criteria and three recommendations (Hawaii State Commission on

Performance Standards, 1994, pp. 364–367). Furthermore, a model cited as a promising one for implementing standards-based education in Hawaii was the relationship between teaching and research inherent in the University of Hawaii's Curriculum Research & Development Group's partnership with the University Laboratory School (Hawaii State Commission on Performance Standards, 1994, pp. 375–376).

The work of the commission was published in 1994 as the *Hawaii Content and Performance Standards* (HCPS). Commonly known as the "Blue Book," it provided "standards for students completing the final year in each of four sets of grades—K–3 (primary), 4–6 (elementary), 7–8 (middle school), and 9–12 (high school)" (Hawaii State Performance Standards Review Commission 1999, p. 7). These standards were adopted by the Board of Education (BOE) in October 1994 (Standards: setting, 1995).

They were voluminous: 1,544 standards in all including "495…in language arts, 119 in mathematics, 418 in science, 133 in social studies, 113 in health and fitness, 89 in fine arts, 101 in home and work skills, and 76 in world languages" (Hawaii State Performance Standards Review Commission 1999, p. 8).

During the 1994 session, the Hawaii State Legislature passed a law that would become Section 302A-201, Hawaii Revised Statutes. This statute called upon the BOE to appoint a "performance standards review commission, to be convened at the beginning of the 1997–1998 school year, and every four years thereafter" composed of various education stakeholders and professionals (Hawaii State Legislature, 1994). In addition to the representatives of the Hawaii State Parent Teacher Student Association, the Hawaii State Student Council, the State Superintendent of Education, the Dean of the University of Hawaii College of Education, and the professional education committee seats required by statute, the BOE also appointed "a principal, a School Renewal Specialist, an intermediate school teacher, a Title I teacher, a business community representative, and a representative of the community-at-large" (Hawaii State Performance Standards Review Commission, 1999, pp. 9–10). The commission was charged to "review the implementation of the performance standards by the board and the schools to determine whether or not the standards should be modified" (Hawaii State Legislature, 1994).

Hawaii's momentum and pioneering role were maintained at the national level when Hawaii became the first state to receive federal money to develop standards under President Clinton's *Goals 2000* legislation in July 1994 (A Goals 2000 time line, 1998 para. 6).

Through a partnership between the Hawaii Department of Education, the University of Hawaii system, and the Hawaii Business Roundtable, Hawaii joined the American Diploma Project (ADP) network in 2006 and was (and remains) committed to raising high school standards, strengthening assessments and curriculum, and aligning high school requirements with the expectations of employers and colleges (Hawaii Department of Education, 2010, p. 118).

The Performance Standards Review Commission (PSRC), created by Hawaii Revised Statutes 302A-201 in 1994, came together in 1998 to fulfill it duties. It convened public fora, received testimony, visited schools, gathered expert opinion, made presentations to key stakeholders, conducted an extensive review of "more than 50 standards documents," and was briefed on "the significance of standards in regard to federally funded programs, particularly Goals 2000 and Title I" (Hawaii State Performance Standards Review Commission, 1999, pp. 1, 10).

Perhaps the most crucial finding of its January 1999 final report was that "standards-based education is an extremely effective way to improve student learning"; other key findings were that the "Blue Book" lacked performance standards, didn't cover some academic areas, and wasn't "user-friendly" (Hawaii State Performance Standards Review Commission 1999, p. 2). The lack of an "overarching vision" and "systematic implementation plan" hampered utilization of standards as well (Hawaii State Performance Standards Review Commission, 1999, p. 2). Furthermore, the report stated that "a statewide assessment system is lacking" and should be developed, in alignment with the standards (Hawaii State Performance Standards Review Commission, 1999, p. 2). The report also contextualized Hawaii's efforts by noting that "as of 1995, 48 states were engaged in developing academic standards." (Hawaii State Performance Standards Review Commission, 1999, p. 5). To address one of these major concerns, the Hawaii Department of Education drafted a *Strategic Plan for Standards-Based Education* (1999a), followed up by a *Strategic Implementation Plan* in 2003.

In its discussion of the school community fora held by the commission, the report noted that public feedback indicated that there were too many standards, most of the performance standards are actually content-oriented, [and] many standards are duplicative and difficult to understand" (Hawaii State Performance Standards Review Commission, 1999, p. 13). A tremendous need for additional time, resources, and guidance in understanding and using the standards came up again and again as well (Hawaii State Performance Standards Review Commission, 1999, p. 15).

The Curriculum Research & Development Group at the University of Hawaii at Mānoa executed a Memorandum of Agreement to "organize, analyze, and summarize each school's review of the standards and to study instructional modules or standards applications that have been developed by individual schools or several schools grouped in a complex" (Hawaii State Performance Standards Review Commission, 1999, p. 18). The ensuing report, *Hawaii Content and Performance Standards: Schools' Review of Standards and Instructional Module Development* (Lai, 1998) was provided to the commission by principal investigator Dr. Morris Lai during a February 27, 1998 meeting. It proved to be "very useful to the Commission's deliberations" and helped the commission to understand "that schools and complexes vary considerably both in their understanding of the assigned tasks and in the extent to which they tried to accomplish them" (Hawaii State Performance Standards Review Commission, 1999, p. 18).

In their literature review, the commission was especially interested in "criteria for judging standards," which led them to give careful consideration to the work of "the American Federation of Teachers (AFT), Council for Basic Education, Mid-continent Regional Educational Laboratory (McREL), Southern California Comprehensive Assessment Center, U.S. Department of Education, and the state of California Academic Standards Commission" (Hawaii State Performance Standards Review Commission, 1999, pp. 18–19). They examined model programs for implementation as well, especially the National Center on Education and the Economy's New Standards Project, which had already certified 15 trainers through the Department of Education's (DOE) Office of Accountability and School Instructional Support. Model material from other states was examined, "particularly Vermont, Delaware, Kentucky, and Virginia—states regularly lauded for their progress by such organizations as the Educational Commission of the States and cited for their programs by the U.S. Department of Education" (Hawaii State Performance Standards Review Commission, 1999, pp. 18–19).

In 1999 the DOE drafted "a comprehensive needs assessment of the public schools system" that "found that the 'Blue Book' did not adequately reflect some important dispositions, attitudes, and skills that students should achieve" (Hawaii State Auditor, 2001, p. 3).

In response to the 1999 Hawaii State Performance Standards Review Commission report and the DOE's 1999 "comprehensive needs assessment," the DOE promulgated the HCPS II, often referred to as the "rainbow series" after the differently colored booklets of standards for 10 academic subjects (Hawaii

State Auditor, 2001, pp. 2–3). In August 1999 these were approved by the BOE (Hawaii State Performance Standards Review Commission, 2003, p. 20). This second round of standards not only covered a more comprehensive array of subject matter areas, but it also included true performance standards and reduced the number of standards considerably from 1,544 to 139, although these performance standards were not entirely complete upon publication (Hawaii State Auditor, 2001, p. 3). It also grouped them "into grade clusters, rather than grade levels" (Hawaii State Performance Standards Review Commission 2003, p. 20). In addition, the DOE also drafted the booklet *Making Sense of Standards, Moving From the Blue Book to HCPS II* in 1999 (Hawaii Department of Education, 1999b) to enhance the user friendliness of the standards, as suggested by the commission's January 1999 report. The report noted that "placing standards at the core of the system unified curriculum, instruction, assessment/accountability, and staff development" (Hawaii State Performance Standards Review Commission, 1999, p. 6). It also reiterated the importance of General Learner Outcomes as an important set of goals for standard-based learning. These outcomes are as follows: "The ability to be responsible for one's own learning; the understanding that it is essential for human beings to work together; the ability to be involved in complex thinking and problem solving; [and] the ability to recognize and produce quality performance and quality products" (Hawaii State Performance Standards Review Commission, 1999, p. 7).

An important national conference held in 1999 by the Council for Basic Education in collaboration with the Johnson Foundation with key stakeholders nationwide, the "Wingspread Conference," helped Hawaii change agents "identify the key issues related to the implementation of the Hawaii Content and Performance Standards in a standards-based system" (Hawaii Department of Education, 2005b, para. 7). Prominent among these key issues was a recognition of the need to enhance teacher support and improve alignment of assessments with standards.

In addition to participating in the conference, the DOE also consulted "guidelines developed for the U.S. Department of Education and the Council of Chief State School Officers" (Hawaii State Auditor, 2001, p. 3). All of this work culminated in the final drafting of revised content standards by June 1999, which were adopted by the BOE during August 1999. That same month, the DOE began writing performance standards (Hawaii State Auditor, 2001, p. 3).

During the 2000 session, the Hawaii State Legislature passed Senate Concurrent Resolution 57, which requested the Legislative Auditor "to review and assess the Department of Education's development of educational standards for public schools statewide to ensure that Hawaii's standards for competency in the basic educational skills are on par with the standards of other states" (Hawaii State Legislature, 2000, para. 5). The resolution also mentioned that a primary motivation for requesting this study was that "a national study on the development of educational standards by states, indicat[ed] that Hawaii's overall grade was D-minus and ranked 44 in its English, History, Geography, Science, and Math standards" (Hawaii State Legislature, 2000, para. 3). The study referred to appears to be the 1999 edition of the *Education Week* annual national review, *Quality Counts*. The 1999 *Quality Counts* assessment gave the state a D- for standards and assessments in large part because "the state got a failing grade for the clarity and specificity of its standards from the American Federation of Teachers" (Education Week, 1999, para. 1).

The Hawaii State Auditor has a policy of not responding to single body resolutions requesting reports from the state Senate or House alone. It does, however, respond to concurrent resolutions that have passed both the House and Senate, as Senate Concurrent Resolution 57 did during the 2000 session. To facilitate its analysis, the Auditor contracted with a firm nationally known in the field of standards, McREL. McREL was tasked to assess "each content standard for coherence, clarity, and comprehensiveness" (Hawaii State Auditor, 2001, summary section para. 3). The report summary defined their use of the terms as follows:

> Coherence refers to how well each standards document is organized so that the material will make sense to the reader and will be easy to use. Clarity refers to how clearly the standards describe the concepts and skills that students should learn and can demonstrate. Comprehensiveness refers to whether the concepts and skills address significant concepts and skills for each subject area, whether the concepts and skills are presented at the appropriate level of difficulty, and whether the content and skills described are specific enough to be meaningful (Hawaii State Auditor, 2001, summary section para. 3).

The standards were determined to be generally "coherent and well organized" in the core academic areas of language arts, mathematics, science, and social studies, although "the level of specificity of some benchmarks is inconsistent" (Hawaii State Auditor, 2001, summary section para. 3). Improvement of the clarity of the standards was recommended. While the core subject matter area standards covered "significant concepts and skills," it was noted that they could nevertheless "benefit from the inclusion of skills and concepts found in highly regarded state and national documents" (Hawaii State Auditor, 2001, summary section para. 6). Other more concrete, specific revisions were urged as well. Mathematics received special praise; "the job is nearly complete" (Hawaii State Auditor, 2001, p. 36).

The Auditor's examination of the DOE's strategic plan for the implementation of standards (Hawaii Department of Education, 1999a) also noted that they field tested standards-based "student assessments in reading, writing, and math" on 51,000 students in May 2000 for a statewide rollout during Spring 2001 (Hawaii State Auditor, 2001, p. 6). This instrument would be complemented "with a portion of the Stanford Achievement Tests, 9th edition" (Hawaii State Auditor, 2001, p. 6). As assessment would be linked to standards, so, too, would professional development and curricular support, according to Superintendent Paul LeMahieu's address at the Annual Leadership Conference in August 2000. The audit noted that concrete steps were beginning to be taken in this area.

In 2002 the Hawaii State Performance Standards Review Commission convened again under the mandate of Hawaii Revised Statutes 302A-201, assisted by "ample logistical and technical support" from Pacific Resources for Education and Learning (Hawaii State Performance Standards Review Commission, 2003, p. 6). They issued their final report in January 2003, which made a wide variety of findings and recommendations designed to support the ongoing improvement of the reform model. Among the most salient was that "the DOE had made appropriate revisions suggested in the state audit of the HCPS II's core content areas (language arts, mathematics, social studies, and science), conducted by the Mid-continent Research for Education and Learning" (Hawaii State Performance Standards Review Commission, 2003, p. 2). The commission also noted that "performance standards are in the final stages of development" (Hawaii State Performance Standards Review Commission, 2003, p. 2). Furthermore, the BOE and DOE came under criticism for failing to establish a system

> to attend or respond to the seven recommendations of 1998 PSRC report. This has made it difficult for the current Commissioners to evaluate the quality of the BOE's and DOE's responses to the PSRC's first recommendations" (Hawaii State Performance Standards Review Commission, 2003, p. 3).

In spite of a variety of concrete criticisms, the report did cite the Standards Implementation Design System and the Strategic Implementation Plan as valuable tools for establishing standards on a firmer footing (Hawaii State Performance Standards Review Commission, 2003, p. 49). Finally, the report issued in January 2003 continued to vigorously support the notion that standards-based education would "produce consistently high results for all children across Hawaii" (Hawaii State Performance Standards Review Commission, 2003, p. 5). While the report was generally positive, it stated that HCPS II was still "a 'work in progress' when it came to direct linkages to the General Learner Outcomes, clear criteria or rubrics, samples of student work, and strategies to meet diverse learner needs" (Hawaii State Performance Standards Review Commission, 2003, pp. 21–22).

After working with the Auditor to identify shortcomings in HCPS II, McREL was contracted by the DOE to implement their findings by revising the standards to create HCPS III. Over the course of 2003–2005, McREL once again supported standards development in Hawaii by working with the DOE to develop "recommendations for revision of Hawaii state standards in English language arts, mathematics, science, social studies, the arts, educational technology, health, physical education, career and life skills, and world languages" with particular attention given to the development of performance standards (Mid-continent Research for Education and Learning, 2009, para. 6). In addition, "revisions included a consistent grain size for standards and benchmarks, the use of Marzano's New Taxonomy to develop benchmarks, and alignment with instructional time available in the classroom" (Hawaii State Performance Standards Review Commission, 2006, p. 15).

During this period, the DOE also moved to address the commission's concern from their 2003 report for enhanced standards-based teacher training by developing a train-the-trainer model in which "state level staff train district/complex area cadre who then work with schools" (Hawaii Department of Education, 2006, p. 15). DOE also developed a "professional development series of modules, entitled Transforming Our Teaching and Learning (TOTAL)" (Hawaii State Performance Standards Review Commission, 2006, p. 16), and DOE produced a video shown on Olelo public access television and the Internet (Hawaii Department of Education, 2006, p. 15).

External policy developments during this period also impacted standards-based education. Most notably this is included Act 51, Session Laws of Hawaii 2004, which "replaced the Standards Implementation Design (SID) school improvement plan with the Academic and Financial Plan which required closer alignment of funds with student achievement of the HCPS" (Hawaii State Performance Standards Review Commission, 2006, p. 16).

Recommendations for the ongoing improvement of the standards culminated in BOE approval between April and August 2005 of the Hawaii Content and Performance Standards III in nine content areas. These documents include K–12 content standards, grade level/course benchmarks, a sample performance assessment for each benchmark, and a rubric that enables teachers to judge the performance of students with respect to the expected level of rigor of the benchmark (Hawaii State Performance Standards Review Commission, 2006, p. 15).

Among the reasons for the transition from HCPS II to HCPS III were reports from teachers "that HCPS II lacked the specificity by grade level and courses, was unrealistic—due to the sheer number of standards—to teach and students to learn in one year, [and] lacked performance standards (measures of quality)" (Hawaii Department of Education, 2006, p. 2). Other key motivators for change included external reviews from nationally recognized experts, and the 2003 PSRC report.

Among the national experts whose opinions seemed to carry some weight were those of W. James Popham of the University of California at Los Angeles, who gave a presentation to Superintendent Patricia Hamamoto and staff in Honolulu on April 17, 2003. In this presentation, Popham (2003) urged adoption of what he termed "instructionally sensitive NCLB tests." These would "(1) measure only a modest number of super-significant curricular aims, (2) supply lucid teacher-palatable descriptions of what's to be assessed, and (3) provide instructionally informative results so that a student's mastery of each assessed curricular aim can be determined" (Popham, 2003, para. 1). Absent achievement of these objectives, Popham argued, states risk "failure to make adequate yearly progress on tests whose very nature makes such progress essentially unattainable." The solution he suggests is the division of existing standards into those that are "desirable, very desirable, and essential" and to "focus on only the essential standards" (Popham, 2001, pp. 30–36).

In response to the feedback from all of these sources, the DOE's Office of Curriculum, Instruction and Student Support (OCISS) developed several criteria that would be used to guide the transition from HCPS II to HCPS III. Presented to the Board of Education on March 14, 2006, these were to

- Provide specificity of expectations by grade level and courses…
- Communicate expectations for ALL students…
- Identif[y] grade level and course standards… implementable… within the instructional time frame.

- Be comparable to national and highly regarded state standards.
- Provide rubrics to assess student's learning which are based on the taxonomic levels of thinking (rigor) (Hawaii Department of Education, 2006, p. 7).

By 2006 it was again time for the Hawaii State Performance Standards Review Commission to reconvene, as per statute. As in 2003, they issued a thorough report (Hawaii State Performance Standards Review Commission, 2006) with numerous findings and recommendations. Perhaps the two most notable ones were that "the 2006 PSRC recommends that the Hawaii Content and Performance Standard III has undergone rigorous development and that it need not be modified at this time" (Hawaii State Performance Standards Review Commission, 2006, p. 5) and that "national organizations have found the HCPS to be valid and rigorous" (Hawaii State Performance Standards Review Commission, 2006, p. 4).

In the course of its three successive versions, the Hawaii Content and Performance Standards have indeed undergone extensive review by nationally respected external entities for well over a decade. In 1995 one of the leading proponents of standards-based education, the American Federation of Teachers led by then-president Albert Shanker, issued the first in an annual series of "comprehensive [analyses] of education standards in the states" (American Federation of Teachers, 1999, p. 2). This report, *Making Standards Matter*, would become an influential annual review of the state of standards in the states, one that continued through 2001 (American Federation of Teachers, 1996, 1997, 1998, 1999, 2001). *Making Standards Matter* sought to evaluate whether or not state standards in four core academic subjects (English, math, science, and social studies) were clear and rigorous, and to briefly examine their relationship to assessments, student incentives, and academic intervention. The report suffers from an inconsistent reporting format that changed over time, making a longitudinal comparison somewhat difficult. Generally, however, assessments were not especially positive, although mathematics and science did well between 1995–1997.

The other most significant ongoing annual national review of the states' educational standards has been that conducted by the national newspaper of record for K–12 education, *Education Week*. This review, *Quality Counts*, began in 1997 and continues to the present day. The initial 1997 edition mentioned that work on standards-based education began in Hawaii in 1994. It also quoted the chair of the state's Goals 2000 Panel on Assessment,

Teaching, and Learning, Lois-ellin Datta, that she felt "it is doubtful that many teachers know about the new standards, have copies of them, and have done much to link specific curriculum elements and assessments to the framework" (Trotter, 1997, p. 96). Instead, the report stated that "the school system considers its most important recent reform to be the movement to school- and community-based management" (Trotter, 1997, p. 96). In 1998 it was noted that, while standards were in their third year, "there still is no funding to develop the accompanying assessment" and that "the standardized test used in math and reading is not aligned to state standards" (Manzo, 1998, p. 138). In 1999 the state's grade from *Quality Counts* dropped considerably to a D-: "the state got a failing grade for the clarity and specificity of its standards from the American Federation of Teachers" (Education Week, 1999, p. 140).

While the state's grade improved only marginally in 2000, that year's report did mention Superintendent LeMahieu's concerted effort "to make Hawaii's content and performance standards the centerpiece of the education system" (Jacobson, 2000, p. 112). That year's assessment also made reference to the criticisms of the PSRC 1999 report: vagueness, lack of standards for certain content areas, and an absence of performance standards. Further noted was LaMahieu's call for a system-wide needs assessment. Delivered in February 1999, it cited the "need to improve standards-based learning" in addition to five other core needs (Jacobson, 2000, p. 112). In conjunction with the commission's report, the two documents were "being used to point the department in the direction of standards-based reform" (Jacobson, 2000, p. 112). Steps to come included the development of performance standards and piloting that year of the Hawaii Assessment Program of Outcomes.

By the 2001 edition of *Quality Counts*, Superintendent LeMahieu was able to claim that "we're starting to gain some serious momentum" (Jacobson, 2001, p. 130). "Standards alliance teams" fanned out from the DOE to provide training in standards implementation at nearly half of the DOE schools by the time of the report (Jacobson, 2001, p. 130). Furthermore, that year each school was "expected to turn in its first 'standards implementation design', a standards-based document that replaces various other school-level planning activities" (Jacobson, 2001, p. 130). As had been the case since the inception of the *Quality Counts* review, Hawaii's assessment practices remained an area in need of improvement, which was being addressed by "the development of a new program of criterion-referenced assessments aligned with the state standards" (Jacobson, 2001, p. 130).

Not until HCPS III was adopted by the BOE in 2005 did Hawaii's score on the *Quality Counts* report rise above the C and D level, to a B+ for the years 2005 and 2006. However, since *Quality Counts* is typically issued in January of each year, and HCPS III was adopted by the BOE between April and August 2005, Hawaii's much-improved grades from *Education Week* between 2003–2005 may have been an increasingly positive response to the performance standards that were released after HCPS II was approved by the BOE in August 1999. It only achieved a B+ in 2005 and 2006. In 1999 it was as low as a D-.

Other important external reviews of Hawaii's standards over the years have come from the Thomas Fordham Foundation, the American Federation of Teachers (distinct from its previous *Making Standards Matter* review), Achieve, Inc., and the Hoover Institution.

Like the American Federation of Teachers and *Education Week*, the Thomas Fordham Foundation has a relatively long history of analyzing state standards. This took the form of either analyzing specific subject matter areas across the country or examining a group of core academic subject matter areas across the country. For example, in 1997 Hawaii's HCPS I English standards were reviewed. Their report was ambiguous. Fordham determined that the standards "do not express high academic standards" and yet elsewhere in the report called them "clear" and "demanding" (Stotsky, 1997, pp. 2, 5). In 1998 Fordham issued a number of reports on individual subject matter areas that were later consolidated into a single report. The 1998 report of the states' history standards found that in Hawaii "no standards were available for review" (Saxe, 1998, p. 29). Similarly, geography was graded "incomplete." What they could find about geography was "embedded in Hawaii's social studies framework" and judged "neither comprehensive nor rigorous" (Munroe and Smith, 1998, para. 1). Mathematics standards in 1998, graded on "clarity, content, reason, and negative qualities," were called "vague" and given no points at all in the categories of clarity and reason (Raimi and Braden, 1998, p. 30).

The bright spot was science. Even though Hawaii science standards were criticized for suffering "from the limitation of lists" and failure to emphasize "the connectedness that is so essential to science," they were still given an A grade and tied for second place in the nation (Lerner, 1998, pp. viii, 21). In the cumulative report issued later that year, Hawaii received a combined score of D+ for its F grades in English and Math and its A in Science (Finn, Petrilli, and Vanourek, 1998). In spite of such a low grade, however, Hawaii's score was still slightly above the median, coming in at 21st place.

In Fordham's second multi-disciplinary nationwide review, released in 2000, Hawaii did worse, coming in 44th place on a review of HCPS II. The report card yielded an F in English, geography, and history, a C in Math, a D in science, and a D- cumulatively. A common complaint was vagueness, too much breadth, and a lack of specifics. The drop in the science grade from an A to a D was a dramatic change, although the analysis commented positively that "a competent committee assigned to flesh out" the science standards might result in "one of the finest science standards in the nation" (Finn and Petrelli, 2000, pp. 49–50).

In 2003 U.S. history standards were examined by Fordham nationwide. As in 2000, Hawaii received an F. Fordham noted that Hawaii's standards reflected "the outlook of 'Meeting the Challenge: A Framework for Social Studies Restructuring' published in 1992 by the National Council for the Social Studies," a model that was apparently none too popular with Fordham. The report further criticized Hawaii's U.S. history standards for an "ambivalent and almost anti-intellectual approach to historical knowledge" (Stern, Chesson, Klee, and Spoehr, 2003, p. 36).

In 2005 Fordham's analysts turned their attention to state math standards nationwide. Here, Hawaii's math standards grade reverted from a C back to the F it had originally received in Fordham's first national report on the subject in 1998. The 2005 Fordham math report blasted Hawaii's standards saying, "There is little that can be salvaged in Hawaii's mathematics standards" (Klein, Braams, Parker, Quirk, Schmid, Wilson, Finn, Torres, Braden, and Raimi, 2005, p. 56). In math, as with U.S. history mentioned above, a portion of Fordham's negative appraisal stemmed from their dissatisfaction with the models promulgated by the national disciplinary organizations. In a response defending their HCPS II math standards, the DOE noted that they were "modeled after National Council of Teachers of Mathematics (NCTM) Principles and Standards for School Mathematics (PSSM) 2000" (Hawaii Department of Education, 2005a, para. 2). States that built on this organization's work were criticized by Fordham for an "unfortunate embrace of the advice of the National Council of Teachers of Mathematics" (Klein, Braams, Parker, Quirk, Schmid, Wilson, Finn, Torres, Braden, and Raimi, 2005, p. 7). In its further defense, the DOE noted that "while California received the Fordham Institute's highest rating and Hawaii received one of its lowest, both states scored equally well on the 2003 NAEP mathematics assessment for grades 4 and 8" (Hawaii Department of Education, 2005a, para. 4).

In 2005 Fordham also looked at English and science standards. In science, Fordham's earlier optimism that Hawaii's science standards could be "among the finest in the nation" with a little improvement had apparently fallen by the wayside. Hawaii's science standards were called "bloated," "poorly organized," "with a quality of writing... so weak that one wonders if there has even been a single proofreading" (Gross, Goodenough, Lerner, Haack, Schwartz, Schwartz, and Finn, 2005, p. 35). Hawaii's grade in that subject dropped from a D in 2000 to an F in 2005 (Gross, Goodenough, Lerner, Haack, Schwartz, Schwartz, and Finn, 2005, p. 20). Unlike math, the grade for Hawaii's English standards improved from 2000 to 2005, from a D to C. Furthermore, Fordham's report said that, overall, the addition of performance standards to HCPS II "considerably strengthen[ed] understanding of the 1999 standards" (Stotsky and Finn, 2005, p. 39). Nevertheless, they were still judged in the main to be "vague, undemanding, and unmeasurable" (Stotsky and Finn, 2005, p. 39).

Fordham rated state world history standards in 2006. Hawaii did poorly yet again, earning an F for standards that were "truly weak" and presented in such a way so that "it is not clear that Hawaii's students will learn anything about world history" (Finn, Davis, and Mead, 2006, pp. 43–44). Hawaii continued to rank poorly in Fordham's 2006 nationwide assessment of standards in core academic subject areas, receiving an F and a ranking of 47, down from a grade and ranking of D- and 44 in the previous report in 2000, and a D+ and 21st place finish in 1998. Hawaii was given a C in English and an F in all other remaining subjects: math, science, U.S. history, and world history, although the report held out hope that "more specificity would go a long way" (Finn, Petrilli, and Julian, 2006, p. 62).

The American Federation of Teachers quit publishing their annual *Making Standards Matter* series in 2001. In 2006, however, they revisited the issue of the alignment of state tests required under *No Child Left Behind* with state standards. They identified "strong" criteria for content standards in math and science but not reading. In Hawaii, however, they didn't see assessment aligned with standards in any of these subjects, making Hawaii one of only nine states to earn a 0% in this category (American Federation of Teachers, 2006, pp. 8, 13). This judgment, however, was probably because American Federation of Teachers found that "there are no test documents available online that identify the standards to be assessed by the states," not because such instruments didn't exist (American Federation of Teachers, 2006, p. 1). In fact, contrary to their claims, the DOE had already rolled out standards-aligned tests for grades 3, 5, 8, and 10 in 2002 (Jacobson, 2003, p. 125).

In any event, this perception has perhaps been laid to rest by "new, grade-level specific tests that are closely aligned with the latest Hawaii Content and Performance Standards III. The new tests, developed and administered by American Institutes for Research (AIR), provide a better measure of how well students are learning what they are expected to learn in reading and mathematics in grades 3 through 8 and grade 10" (McClelland, 2007, para. 1–2).

Achieve, Inc. is a business-oriented education reform organization that focuses on helping states graduate high school students who are "college and work ready." In the early 2000 decade, they offered the business community their primary vehicle to stay engaged consistently with their preferred vision of education reform. For example, in 2004, they compared "the graduation exams in six states—Florida, Maryland, Massachusetts, New Jersey, Ohio, and Texas"—to assess the tests' "content and rigor" and the appropriateness of their "cut scores," (what is judged sufficient to pass) (Achieve, Inc., 2006, p. 1). The resulting report, *Do High School Graduation Exams Measure Up?*, drew the attention of the DOE as a means of evaluating one of their primary assessment instruments. In 2005 the DOE asked Achieve, Inc. to utilize the same methodology to compare Hawaii's "grade 10 Hawaii State Assessment in reading and mathematics with the six states' exams" (Achieve, Inc., 2006, p. 1). Their report on Hawaii concluded that "the reading test is generally less demanding than those of other states, [while] the mathematics test contains considerably more challenging content than tests from other states" although "neither assessment is overly rigorous" (Achieve, Inc., 2006, p. 1).

More specific findings included the sense that "Hawaii's reading test puts a premium on comprehension of informational text" over literature, which Achieve claims is preferred by colleges and business. However, the expository prose given emphasis in the testing instrument tended to be of "relatively low cognitive complexity," making it "among the least rigorous" of the states tests' they examined (Achieve, Inc., 2006, p. 2). Cut scores for "meets proficiency" in reading were comparable to those of other states, although they opined that this was nevertheless a relatively low bar, more comparable to ACT's test for 8th and 9th graders than ACT's test for college admissions (Achieve, Inc., 2006, p. 2). In math, Hawaii's test was considered "well balanced" and "rigorous"; in fact, "more rigorous than all but one of the states analyzed in Achieve's earlier study" (Achieve, Inc., 2006, p. 2). They gave special praise for Hawaii's emphasis on advanced algebra, especially in light of their sense "that Algebra II is fast replacing Algebra I as the gatekeeper course for success in college and the high skills workplace" (Achieve, Inc., 2006, pp. 2–3). They also found "the content demand" to be "higher than those in other states," while "the test items themselves are less cognitively demanding" (Achieve, Inc., 2006, p. 3). On balance, this put the cut scores for "meets proficiency" in math slightly above those of the other states they looked at. As with reading, however, a caveat was added: meeting proficiency in this test was equivalent to 8th grade math "in most other countries" (Achieve, Inc., 2006, p. 3).

Achieve recommended that "the overall rigor of the grade 10 reading test" be raised, the cut score of the reading test be raised over time, and "the level of performance demand of the mathematics items" be raised (Achieve, Inc., 2006, p. 3).

In another important external review of Hawaii's standards made by the Hoover Institution in 2005 comparing the "strength of state proficiency standards," Hawaii ranked 6th out of 40 states, receiving a B grade (Peterson and Hess, 2005, p. 53). As the study co-author Frederick M. Hess remarked, "We want to be sure that states that are really stepping up to the challenge like Hawaii are being recognized" (Hess cited in Essoyan, 2005, para. 8).

"States such as California, Kentucky, Maryland, Massachusetts, North Carolina, and Texas had all begun to implement standards-based reform in the 1980s using their own funds" (Hamilton, Steecher, and Yuan, 2008, p. 24). While not among these pioneers, Hawaii does appear to have been ahead of the curve on standards-based education in the United States. Passage of Act 334, Session Laws of Hawaii 1991, created the Hawaii Commission on Performance Standards and set the state on the road to implementing this reform model prior to the passage of the federal *Goals 2000* legislation and well before most of the disciplinary organizations had even begun drafting model standards. Furthermore, Hawaii was the first state to receive *Goals 2000* funding for work on standards (A Goals 2000 time line, 1998, para. 6). Under Superintendent Paul LeMahieu's leadership, the DOE made a concerted effort "to make Hawaii's content and performance standards the centerpiece of the education system" (Jacobson, 2000, p. 112). Superintendent Patricia Hamamoto continued this commitment during her tenure. In spite of this early start, however, Hawaii has never been among those states consistently lauded by external reviewers as having exemplary standards across the board. One early bright spot was the initial reception of HCPS I science standards by the Fordham Institute in 1998.

Nevertheless, it should be noted that Hawaii's efforts to continually refine the state standards documents have certainly born fruit. Since HCPS III was released in 2005, Hawaii has received consistent B+ ratings from the *Education Week Quality Counts* survey, with particular praise directed at English standards and middle and high school level social studies/history standards (Quality Counts, 2005, para. 3). In fairness to Hawaii, many external reviewers were harsh judges of many other states' efforts in the early years of the movement. For example, Hawaii's overall grade of D+ from Fordham in 1998 was still good enough for a 21st place ranking (Finn, Petrilli, and Vanourek, 1998).

Kathryn Matayoshi was hired away from the Hawaii Business Roundtable, where she served as executive director since 2007, in July 2009 "to serve as the deputy superintendent" in the Hawaii DOE "and assist in the department's bid for federal Race to the Top funds" (Honolulu Civil Beat; Hawaii Department of Education, *Leadership profiles and staff*, para. 2). In June 2010 Hawaii adopted the Common Core State Standards (KHON Channel 2, 2010). Matayoshi was appointed superintendent in September 2010, (Hawaii Department of Education, *Leadership profiles and staff*, para. 2). Dan Horner, a Hawaii banker and former chair of the Hawaii Business Roundtable, was "sworn in as Governor Neil Abercrombie's first selection" in February 2011 to the newly-appointed state Board of Education, which was then in a transition from being an elected body to an appointed one (Koga, 2011, para. 5, 29).

Hawaii was chosen as "one of 10 states" to "serve as a national model for implementing Common Core State Standards and associated assessments to improve students' readiness for and success in college" in December 2011 under the Core to College program, which was partially funded by the Bill and Melinda Gates Foundation (University of Hawaii, 2011, para. 1, 7–8). That same month, Hawaii's Race to the Top grant was labeled as "high risk" by the U.S. Department of Education, primarily because of "teacher evaluation problems" (Kalani, 2014, p. B1; McNeill, 2014, para. 7).

During the 2012–2013 school year, "the Hawaii State Department of Education began its implementation of the Common Core in 2012–2013 with grades K–2 and 11–12, with implementation in all grade levels" begun in 2013–2014 and with student evaluation "transitioning from the Hawaii State Assessment to a new statewide test aligned to the Common Core" as a member of the Smarter Balanced Assessment Consortium, with initial trials held during the 2013–2014 school year and a full roll-out to follow during the 2014–2015 school year (Hawaii Department of Education, *Hawaii Common Core Standards*).

When Hawaii applied for a Round 1 grant under Race to the Top, Secretary Duncan said that initially "there was a huge amount of skepticism in the outside world, and frankly, internally" within the United States Department of Education (Hawaii Department of Education, 2014, para. 2). Despite these qualms, Duncan tapped Hawaii as the winner of a four year "$75 million federal Race to the Top grant" in 2010 (Hawaii Board of Education, 2014, para. 1). Hawaii faced a number of challenges during the first year of its grant. These included internal matters within the DOE, a new superintendent being appointed, and the transition of the Board of Education from being elected to being appointed by the governor (United States Department of Education, 2012, p. 4). After nearly two years on the job, Matayoshi was given the "top rating of 'exceptional' from the DOE in her annual job performance evaluation" during July 2013 (Hawaii Department of Education, 2013, para. 1).

The high risk warning label attached to Hawaii's Race to the Top award "was partially lifted in February 2013 and completely lifted" that summer (Kalani, 2014, p. B1). In March 2014 Secretary Duncan visited Hawaii and called it a "model for other states" (Kalani, 2014, p. B1). Secretary Duncan and Governor Abercrombie penned an editorial published in the local daily newspaper calling Hawaii "a rising star in education reform," noting that Hawaii was also "one of the top five fastest improving states in the country" in 2013 National Assessment for Educational Progress results (Duncan and Abercrombie, 2014). Stephen Schatz, brother of the senior U.S. Senator from Hawaii, Brian Schatz, led implementation of Hawaii's Race to the Top award as an Assistant Superintendent of the DOE (Hawaii Department of Education, *Leadership profiles and staff*, para. 7). Superintendent Matayoshi has said that "Race to the Top was an important step in the transformation of our public school system and we are staying the course" (Kalani, 2014, p. B4).

This is very similar language to that used by John Engler (chair of the Business Roundtable) and Randi Weingarten (president of the American Federation of Teachers) in 2013 when they urged governors "to stay the course and oppose attempts to impede the successful implementation of the Common Core State Standards" (Engler and Weingarten, 2013, para. 5). Hawaii is very likely to "stay the course" because, as Hawaii Board of Education chair noted, he used to

> chair the [Hawaii] Business Roundtable [and] the superintendent was the executive director, so [they've] known each other for a lot of years...But having said that, the key to any organization is your common core values. Business without core values is not a good business model. It's the job of the appointed board to set the tone of those core values, and within those core values you set the priorities (Koga, 2011, para. 29).

On April 23, 2014, the Hawaii State Legislature voted to confirm Horner for a second term on the BOE (Hawaii State Legislature, 2014).

In this chapter, I outlined the political context that made Hawaii one of the early adopters of standards-based education by examining a number of important local initiatives that took place during the late 1980s and early 1990s in the context of relevant and comparable initiatives occurring on the "mainland" United States. Having set the stage in this way, I was then able to closely examine the historical evolution of numerous iterations of standards in Hawaii. Next, I summarized the local and national evaluation literature revolving around Hawaii's standards, which gave Hawaii a mixed grade. Finally, I examined recent developments in Hawaiian education policy as it related to Race to the Top and Common Core.

· 6 ·

NO CHILD LEFT BEHIND, RACE TO THE TOP, AND COMMON CORE

In this chapter I will examine alternative legislative proposals that competed with No Child Left Behind (NCLB), the politics of the passage and implementation of NCLB, and the emergence of a bipartisan elite consensus among the mainstream educational establishment that led to the creation of Race to the Top and Common Core. A number of different education plans were floating around during the 106th Congress, as Gore and Bush battled for the presidency. Conservative education interests coalesced around the collaboration between the EXPECT coalition and House Education Committee chair Representative Bill Goodling (R-PA) with the Academic Achievement for All Act (the "Straight A's" bill). It sought to consolidate the categorical programs of the Elementary and Secondary Education Act (ESEA) into block grants and enhance opportunities for school choice, especially through vouchers. The National Governors Association and the National Council of State Legislators appreciated the flexibility (Hess and Petrilli, 2006, p. 16; Debray-Pelot, 2007, pp. 73–74). Another bill was the Student Results Act. It was drafted by Representative George Miller (D-CA) and Senator Edward Kennedy (D-MA) with the help of the Education Trust. Executive Director of the Education Trust, Kati Haycock, noted that Miller and Kennedy "were bonkers about what happened to the IASA," in that the

Clinton administration kept scaling back implementation responsibilities at the state level (cited in Rhodes, 2012, pp. 142–143). Yet another bill was the Public Education Reinvestment, Reinvention, and Responsibility Act (the "3 R's" bill) floated by Centrist Senate Democrats led by Joseph Lieberman (D-CT) and Evan Bayh (D-IN).

Bush and Gore both needed a comprehensive education plan. In campaigning as a "compassionate conservative," Bush shifted from the antigovernment rhetoric of Reagan, from saying "the problem of government is government," to saying that this approach was a "destructive mindset" encapsulating "the idea that if government would only get out of the way, all our problems would be solved… An approach with no higher goal, no nobler purpose than 'leave us alone'" (cited in Sorin, 2012, para. 62).

As Clinton essentially borrowed George H. W. Bush's ideas, so too did George W. Bush borrow them back from Clinton via the Democratic Leadership Council's Progressive Policy Institute (as well as utilizing some of his own standards-based education efforts while governor of Texas) (Gorman, 2002, para. 20–21). This encroached on an issue that had been firmly controlled by the Democrats for decades, in much the same way Clinton encroached on "Republican issues" of crime and welfare in his process of "triangulation." Gore was left to play catch up. Both campaigns utilized many of the ideas from the 3 R's bill (Rotherham, 2001, para. 15).

While still president elect, Bush invited a number of key education policy players in Congress from both sides of the aisle to meet with him in Texas, Senator Edward Kennedy excepted. He was later invited to a separate gathering at the White House, a private screening of *Thirteen Days*, a film about Kennedy's brother's management of the Cuban missile crisis (Baker, 2007, para. 15). With this meeting, Bush secured Kennedy's agreement to work together on reform legislation. Bush also "later renamed the Justice Department headquarters after Robert F. Kennedy" (Baker, 2007, para. 15).

After Bush took office, he moved quickly to lay the groundwork for what he hoped would be his signature piece of domestic legislation, a bipartisan education bill. He sent an outline for NCLB up to Capitol Hill soon after his inauguration (Gorman, 2001, para. 28). It was simply a sketch, not an actual bill. While the document was short, it was still substantive and supple enough to provide a firm basis for negotiations. Lieberman and Bayh reintroduced the 3 R's bill the same day Bush released his outline. Many of the states that had the most stringent standards-based education regimes prior to NCLB failed to improve much on the National Assessment of Educational Progress in the

1990s. Nevertheless, this didn't matter much while NCLB was being negotiated. Liberal democrat frustration with how thoroughly Clinton had watered down the state implementation requirements of the Improving America's Schools Act (IASA) made them receptive to stringent federal solutions. It also made them willing to go to bat against the teacher unions.

Some thought that if states and smaller subdivisions of government failed to reform their educational systems according to standards-based education, perhaps the problem was not with standards-based education per se but rather with the heterogeneity, incoherence, lack of leadership, and slack implementation of state initiatives. Kati Haycock of the Education Trust said that "going state-by-state on standards and accountability was a very slow strategy;" better "to get the feds to make them do it" (cited in Rhodes, 2012, p. 142). Of course, it did not hurt the bill's chances for passage; it "increased the Department of Education's overall discretionary budget by 15.9 percent, to $48.9 billion, the largest dollar increase in the department's two-decade history" (Vinovskis, 2009, p. 170). In an era of tight resources, this was enough to gain the attention of and compliance by the states, even though the federal share of education spending was only running about 7% at this time. In spite of momentum in support, the testing provisions united left Democrats and conservative Republicans in opposition. In the House, Barney Frank (D-MA) and Peter Hoekstra (R-MI) combined to fight against these provisions, although the effort failed (Fine, 2001, para. 7–8). The Business Roundtable called on its members to contact Congress in opposition to the proposed amendment (McGuinn, 2006, p. 174).

Secretary of Education Rod Paige was largely left out of negotiations, in favor of Bush's long-time education advisor Alexander "Sandy" Kress (a veteran Texas business lobbyist Bush knew from his time as governor) and the White House's Domestic Policy Council. The membership of the seven-person group holding the new administration's education portfolio included

> Margaret LaMontagne, senior education advisor, Office of the Governor of Texas; William Hansen, executive director, Education Finance Council (and a Department of Education official in the previous Bush administration); Sandy Kress, a partner in Akin, Gump, Hauer, and Field, as well as an education advisor to the Bush campaign; Sarah Youssef, education policy advisor to the Bush campaign and former education analyst at the Heritage Foundation; Christine Wolf, professional staff member, House Education and the Workforce Committee and former education analyst at the Heritage Foundation; Becky Campoverde, communications director, House Education and Workforce Committee (and Department of Education official

in the previous Bush administration); and Nina Shokraii Rees, senior education policy analyst at the Heritage Foundation and education advisor to the Bush campaign. These individuals, and a few other advisors, oversaw the education transition and filled key White House and Department of Education jobs in the new administration (Vinovskis, 2009, p. 159).

Again, the involvement of big business proved crucial in sustaining the momentum of standards-based education, this time as legislative negotiations on NCLB began. Kress sought the counsel of the Business Coalition for Excellence in Education in regular meetings, "a larger successor organization to the Business Coalition for Education Reform" (Rhodes, 2012, p. 140). The Business Coalition for Excellence in Education also mounted a multi-faceted lobbying effort with Congress, including sending 30 CEOs to lobby Congress on April 4, 2001 (As the school-reform debate heats up, Where's business?, 2001, para. 2). As Rotherham of the Democratic Leader Council said, "You need business to do some heavy lifting if you want to get a strong bill passed" (As the school-reform debate heats up, Where's business?, 2001, para. 3).

State-level Business Roundtable members also penned letters and worked the phones to convey state-level experiences to "share lessons learned at the state level" with their Congressional delegates, emphasizing the relationship between passing bipartisan education reform and maintaining America's global economic competiveness in the new millennium (Business Roundtable, 2001, para. 4). Paige's successor, Margaret Spellings (2009) admitted that these types of big business entities were "a huge ally in the development, implementation, and support for No Child Left Behind."

In the midst of all of this, a political earthquake shook Washington, DC on May 24, 2001 when Senator James Jeffords (R-NH) announced his resignation from the Republican party to serve as an independent, and that he would be caucusing with the Democrats. This tilted the balance of power in the Senate from 50–50 (with Vice President Dick Cheney as the tie-breaking vote) to 51–49 in favor of the Democrats. Jeffords assumed the chairmanship of the Senate Environmental committee and Edward Kennedy become chair of the Senate Education Committee.

Bush's earlier cultivation of Kennedy now began to pay off. Now Bush had a liberal icon eager to deliver recalcitrant groups like the teacher unions. Kennedy's job was also made easier because numerous high profile civil rights organizations saw the bill as an extension of the long-standing civil rights and equity regime in education policy, a means of helping traditionally disadvantaged groups and closing the achievement gap between Caucasians and

Asians, and Hispanics and African Americans. They saw it as a means of giving the poor and disadvantaged a path to a better life. Early talks on the substance of the bill among Kennedy, Miller, and the White House caused the executive branch to break with educational conservatives and abandon vouchers in favor of letting parents and schools use Title I funding for private tutoring. Bush was able to weather criticism from conservatives on education because he was strong on "issues like taxes, the military, and business regulation" (Hess and Petrilli, 2006, pp. 18–19). A more difficult issue for negotiations was how to define "annual yearly progress": how to determine whether schools were failing or not.

The Business Roundtable education director, Susan Traiman, noted that "Bush really reached out to the Business Roundtable and asked for our support. He asked us to work with him, arguing that additional federal involvement really could make a difference" (cited in Rhodes, 2012, p. 140). This outreach was channeled in part through the Business Coalition for Excellence in Education.

After conservatives, business groups, civil rights advocates, and teacher unions all had their initial say, access to the actual drafting of the bill and decision-making process as the kinks were worked out became quite restricted, especially as law-makers felt the need for quick passage of a major bipartisan legislation after the September 11th attacks (DeBray-Pelot, 2007, p. 80). The conference committee report reconciling the differences between the House and Senate versions passed 381–41 in the House on December 13, 87–10 in the Senate on December 18, and was signed into law by President Bush on January 8, 2002 (Govtrack.us, H.R. 1 107th).

A more detailed history of NCLB can be found in such excellent volumes as McGuinn (2006), Vinovskis (2009), and Rhodes (2012). By necessity of the structure of my book, I will be offering a more concise version of the law. While some scholars argue that state efforts led federal initiatives for standards-based reform, others argued that federal initiatives led state efforts. On balance, I would have to side with those who argue that state efforts guided federal initiatives. To be sure, George H. W. Bush's efforts and Clinton's enacted legislation were at the federal level. Furthermore, these initiatives did goad some states along. However, these federal efforts would not have occurred unless the activities of early adopter states like Minnesota, California, Texas, North Carolina, Massachusetts, and Hawaii had not provided the blueprint; in terms of specific interventions by the Business Roundtable and favored contractors and associates like the consulting firm Bernard Weiler in the early days of standards-based education in Minnesota, California, and Hawaii.

Although the American Federation of Teachers and National Education Association had been supportive of standards-based reform, they were "lukewarm" regarding NCLB (Blair, 2002, para. 8). Both lobbied to dilute certain mandates they saw as inimical to the needs of their members. The National Education Association even announced in 2003 that it would file a lawsuit claiming NCLB was an unfunded mandate (Keller, 2003, para. 4, 10).

It could be said that public opinion was equally lukewarm. In 2004 a poll had Americans "evenly divided between those who feel favorable (39%) and those who feel unfavorable (38%);" 20% said "they did not know enough about the No Child Left Behind Act to form an opinion about it" (Education Testing Service, 2004, p. 2). As NCLB began to be implemented, many rank and file teachers and administrators had difficulty grasping the extent of the changes afoot. The more they came to understand the bill, the less they believed it was practical, or that it had even passed.

While the law required states to develop firmer sanctions than those provided for in the IASA, it also said that nothing in it allowed any branch of the federal government to "mandate, direct, or control a State, local educational agency, or school's specific instructional content, academic achievement standards and assessments, curriculum, or program of instruction" (Elementary & Secondary Education Part I – General Provisions, para. 1905). This preserved some degree of local autonomy in education policy-making, but also opened the door for states and districts to manipulate performance numbers in a variety of ways as well, especially regarding restructuring, assessments, and what counted as annual yearly progress (Scott, 2008). Even with these loopholes and the chorus of "unfunded mandate" growing ever louder, many states began to rebel. By the time of Kerry vs. Bush in 2004, this had become a campaign issue.

While agreeing with the law's substance, Kerry also called NCLB an unfunded mandate, claiming that NCLB fell "$27 billion short and implemented the law with a top-down, Washington-knows-best attitude that hurts students" (Robelen, September 20, 2004, para. 9). Civil rights groups like the NAACP added that it "'fostered a kind of drill-and-kill curriculum' that encouraged teaching to the test" (Reid, 2004, para. 10). This prompted significant push-back from Paige. He called the NAACP rhetoric "hateful" (Reid, 2004, para. 10). Bush said "we're not backing down…I don't care how much pressure they try to put on the process, I'm not changing my mind about high standards and the need for accountability" (Cavanagh, 2004, para. 2).

After Bush managed to retain the presidency in 2004, he moved quickly to fire Paige. Even though Paige had not been at the table in negotiating NCLB with Congress, he became associated with the difficulties in implementing it. The replacement of Paige with long-time advisor Margaret Spellings provided Bush with a fresh start of sorts but did little to squelch ever-increasing resistance. Shortly after Spellings' confirmation as the new Secretary of Education by the Senate on January 20, 2005, she introduced new regulations that allowed for greater flexibility for states and local education agencies in an April 2005 address calling for "a new common sense approach" (Hoff, April 7, 2005, para. 1, 4). In a November 2005 announcement Spellings allowed 10 states to develop these new types of assessment models (Hess and Petrilli, 2006, p. 41). There were also technical changes that waived testing requirements for very small groups of students and a number of other tweaks as well.

In spite of these changes, the political establishment continued to defend the substance of the law. From the right, Spellings said that "this law is a bipartisan expression of the fact that we as a nation no longer find it acceptable to let some children remain in the shadows, without the skills to achieve the American dream" (Spellings, 2005, para. 11). From the left, Robert Gordon, a Kerry education advisor, portrayed Democratic and civil rights-based criticism of NCLB as blind to the equity features inherent in the law's attempt to close the achievement gap (Gordon, 2005). Still, the common equity regime claim that NCLB was a fundamentally good law nonetheless came under attack. While president of the National Academy of Education, Noddings wrote that

> No Child Left Behind Act is a bad law and a bad law is not made better by fully funding it... The law employs a view of motivation that many of us in education find objectionable. As educators, we would not use threats, punishments, and pernicious comparisons to 'motivate' our students. But that is how the No Child Left Behind law treats the school establishment (2005, para. 1, 3).

Furthermore, a large number of critics noted that an immense amount of factors (especially students' social-economic status) affected their performance in school. Some claimed that it was unfair to put on all of the blame of student achievement on their classroom experience (Rothstein, 2004).

After Democrats regained the House in the 2006 elections, Representative George Miller assumed chairmanship of the House Education and Labor Committee. In July 2007 he said "I can tell you that there are no votes in the U.S. House of Representatives for continuing the No Child Left Behind Act without making serious changes to it" (Miller, 2007, para. 27). Popular opinion at this time was ambivalent-to-unsupportive; 68% believed "the law is hurting the performance of schools or making no difference" (Rose and Gallup, 2007, p. 34). Still, Miller was committed to an overhaul. He circulated a discussion draft in August 2007 that he hoped would strike common ground between supporters and detractors, and address the concerns of the various interest groups, while still retaining much of the law's original accountability provisions. In exchange for his efforts, he said his draft was treated "like a piñata" (cited in Baker, 2007, para. 37).

Criticism came from every corner: the Senate, big business, the Education Trust, state organizations, and educational conservatives. On February 15, 2007, 10 Democratic senators sent the Senate Education Committee leadership a letter that stated they "have concluded that the testing mandates of No Child Left Behind in their current form are unsustainable and must be overhauled significantly during the reauthorization process" and that the "requirements of NCLB are pressuring schools and teachers to narrow curriculum," (Feingold, Leahy, Cantwell, Nelson, Levin, Stabenow, Salazar, Klobuchar, McCaskill, and Durbin, 2007, para. 6–7). During the reauthorization process the Business Coalition for Student Achievement testified before Miller's committee "that improving the performance of the K-12 education system in the United States is necessary to provide a strong foundation for both U.S. competitiveness" (Business Coalition for Student Achievement, 2007, para. 2). They also noted that they had "deep concern" about "provisions included in the draft that we believe would undermine the current accountability for all students to reach proficiency and would provide a path by which states would create accountability system so complex as to be rendered meaningless" (Business Coalition for Student Achievement, 2007, para. 7). Amy Wilkins, vice president for government affairs and communication for the Education Trust, provided written testimony to the Senate asserting that

> it's hard from a policy point of view to make sense of the accountability provisions in [Miller's] draft, but their political meaning is quite clear. The efforts to dumb-down the definitions of progress and success by well-financed and ill-informed defenders of the status quo are gaining traction (Education Trust, 2007, para. 2).

Joan Wodiska, Education, Early Childhood, and Workforce Committee director for the National Governors Association, noted in testimony to Miller's committee that "the discussion draft does not recognize the leading role of governors in education reform" (Wodiska, 2007, para. 12). The National Governors Association, Council of Chief State School Officers, and National

Association of State Boards of Education combined to argue for greater flexibility at the state level. Educational conservatives were torn. Some had the traditional concern for states' rights, like the Heritage Foundation (Lips, 2007). Others were generally in favor of the law but sought numerous and detailed technocratic tweaks, like those suggested by policy entrepreneurs and scholars at the Hoover Institution, especially John Chubb, Chester Finn, and Rick Hess (Chubb, 2008). Other conservatives' camps simply wanted to end NCLB altogether, like Representative Peter Hoekstra (R-MI) and the libertarian Cato Foundation (Hoff, 2007, para. 8; McCluskey and Coulson, 2007).

As 2007 passed into 2008, Sam Graves (R-MS) and Tim Walz (D-MN) proposed a unique solution, a moratorium: the NCLB Recess until Reauthorization Act. This coalition was reminiscent of the liberal-conservative alliance against testing provisions that came together in 2001. Although it had the vocal support of the National Educational Association, Craig Barrett of Intel and Edward Rust of State Farm Insurance wrote an op-ed piece against the bill in the *Wall Street Journal* (Barrett and Rust, 2008). While the draft was written, circulated, and discussed, business leaders and organizations urged states to develop "college and career ready" standards. These leaders and organizations included:

1) The U.S. Chamber of Commerce and the Center for American Progress in their *Joint Platform for Education Reform* (2007);
2) Arthur Rothkopf, senior vice president of the U.S. Chamber of Commerce in testimony before the House and Senate in March 2007 (Rothkopf, 2007);
3) Thomas Donohue, U.S. Chamber of Commerce president, in a speech given in December 2007 (Donohue, 2007);
4) The Business Coalition for Student Achievement's Framework for Reauthorizing the No Child Left Behind (NCLB) Act (Business Coalition for Student Achievement);
5) Secretary of Education Margaret Spellings, the Business Roundtable's John Castellani of the Business Roundtable and the Citizens' Commission on Civil Rights' William Taylor at a January 2008 roundtable meeting at the National Press Club (Spellings, 2008); and
6) Hoover Institution scholars (Chubb, 2008).

During the 2008 campaign, Obama sought to distinguish himself from the Republicans on many key issues: Gulf War 2.0, the economy, social policy, and health care. On education, however, his desire for differentiation was less urgent, and his overall rhetoric on standards, assessments, and sanctions was essentially laudatory. In a May 2008 speech in Denver, for example, candidate Obama argued in favor of fixing NCLB instead of radically changing it (Obama, 2008). NCLB just needed to be better funded and managed, perhaps tweaked here and there (Hoff, 2008). The coalition of "compassionate conservatives," educational liberals, New Democrats, civil rights groups, and technocratic policy entrepreneurs that made NCLB possible seemed to be holding firm. The paradigm remained stable because it was able to conflate social justice for poor and minority students with human capital issues relating to national economic competitiveness (Maranto and McShane, 2012, p. 1).

In spite of the diverse criticism of NCLB from a variety of quarters many states worked diligently and quickly to meet the mandates of the law, even as implementation guidelines changed. Just as many states were finally starting to get a handle on NCLB compliance many of them found their initiatives thrown into limbo by the relatively sudden appearance of a quasi-national system of standards-based education in the waning years of the Bush administration. I use the phrase "quasi-national" because, even though proponents envisioned a holistic, technocratic, expertise-based system embracing virtually every aspect of public K–12 education they realized that it would have to be enacted and implemented on a state-by-state basis.

McGuinn defines a policy regime as "the set of ideas, interests, and institutions that structures governmental activity in a particular issue area" (2006, p. 11). Early proponents began advocating for the idea of national standards years ago (Kendall and Marzano, 1996; Tucker and Codding, 1998; Barth, 2003). In 2003 Haycock wrote, "it's a new century. It's time to set aside our Industrial Age curriculum and agree on a common core curriculum for the Information Age" (p. 2).

A policy regime in favor of a quasi-national system of standards-based education capable of taking this idea into the realm of action did not start coalescing in earnest until the February 26–27, 2005 National Education Summit on High Schools, co-sponsored by Achieve, Inc. and the National Governors Association "in partnership with the Business Roundtable" (Achieve, Inc., 2005, para. 11). It brought "together governors from the 55 U.S. states and territories along with top business executives and prominent K-12 and higher education leaders" to set "common expectations," which included a keynote address from Bill Gates (Achieve, Inc., 2005, para. 2, 11, 12). This was the fifth education summit pairing business leaders with politicians organized by the Business Roundtable since 1989, which cumulatively "were instrumental in creating political momentum and public support for raising academic standards and performance in the nation's schools" (Achieve, Inc., 2005, para. 9). A consensus emerged from the conference that schools were not adequately preparing students for college and 21st century jobs. As a result of the Summit, 29 states joined with Achieve to form the American Diploma Project Network—a coalition of states committed to aligning high school standards, assessments, graduation requirements, and accountability systems with the demands of college and the workplace (Achieve, Inc., 2007, p. 2).

In an April 2007 report, Achieve, Inc. noted that 12 states had aligned their high school standards with "college and workplace expectations," 27 states were in the process of doing so, 5 states planned to do so, and 6 states did not plan to do so (Achieve Inc., 2007, p. 9). Later, in November 2007, the Council of Chief State School Officers continued the discussion on at their annual Policy Forum. Although the trend towards Common Core State Standards seemed inexorable at this point, still, not everyone agreed. James Harvey, a member of the commission that produced *A Nation at Risk*, expressed concern that

> educational decisions have been moved as far as possible from the classroom. Federal officials are now in a position to make decisions that would have been unimaginable even two years ago. They've established the criteria for disciplining schools, removing principals and teachers, and even defining appropriate curriculum for American classrooms (Ansary, 2007, para. 35).

In spite of the concerns of people like Harvey and others, the momentum in favor of quasi-national standards-based education continued to grow. It was usually discussed in conjunction with a professed need for benchmarking against other strong-performing countries (Ravitch, 1995a; Achieve, Inc. 2007; Jerald, 2008; Schmidt, Houang, and Shakrani, 2009). Such internationally cross-referenced data could include that collected by the Project to Increase Mastery of Mathematics and Science (PIMMS), Trends in International Mathematics and Science Study (TIMSS), Progress in International Reading Literacy Study (PIRLS), and the Program for International Student Assessment (PISA). As usual, this international benchmarking was almost always explicitly justified by the need "to meet the realities of the 21st century global economy and maintain America's competitive edge into the future" and to help design any quasi-national system with a systems-oriented approach that coordinated a number of typical components, like "standards, accountability, educator workforce, and assessments" (Jerald, 2008, p. 1).

In the interim between Obama's election on November 4, 2008 and his inauguration on January 20, 2009, academics began actively pitching "policy ideas" in an incredibly broad, thorough, concrete and "rare consensus" (Viadero, 2008, p. 11). The National Academy of Education issued a report *Common Standards for K-12 Education? Considering the Evidence*, which encouraged a "national renaissance" to recover "the promise in standards-based education," particularly by examining standards holistically in conjunction with assessments, professional development, and teacher training (Viadero, 2008, p. 11). They also recommended the "federal government, in coordination with partnerships among state, universities, groups of teachers, scholars, and the private sector redesign... content standards—and the curricula, professional development that go with them—to present clear progressions for teaching and learning" (National Academy of Education, 2008, para. 7). Jane Hathaway, director of the Education Policy Center at the Urban Institute and "co-chairwoman of the academy working group that developed the recommendations on standards" took a close look at states' standards and found them wanting: "too voluminous, superficial, and repetitive," offering "little coherent direction for instruction" (Viadero, 2008, p. 11). The proposals that these scholars unveiled at a November 18 conference in Washington, DC had been developed over the course of 2008 at the goading of the nonpartisan group Strong American Schools and appeared to come right up to but stop just "short of a call for a national curriculum" (Viadero, 2008, pp. 11–12). The fact that they were developed throughout 2008 (well before the general election in the midst of a relatively close campaign) implies that their architects felt the ideas were likely to have bipartisan appeal no matter who won the White House.

From the day Obama took office and Arne Duncan was confirmed as Secretary of Education by the Senate on January 20, 2009, these ideas seemed to be a settled consensus, with the full weight of the entire mainstream bipartisan education establishment behind them: influential education researchers, Obama, Duncan, the National Governors Association, the National Academy of Education, the National Research Council (2008), the Council of Chief State School Officers, the National School Board Association, numerous state governments, and key charitable foundations (like Gates, Broad, and Walton, among others).

When Obama signed the American Recovery and Reinvestment Act into law on February 17, 2009, it provided "$4.35 billion for the Race to the Top

Fund" (United States Department of Education, November 2009), which "was designed by people from the New Schools Venture Fund" whose CEO went on to become number two at the U.S. Department of Education (Eidelson, 2014, para. 47).

During his tenure as Chicago's school chief, Duncan had already experienced success in cultivating significant business support. He also brought 23 "Broad Residents and alumni" of Broad Foundation leadership programs into his municipal administration and 5 into his federal department (Pelto, 2014, para. 17). In fact, Duncan was even on the Board of Directors of the foundation. The Broad Foundation is noted for bringing people from outside of professional education, giving them training in data-driven, business-oriented management techniques and sending them out into positions of high authority in education.

Meanwhile, as Race to the Top emerged as policy, so too did the Common Core State Standards Initiative. In April 2009 the National Governors Association and the Council of Chief State School Officers gathered together "governors' education policy advisors and chief state school officers in Chicago to discuss creation of the Common Core State Standards Initiative" (Common Core State Standards Initiative, 2014, para. 1). State leaders proved receptive to the development of "common standards in English language arts/literacy and mathematics," and began work to develop them (Common Core State Standards Initiative, 2014a, para. 1).

On June 1, 2009 NGA Vice Chair and Vermont Governor Jim Douglas framed his announcement of the creation of the Common Core States Standards Initiative in terms of global competiveness ideology. "To maintain America's competitive edge" 46 states, the District of Columbia, Puerto Rico, and the Virgin Islands formed "a state-led process to develop a common core of state standards in English language arts and mathematics for grades K-12" (National Governors Association, 2009, para 4–5). Governor Douglas also noted that "these standards will be research and evidence based, internationally benchmarked, aligned with college and work expectations, and include rigorous content and skills" (National Governors Association, 2009, para 4–5). The only states abstaining were Alaska, Missouri, South Carolina, and Texas.

In a speech Obama made on July 24, 2009 to announce the Race to the Top, he said that "this competition will not be based on politics, ideology, or the preferences of a particular interest group… America's economy… will be better for it" (United States Department of Education, July 24, 2009, para. 1).

These statements imply that Race to the Top was based on one particular set of politics (the "Washington Rules"), one particular ideology (neoliberal economic globalization), and the preferences of one particular interest group (big business, especially as led by Wall Street and the financial sector) (Bacevich, 2010). Obama further defended it as "the single most important thing we've done" (Klein, 2010, para. 2).

By November 2009 the U.S. Department of Education issued guidelines as to how to apply for these funds. It was much like NCLB, except in that 1) it was competitive and not automatically granted to states, 2) the efforts of the recipients were meant to serve as pilot projects for other states, 3) the competition coaxed states into legal compliance with a variety of qualifying criteria, which would probably still be on the books whether the state's application was successful or not, and 4) it required adoption of Common Core (although not by naming the initiative outright). In the words of the Race to the Top executive summary, the program was

> designed to encourage and reward States that are creating the conditions for education innovation and reform; achieving significant improvement in student outcomes, including making substantial gains in student achievement, closing achievement gaps, improving high school graduation rates, and ensuring student preparation for success in college and careers; and implementing ambitious plans in four core education reform areas:
> – Adopting standards and assessments that prepare students to succeed in college and the workplace and to compete in the global economy;
> – Building data systems that measure student growth and success, and inform teachers and principals about how they can improve instruction;
> – Recruiting, developing, rewarding, and retaining effective teachers and principals, especially where they are needed most; and
> – Turning around our lowest-achieving schools (United States Department of Education, November 2009, para. 2).

In the executive summary, "reform plan criteria" was defined as

> The extent to which the State, in collaboration with its participating [local education agencies]... has a high-quality plan for supporting a statewide transition to and implementation of internationally benchmarked K-12 standards that build toward college and career readiness by the time of high school graduation, and high-quality assessments... tied to these standards (United States Department of Education, November 2009, p. 8).

Furthermore, a "common set of K-12 standards" was defined as a set of content standards that define what students must know and be able to do and that are substantially identical across all States in a consortium. A State may supplement the common standards with additional standards, provided that the additional standards do not exceed 15 percent of the State's total standards for that content area. (U.S. Department of Education, November 2009, p. 12).

By defining acceptable standards so narrowly, the application guidelines left Common Core as the only plausible candidate. Even before Round 1 winners of Race to the Top were announced or Common Core State Standards released, many people were already evaluating the trajectory of federal standards-based education policy. This included such luminaries as Diane Ravitch and Linda Darling-Hammond, and two camps.

Diane Ravitch called "the governing philosophy of NCLB" one of "measure and punish," and claimed that Obama's "administration has embraced some of the worst features of the George W. Bush era" (Ravitch, 2010a, para. 5, 20). She also claimed that "accountability, narrowly focused as it is, dumbs down education" (Ravitch, 2010a, para. 23). While Ravitch supported curriculum reform, Darling-Hammond wanted to "improve the whole system" (Darling-Hammond, 2010, p. 14). Darling-Hammond reiterated the oft-made point that "conservatives introduced a new theory of reform focused on outcomes rather than inputs—that is, high-stakes testing without investing" (Darling-Hammond, 2010, p. 18). Instead of "competition and sanctions," she favored "capacity-building and strategic investments" (Darling-Hammond, 2010, p. 19).

On May 2010 ASCD issued a press release declaring that they "had become an endorsing partner of the Common Core State Standards Initiative" and expressed their commitment to "helping educators understand the new standards and how to implement them in their schools and classrooms" through professional development (ASCD, 2010, para. 1–2). The standards would "prepare our children for college, the workforce, and success in the global economy" (ASCD, 2010, para. 1).

In June 2010, almost a year to the day after Governor Douglas announced the formation of the Common Core State Standards Initiative, they released their model K–12 "English-language arts and mathematics standards," which they "developed in collaboration with a variety of stakeholders" establishing "clear and consistent goals for learning that will prepare America's children for success in college and work" (National Governors Association, 2010, para. 1). Not surprisingly, one of the rationales for their adoption was global competitiveness ideology. According to comments made by Georgia governor Sonny Perdue in the press release accompanying the issuance of new standards,

American competitiveness relies on an education system that can adequately prepare our youth for college and the workforce. When American students have the skills and knowledge needed in today's jobs, our communities will be positioned to compete successfully in the global economy (National Governors Association, 2010, para. 5).

In a press release supporting the first iteration of Common Core standards, Arne Duncan used almost identical language when he lauded the claim that they "are internationally benchmarked and include the knowledge and skills that students must learn to succeed in college and career" (United States Department of Education, June 2, 2010, para. 2), as well as their contribution to maintaining America's "international competitiveness" and preparing "all students for college, work and citizenship" (United States Department of Education, June 2, 2010, para. 5).

On July 29, 2010, the final state in America to adopt state standards, Iowa, "voted to adopt the Common Core State Standards as part of the Iowa Core" (Iowa State Department of Education, 2010, para. 1). This shows that even a late adopter of standards-based education when it was within the purview of the states could wind up being a early adopter of the reform model as it became more quasi-national. Again, the rationale was in large part because of global competitiveness ideology. In the press release announcing Iowa's decision, the Iowa Board of Education president said "we want our students to not only be competitive in our own state, but in the nation and the world" (Iowa State Department of Education, 2010, para. 1).

Since both Race to the Top and Common Core had so many of the same ideological and empirical drivers, were both rolled out almost simultaneously in 2009–2010 and depended upon each other in so many integral ways, it is difficult to analyze them in a compartmentalized fashion, separate from one another. Both must be considered together.

Duncan used the leverage available to the federal government in offering a competitive state-level grant to push for state-level policy changes, such as breaking down traditional fire walls between the test scores of specific students with the evaluation of specific teachers (Dillon, 2009; Associated Press, 2010). "The Secretary announced the winners for Phase 1 of Race to the Top on March 29, 2010, the winners for Phase 2 on August 24, 2010, and the winners for Phase 3 on December 22, 2011" (United States Department of Education, March 18, 2013, para. 1). In announcing the Phase 2 winners, the U.S. Department of Education noted that "35 states and the District of Columbia have adopted rigorous common, college- and career-ready standards in reading and math, and 34 states have changed laws or policies to improve education" (United States Department of Education, August 24, 2010, para. 6). Phase 1 applications were submitted by:

> Alabama, Arizona, Arkansas, California, Colorado, Connecticut, Delaware, District of Columbia, Florida, Georgia, Hawaii, Idaho, Illinois, Indiana, Iowa, Kansas, Kentucky, Louisiana, Massachusetts, Michigan, Minnesota, Missouri, Nebraska, New Hampshire, New Jersey, New Mexico, New York, North Carolina, Ohio, Oklahoma, Oregon, Pennsylvania, Rhode Island, South Carolina, South Dakota, Tennessee, Utah, Virginia, West Virginia, Wisconsin, Wyoming (U.S. Department of Education, February 15, 2012a, Phase 1).

Of these 40 states and the District of Columbia, only two states were slated to receive funding: Delaware, "approximately $100 million and Tennessee $500 million" (U.S. Department of Education, March 29, 2010, para. 3). Phase 2 applications were submitted by:

> Alabama, Arizona, Arkansas, California, Colorado, Connecticut, District of Columbia, Florida, Georgia, Hawaii, Illinois, Iowa, Kentucky, Louisiana, Maine, Maryland, Massachusetts, Michigan, Mississippi, Missouri, Montana, Nebraska, Nevada, New Hampshire, New Jersey, New Mexico, New York, North Carolina, Ohio, Oklahoma, Pennsylvania, Rhode Island, South Carolina, Utah, Washington, and Wisconsin (U.S. Department of Education, February 15, 2012b, Phase 2).

Of these 35 states and the District of Columbia, only "the District of Columbia, Florida, Georgia, Hawaii, Maryland, Massachusetts, New York, North Carolina, Ohio, and Rhode Island" won grant money enabling them to participate in a "groundbreaking education reform program that will directly impact 13.6 million students, and 980,000 teachers in 25,000 schools" (U.S. Department of Education, August 24, 2010, para. 1–2).

Shortly after announcing the Round 2 winners in Race to the Top, Duncan announced a closely related initiative, that two multi-state consortia would be awarded a total of $330 million to develop Common Core–aligned assessments. These included the Partnership for Assessment of Readiness for College and Careers (PARCC; $170 million) and the Smarter Balanced Assessment Consortium (SBAC; $160 million) (U.S. Department of Education, September 2, 2010, para. 2).

> The Partnership for Assessment of Readiness for College and Careers is a coalition of 26 states including AL, AR, AZ, CA, CO, DC, DE, FL, GA, IL, IN, KY, LA, MA, MD, MS, ND, NH, NJ, NY, OH, OK, PA, RI, SC and TN…The PARCC coalition

will test students' ability to read complex text, complete research projects, excel at classroom speaking and listening assignments, and work with digital media (United States Department of Education, September 2, 2010, para. 4, 6).

Instead of one single, high-stakes summative test at the end of the year, PARCC will average the scores of a series of tests administered throughout the school year. It is coordinated by Achieve, Inc.

> The SMARTER Balanced Assessment Consortium is a coalition of 31 states including AL, CO, CT, DE, GA, HI, IA, ID, KS, KY, ME, MI, MO, MT, NC, ND, NH, NJ, NM, NV, OH, OK, OR, PA, SC, SD, UT, VT, WA, WI, and WV... The SMARTER coalition will test students using computer adaptive technology that will ask students tailored questions based on their previous answers. SMARTER will continue to use one test at the end of the year for accountability purposes (U.S. Department of Education, September 2, 2010, para. 4, 6).

Secretary Duncan announced the program in "remarks to state leaders at Achieve's American Diploma Project leadership team meeting" (Duncan, September 2, 2010). In this speech, he mentioned global competitiveness no less than four times and called state standards an "insidious practice" (Duncan, September 2, 2010, para. 19).

In 2011 both sides debated the issue via manifesto. The more "establishment" manifesto was issued in March. Entitled *A Call for Common Content*, it envisioned a comprehensive national education system with everything linked to a single national set of standards. It defined curriculum as

> academic disciplines, specifying the content knowledge and skills that all students are expected to learn, over time, in a thoughtful progression across the grades. We do not mean performance standards, textbook offerings, daily lesson plans, or rigid pedagogical prescriptions (Albert Shanker Institute, 2011, p. 41).

It also asked the ultimate question: that is "what is it, precisely, that we expect all educated citizens to have learned?" (Albert Shanker Institute, 2011, p. 41). It also acknowledged some of the major grievances of opponents of Common Core. These included "the fear of centralization, institutional rigidity, and narrow-minded political orthodoxy is deeply ingrained in our political sensibility" (Albert Shanker Institute, 2011, p. 41). It even addressed the notion that different children learn in different ways, were in different stages of development in each grade level, and common content should allow teachers to differentiate instruction to those students "achieving above or below grade level" (Albert Shanker Institute, 2011, p. 42). The manifesto praised those nations with high academic achievement that already had national education standards such as "Finland, Singapore, and South Korea" (Albert Shanker Institute, 2011, p. 42).

The counter-manifesto came in May 2011. It leveled strong opposition to the Partnership for Assessment of Readiness for College and Careers and the Smarter Balanced Assessment Consortium and their concomitant efforts to "develop national curriculum guidelines, national curriculum models [and] national instructional materials" (Greene, Stotsky, Evers, Forster, and Wurman, 2011, para. 1). It also reiterated long-standing criticisms that quasi-national standards would be "one-size-fits-all" and lead to a "centrally controlled curriculum" (Greene, Stotsky, Evers, Forster, and Wurman, 2011, para. 3). In fact, this threatened "to close the door on educational innovation, freezing in place an unacceptable status quo and hindering efforts to develop academically rigorous curricula, assessments, and standards that meet the challenges that lie ahead" (Greene, Stotsky, Evers, Forster, and Wurman, 2011, para. 3).

Even though the Albert Shanker Institute mentioned the constitutional problems, it glossed over and passed right by them. The counter-manifesto dwelled upon them again, explicitly stating that "there is no constitutional or statutory basis for national standards, national assessments, or national curricula" (Greene, Stotsky, Evers, Forster, and Wurman, 2011, para. 6). It also noted that nation-states with "centralized national curricula" didn't necessarily do well on tests, while countries without national curricula (like Canada and Australia) did fine (Greene, Stotsky, Evers, Forster, and Wurman, 2011, para. 8). In asserting a need to put curriculum and teaching ahead of testing, however, the Albert Shanker Institute and the signatories of the "counter-manifesto" agreed.

As Secretary of Education Spellings had offered flexibility in the implementation of NCLB during the Bush administration, so too did Secretary of Education Duncan during the Obama administration, under "section 9401 of the Elementary and Secondary Education Act of 1965" (Duncan, 2011, para. 1, 4). Among the most significant waivers available were the ability of state education agencies "to develop new ambitious but achievable" annual measurable objectives and greater flexibility in Title I schools and local education agencies that failed to make Annual Yearly Progress "for two consecutive years or more" (United States Department of Education, September 28, 2011, p. 1). The quid pro quo for this "temporary flexibility" was adoption of Common Core State Standards and big data "systems of differentiated recognition, accountability, and support; and evaluating and supporting teacher and principal effectiveness" (Duncan, 2011, para. 3). These data collection protocols were largely based on those under development by the Data Quality Campaign and National Education Data Model. By 2014 virtually every state in the union had received ESEA flexibility, except Wyoming, Iowa, and the Bureau of Indian Affairs school system all of which had applications under review. California, Montana, Nebraska, North Dakota, and Vermont never applied (United States Department of Education, *Elementary & secondary education, ESEA flexibility*).

The nine runner-up states in the 2010 Race to the Top competition were eligible to apply for Round 3 funding. South Carolina chose not to apply and California's application was incomplete. On December 23, 2011, the U.S. Department of Education announced that the seven remaining states (Arizona, Colorado, Illinois, Kentucky, Louisiana, New Jersey, and Pennsylvania) had each won a portion of the $200 million available. By now, Race to the Top awards were reaching "65 percent of the nation's children and 59 percent of the low-income students in the country" (United States Department of Education, December 23, 2011, para 3).

Shortly after the announcement of the winners of Rounds 1 and 2, Peng and Guthrie claimed that the federal share of education spending had reached "close to 15 percent" by 2009 (2010, para. 33). While individual sources may vary on precise figures, the Race to the Top does seem to have increased federal spending above the 7% level it had been at for many years.

The American Principles Project, founded by Princeton professor Robert Scott, was one of the earliest and most vociferous critics of Common Core. Beginning in February 2012, they issued a series of white papers with the Pioneer Institute. The first in this series, *The Road to a National Curriculum, the Legal Aspects of the Common Core Standards, Race to the Top, and Conditional Waivers*, argued that these programs representing a statutory overreach on the part of the federal government into education policy (Eitel, Talbert, and Evers, 2012). In their next paper in May 2012, they asked "the American Legislative Exchange Council" (a Koch brothers-funded bill mill designed to give state legislators material to introduce) to develop legislation "opposing the Common Core State Standards Initiative" (McGroarty and Robbins, 2012, p. 1). A September 2013 report from the Pioneer Institute reiterated their concern that "Common Core undermines state and local autonomy over K–12 education" (Scott).

One key technical assistance provider in support of Common Core, ASCD (funded in part by the Bill and Melinda Gates Foundation) issued a report in March 2012 entitled *Fulfilling the Promise of the Common Core State Standards*. In this report, they made the now-routine references to global competitiveness and college- and career-readiness (ASCD, 2012, p. 5). By then, the focus of ASCD's preferred method of supporting the "implementation of the Common Core State Standards through "professional development" had shifted from "raising awareness and understanding of the Common Core standards to implementation and sustainability of them" through a variety of means (ASCD, 2012, p. 6).

By 2013 the Bill and Melinda Gates Foundation had already invested "more than $160 million into developing and promoting the Common Core" (Simon and Shah, 2013, para. 3). Other analysts put the figure closer to $170 million (Berry, March 20, 2014, para. 15) or even $200 million in 2013 alone (Home School Legal Defense Fund, 2014). Few groups associated with the development and promotion of Common Core escaped the largess of this influential foundation. In 2013 the U.S. Chamber of Commerce "received $1.3 million in funding" from them to help launch "an ad campaign with other business groups" (Berry, March 20, 2014, para. 15). The Broad, Walton, and Joyce foundations also made significant contributions to neoliberal, business-oriented education reform initiatives (Pelto, 2014; Lee 2014).

Besides the Pioneer Institute, another right-wing think tank working against Common Core was the Heartland Institute. In a January 2013 report, they wrote that "the notorious Russian communist Vladimir Lenin knew the power of controlling schools. He once said, 'Give me four years to teach the children and the seed I have sown will never be uprooted'" (Pullman, 2013, p. 1). On February 26, 2013, Ravitch weighed in to wonder if standards might "cause the children who now struggle to give up altogether" (cited in Strauss, February 26, 2013, para. 9). Her concern was that the new standards hadn't been properly field tested yet. During the 113th Congress, Republican opposition to Common Core started to grow. On April 12, 2013, the Republican National Committee passed a resolution at their spring meeting stating that Common Core was "an inappropriate overreach to standardize and control the education of our children so they will conform to a preconceived 'normal'" and that the committee "rejects the collection [and sharing] of personal student data for any non-educational purpose… with any person or entity other than schools or education agencies within the state" (Republican National Committee, 2013, para. 8–9).

In an April 17, 2013 letter to Senator Tom Harkin, Chairman of the Subcommittee on Labor, Health and Human Services, Education, Senate

Appropriations Committee urging defunding of Common Core, Chuck Grassley (R-IA) wrote that "current federal law makes clear that the U.S. Department of Education may not be involved in setting specific content standards or determining the content of state assessments" (Grassley, 2013, para. 2). Soon, eight conservative senators signed on to Grassley's letter. These included "Tom Coburn (R-Okla.), Ted Cruz (R-Texas), Deb Fischer (R-Neb.), James Inhofe (R-Okla.), Mike Lee (R-Utah), Rand Paul (R-Ky.), Pat Roberts (R-Kan.), and Jeff Sessions (R-Ala.)" (Nazworth, 2013, para. 3).

On April 30, 2013 Representative Blaine Luetkemeyer (R-MI) and 33 other co-signers sent Secretary Duncan a letter expressing their concerns about how recent administrative changes made for Common Core may have affected the strength of the Family Educational Rights and Privacy Act (FERPA), especially as it relates to the implementation of "State Longitudinal Database System (SLDS) used to track students by obtaining personally identifiable information… a condition of applying for RTTT grant funding" (Luetkemeyer, 2013, para. 8–11). The op-ed pages started to gather sentiments pro and con. An early con was a Washington Post article of May 20, 2013 that said

> resistance to standards puts ideological conservatives in some questionable company. In fighting the Common Core, some tea party activists have made common cause with elements of the progressive education blob that always resist rigor, measurement and accountability. This alliance increasingly constitutes the mediocrity caucus in American politics" (Gerson, 2013, para. 9).

This was an odd editorial in that it started out applauding cross-aisle cooperation and then ended up insulting both sides. Resistance also continued to develop from a variety of grassroots sectors as well, including parents, teachers, and principals. One critique came from a multi-award winning principal, Carol Burris (Strauss, August 26, 2013, para. 1). She feared that students experiencing the plummeting achievement gap seen on the New York Common Core test "between White and Latino students in eighth-grade ELA [as it] grew from 3 points to 22 points… will further internalize defeat" (Burris cited in Strauss, August 26, 2013, para. 3).

Governors started to have an ambiguous and complicated relationship to Common Core at this time too. For instance, Florida governor Rick Scott wanted to support Common Core but felt that the Tea Party was such an important part of his base that he needed to address their concerns, through executive action if need be. This conundrum left him considering executive action but saying nothing more substantial than that testing was "too expensive and it takes too long" (McGrory, Bousquet, and Leary, 2013, para. 4). At an event in support of Louisiana governor Bobby Jindal at the National Press Club, Jeb Bush said (in reference to opponents of Common Core) "'If you're comfortable with mediocrity, fine,' Bush said. 'I'm not'" (McGrory, Bousquet and Leary, 2013, para. 17). Shortly after, Jindal, who harbors presidential aspirations in 2016, switched positions from pro to con (like Scott), and also considered using executive action if need be (O'Donoghue, 2014, para. 2).

Another prominent public appearance by an advocate of Common Core was that of Secretary Duncan on November 15, 2013 at a meeting of the Council of Chief State School Officers meeting in Richmond, Virginia. There, he called critics "white suburban moms" who were disturbed to find out that "all of a sudden, their child isn't as brilliant as they thought they were and their school isn't quite as good as they thought… and that's pretty scary" (Simon, November, 18, 2013, para. 2–3). In spite of all of these criticisms, Common Core was called one of the "education issues to watch in 2014" by a national journalist (Bidwell, 2013).

To bring in the new year of 2014, George Will reiterated the right wing refrain that Common Core was part of a "progressive agenda of centralization and uniformity" in a January 15, 2014 Washington Post editorial; this was also cited this as "yet another" example of "Obama administration indifference to legality" (Will, 2014, para. 3). In addition to criticism from the punditocracy, criticism also started to come from rank and file teachers, albeit for different reasons. During the January 26–27, 2014 weekend "the Board of Directors of the New York State United Teachers, a union with more than 600,000 members, passed a resolution withdrawing support" for Common Core (Strauss, January 27, 2014, para. 1).

In January 2014 New Democrat technocrats in favor of Common Core issued a report calling for a longer school year, one better coordinated with the standards (Farbman, Goldberg, and Miller, 2014, p. 2). In a conference sponsored by the Center for American Progress on January 31, 2014, "Paul Reville, former Secretary of Education for Massachusetts and a Common Core supporter" gave right wing critics a gift when he said that critics of Common Core were misguided because they didn't realize "the children belong to all of us" (Berry, January 15, 2014, para. 10). This remark was widely reported in the rapidly growing right wing media against Common Core. The above-mentioned exceptions notwithstanding, as we entered 2014, many analysts were starting to acknowledge the bipartisan nature of the criticism. Some noted that there's growing backlash to Common Core, and conservatives and liberals increasingly are voicing similar concerns: that the standards take a one-size-fits-all approach, create a de facto national curriculum, put too much emphasis on standardized tests and undermine teacher autonomy (Westervelt, 2014, para. 2–4).

Others cited opponents "ranging from the billionaire Koch Brothers on the right to elements of Occupy Wall Street" (Williams, 2014, para. 2). The "American Federation of Teachers and the National Education Association," which had been leading supporters of standards-based education for a long time, felt their rank and file were drifting away from the leaderships' position (Ujifusa, 2014, para 1–2). They even expressed it at a conclave hosted by the Council of Chief State School Officers, on a panel including "Achieve President Mike Cohen and Education Trust President Kati Haycock"(Ujifusa, 2014, para. 3). Here, union head "Weingarten told the chiefs, 'The field doesn't trust the people in this room to have their backs'" (Ujifusa, 2014, para. 5). Brooks noted that as it was "being attacked by the talk-radio right, the Common Core is being attacked by the interest group left" (Brooks, 2014, para. 11). Some facile liberal critiques claimed that "the Republican revolt against the Common Core can be traced to President Obama's embrace of it" (Martin, 2014, para. 10). Another liberal voice called it a "near-senseless reaction" that was "just one part of a growing tribalism that's consumed the whole of conservative politics. It doesn't matter the issue: If liberals are for it, then—for a large portion of the right—that means it is time to be against it" (Bouie, 2014, para. 6). Obviously, this was not the only source of criticism. To say so was either disingenuous or ignorant. Most critics continued to note the bipartisan flavor of the criticism; "declaring Common Core a tribal war is no help at all" (Bryant, 2014, para. 27–29).

The Bill and Melinda Gates Foundation and Achieve, Inc. were among the prime movers behind the formulation of the Common Core State Standards, although they let the National Governors Association and Council of Chief State School Officers be the lead organizations for marketing and political roll-out. When Obama assumed the presidency, the motive (elite consensus for a quasi-national standards-based education) seemed a settled issue, awaiting only the means and opportunity to put it into action. A grassroots rebellion against Common Core erupted in 2013 and gained momentum in 2014. What seemed a fait accompli to the elite no longer was.

Some of what people say in evaluating Common Core is much like what was said when states developed their own standards, because of the "one size fits all approach" (Ohanian, 1999). Some of what they say is new, because of

Common Core's centralized and quasi-national scope. On the pro side, some assert that Common Core is a civil rights and equity issue that will help close the achievement gap between Whites and Asians, and African-Americans and Latinos; high expectations will help the poor and disadvantaged achieve a better life. Others who argue for the equity regime maintain that student and teacher performance can't be based entirely on the classroom experience when the socio-economic status of students is so important.

On the con side, some say it reverses 400 years of local control and useful heterogeneity in education policy-making. Furthermore, it deprofessionalizes teaching, largely ignores "multiple intelligences" and the differing developmental stages of children in each grade, and masks a corporate agenda to turn students into docile workers, compliant consumers, and apathetic citizens who are just smart enough to do their post-school jobs and just dumb (or willfully ignorant) enough to passively accept how thoroughly the economic and political systems are structured against their interests (Gardner, 2006).

Also on the con side are a wide variety of camps typically (and perhaps unfairly) given the homogenous label of the "far right." These include homeschoolers, Christians, and people who think that Common Core is a means for Obama to get his "socialist" or "globalizing" agenda into the schools by federalizing K–12 education. The Southern Poverty Law Center recently issued a report castigating these interest groups as "far right propaganda" spigots spreading "outright falsehoods and antigovernment conspiracy theories" (Elias, Gunter, van der Valk, and Costello, 2014, p. 7). In fact, Glenn Beck even has a book out against Common Core (2014). Still on the con side, others fear that Common Core will force private, religious, and home schools into alignment with its agenda by alterations expected from the SAT and ACT tests in the near future, and memoranda of understanding between the two multi-state assessment consortia and institutions of higher education in the states of each consortia.

David Coleman was the cofounder of Student Achievement Partners, which "played a leading role in developing the Common Core State Standards in math and literacy. David left Student Achievement Partners in the fall of 2012 to become president of the College Board," which manages and coordinates the SAT (College Board, 2014). In the subtitle to a 2011 report ACT asked "is college and career readiness an internationally competitive standard?" (ACT, 2011). It didn't take them longer than the first page to answer that question in the affirmative. "The US has no choice but to develop a quality educational system that offers a world-class education to all of its students as a centerpiece of our nation's economic competitiveness" (ACT, 2011, p. 1).

The "far right" critics also make the point that the Common Core standards are under copyright by the National Governors Association Center for Best Practices and Council of Chief State School Officers. Furthermore, although it is standard boilerplate legalese, it is ironic that the "National Governors Association Center for Best Practices and Council of Chief State School Officers make no representations… [about the] fitness for a particular purpose" of the standards in their public license, indicating a lack of confidence in the standards, which is somewhat unusual given the extraordinary time and expense put into developing them and convincing states to adopt them (Common Core State Standards Initiative, 2014b, para. 10).

The current executive director of the Council of Chief State School Officers, Chris Minnich, has played a central role in coordinating that organization's establishment of the Common Core State Standards Initiative since 2008 (Council of Chief State School Officers, 2014, para. 1). His ascension to executive director proves how seriously their board of directors take Common Core. The sponsorship of so many companies shows how seriously these companies take Common Core's potential impact on their bottom lines.

Vendors expect Common Core to be an information technology gold mine of the first order. After all, public education is the largest sector of public spending after the military. K–12 spending in America totaled "$632 billion in 2010–11" and virtually every aspect of K–12 education would be computerized under Common Core (United States Department of Education, National Center for Education Statistics, 2013). This includes hardware, software, and online/cloud services; as well as curriculum, student assessment, teacher assessment, school administration at every level, and professional development. The list goes on and on. This is why "Apple, Google, Cisco and a swarm of startups are elbowing in to secure market share. The sector is expected to more than double in size to $13.4 billion by 2017" (Upadhyaya, 2013, para. 2). These vendors include the corporate partners listed on the website of the Council of Chief State School Officers:

> ACT, AdvancED, American Institutes for Research, Amplify, Apple, Battelle for Kids, Blackboard, Cisco, College Board, Data Recognition Corporation, ETS, Generation Ready, Houghton Mifflin Harcourt, inBloom, Intel Corporation, International Business Machines Corporation, IQity, K12 Inc., McGraw-Hill Education, Measured Progress, Measurement Incorporated, MetaMetrics, Microsoft, Northwest Evaluation Association, Pearson Education, Promethean, Questar

Assessment, Inc., Renaissance Learning, Inc., SAS, Scantron, Scholastic, School Improvement Network, TaskStream, Texas Instruments, Truenorthlogic, Wilson Language Training (Council of Chief State School Officers, 2014a, para. 4–41).

In this context, it makes good business sense for the Bill and Melinda Gates Foundation to be promoting Common Core. While they will not be the only vendor, they will certainly be one of the biggest. This savvy long-term strategic action may even raise Microsoft's market capitalization above that of Apple within a decade. As of May 2014, these companies market capitalizations were $327 billion and $510 billion respectively. The technology industry is optimistic that it will soon be signing billions of dollars in contracts annually. The broader business community is optimistic that, after decades of patient and engaged engagement, K–12 education would finally be oriented towards the "college and career-readiness" of high school graduates. Nevertheless, at their moment of seeming triumph, the concerns of the people have come to the fore.

One of the first among these relates to Common Core-aligned instructional materials. There are a plethora of for-profit vendors ready to provide such material and the professional development necessary for teachers to use it effectively. Nevertheless, many teachers feel as though this material was dumped in their laps too quickly without adequate guidance. Some object to the content, not merely to the speed of the rollout or any perceived lack of substantive professional development. Parents and teachers have posted numerous examples of their thoughts on the issue and their childrens' worksheets, homework, and such on the internet and social media like Facebook (Sole, 2014), YouTube, and Twitter. One interesting Twitter protagonist was Ken Libbey whose feed was @kenmlibbey and whose interesting hashtag #corespiracy captured almost all of the leading right wing memes emerging against Common Core (Libbey, 2013). Many of the worksheet and homework examples were strange, unduly complicated, and age-inappropriate. Some of the more civics-oriented example even displayed an overt social agenda of conformity and obedience. Mathematics worksheets and homework seem to be especially absurd to numerous observers; again, especially to parents. The comedian Louis C. K. even issued a series of tweets that went viral (Klein, 2014) and prompted a few editorials as well (Mead, 2014). He followed that up with a humorous critique delivered on the David Letterman show in early 2014 (Ravitch, 2014).

Another major bone of contention is Common Core-aligned assessments (CBS News New York, 2014, para. 3–5). To be sure, formative assessments can help differentiate instruction in the classroom. Summative assessments can help administrators and policy-makers allocate resources wisely and serve the equity regime by assisting in the closure of the achievement gap. At its bare minimum, standards-based education must be considered as three things: standards, testing, and an accountability regime of sanctions and rewards based on testing. Proponents of assessment speak to the positive while appreciating "the differing views and the debate surrounding the common core state standards," as Joe Willhoft, executive director of the Smarter Balanced Assessment Consortium said (cited in Gewertz, 2011, para. 16). Willhoft also stated that his consortium believes that "the assessment system we are developing will provide valuable support to teachers, students, parents, and other educational decision makers to help them improve student learning" (cited in Gewertz, 2011, para. 16).

By the time of NCLB every state had some kind of statewide assessment. Admittedly, in many cases, it took time and effort to align existing instruments with the newly drafted state standards. Sometimes the alignment was not that valid or reliable. The PARCC and SBAC testing consortia can be seen as an effort to leapfrog past any lingering problems that may exist in that realm by simply aligning almost all states' assessments to Common Core. In fact, an ASCD report said that because these "next-generation assessments" are required to "replace current state NCLB tests in the 2014–15 school year" that this is "the de facto implementation deadline of the Common Core State Standards" (ASCD, 2012, p. 11).

Nevertheless, in spite of the confidence of the technocrats and policy-makers, here too rebellion rises. Georgia and Oklahoma have withdrawn their participation in the consortia (Baker, 2014, para. 12). Opposition also comes from parental pressure groups, like the "Mama Bears" in Tennessee (Ravitch cited in Eidelson, 2014, para. 68).

Cut scores are under attack as well. To many, they are at best technically unsubstantiated and at worst politically motivated to label more students and schools as "failures." Some students feel so anxious under Common Core that they lose their zest for learning—or even vomit or urinate during tests. Teachers are rebelling, refusing to give tests throughout the country. Parents are rebelling, refusing to allow their children to take the tests. National conferences on the subject have even been held. A significant and growing "opt-out" movement is spreading throughout the country (Altman, 2014). Administrators are unsure how to react, although their prevailing instinct is to call such opt outs illegal.

New York's experience in rolling out Common Core–aligned tests in early 2014 has been attracting a lot of attention. On February 11, 2014 "the state Board of Regents voted Tuesday to delay Common Core graduation requirements for five years" (Campbell, 2014, para. 1). Also, iconic brands such as Nike,

> Barbie, iPod, Mug Root Beer and Life Savers showed up on the tests of more than a million students in grades 3 through 8 took this month, leading to speculation it was some form of product placement advertising (Matthews, 2014, para. 1–2).

New York education officials said that this was just a coincidence because the written passages had already been published previously elsewhere (Matthews, 2014, para. 3). These officials and Pearson, which has "a $32 million five-year contract to develop New York's tests, said the companies did not pay for the exposure" (Matthews, 2014, para. 15). So far, such a concentrated dose of product placement in Common Core–aligned tests seems restricted to New York (Matthews, 2014, para. 14).

Assessment data in New York were to be collected by inBloom, a Bill and Melinda Gates Foundation–funded non-profit organization, using infrastructure developed over a period of 18 months by "Amplify Education, a division of Rupert Murdoch's News Corp" (Simon, March 3, 2013, para. 8). Privacy concerns were prevalent since the beginning in 2013. FERPA's ambiguities were of little consolation, as it allowed local education officials "to share files in their portion of the database with private companies selling educational products and services," even the personally identifying information of students (Simon, March 3, 2013, para. 4). InBloom's "own privacy policy stated that it 'cannot guarantee the security of the information stored… or that the information will not be intercepted when it is being transmitted" (Simon, March 3, 2013, para. 15). In light of the public uproar over these concerns, the New York legislature recently passed a law against this type of data collection and storage in the cloud (Strauss, April 21, 2014). Because of these legal developments and this backlash, the $100 million inBloom project issued a statement that it was ceasing operations (Strauss, April 21, 2014). None of inBloom's "nine original state partners… are now committed to going forward" (Strauss, April 4, 2014). Other states simply didn't have the computers, bandwidth, and other technological infrastructure necessary to administer these tests. In light of these challenges, the two testing consortiums have adjusted and scaled back their planned evaluation procedures.

State longitudinal data systems are another area of concern. While these data bases may seem invasive, many teachers, administrators, policy-makers and researchers think that student data can help differentiate instruction to customize learning; help schools, districts, and states allocate resources; and inform a wide variety of important policy decisions. When student information is held by for-profit corporations or non-profit organizations in the cloud instead of by the government, privacy protections are hard to maintain. The student privacy rights provided for in FERPA seem weaker and more ambiguous than many students, parents, and civil liberty advocates may hope for. To better understand precisely what these protections are in a rapidly evolving political and technological landscape would be a fruitful avenue for further research.

The two most important student data collection advocates and protocols are the Data Quality Campaign and the National Education Data Model. The Data Quality Campaign is "a nonprofit, nonpartisan, national advocacy organization based in Washington, DC. Launched in 2005 by 10 founding partners," it is one of the prime movers behind big data collection protocols in education (National Data Campaign, 2013, para. 1). It was founded with Bill and Melinda Gates Foundation money, who continue to be a major funder. Achieve, Inc. was one of the founding partners as well. The other prime mover is the National Education Data Model, which is "coordinated by the Council of Chief State School Officers" (National Center for Education Statistics, para. 2). The National Education Data Model is still a conceptual model and holds no data. Therefore, its data points represent a universe of possible ones customizable by individual jurisdictions. The data points are as follows:

Ability Grouped Status Absent Attendance Categories Academic Honors Type Activity Code Activity Curriculum Type Activity Involvement Beginning Date Activity Involvement Ending Date Activity Leadership/Coordinator Participation Level Activity Level Activity Title Activity Type Additional Geographic Designation Additional Post-school Accomplishments Additional Special Health Needs, Information, or Instructions Address Type Admission Date Admission Status Ala Carte Non-Reimbursable Purchase Price Alias Allergy Alert American Indian or Alaska native Amount of Activity Involvement Amount of Non-school Activity Involvement Apartment/Room/ Suite Number Asian Assessment Reporting Method Assignment Assignment Finish Date Assignment Number of Attempts Assignment Type Assignment/ Activity Points Possible At-Risk Indicator At-Risk Status Attendance Description Attendance Status Time Awaiting Initial Evaluation for Special

Education Base Salary or Wage Birthdate Black or African American Boarding Status Born Outside of the U.S. Building/Site Number Bus Route ID Bus Stop Arrival Time Bus Stop Description Bus Stop Distance Bus Stop from School ID Bus Stop to School Distance Bus Stop to School ID Career and Technical Education Completer Career Objectives Change in Developmental Status Citizenship Status City City of Birth Class Attendance Status Class Rank Cohort Year Community Service Hours Compulsory Attendance Status at Time of Discontinuing School Condition Onset Date Corrective Equipment Prescribed Corrective Equipment Purpose Country Code Country of Birth Code Country of Citizenship Code County FIPS (Federal Information Processing Standards) Code County of Birth CTE Concentrator CTE Participant Daily Attendance Status Day/Evening Status Days Truant Death Cause Death Date Developmental Delay Diagnosis of Causative Factor (Condition) Dialect Name Diploma/Credential Award Date Diploma/Credential Type Discontinuing Schooling Reason Diseases, Illnesses, and Other Health Conditions Displacement Status Distance From Home to School Dwelling Arrangement Dwelling Ownership Early Intervention Evaluation Process Description/Title Economic Disadvantage Status Education Planned Electronic Mail Address Electronic Mail Address Type Eligibility Status for School Food Service Programs Emergency Factor Employment End Date Employment Permit Certifying Organization Employment Permit Description Employment Permit Expiration Date Employment Permit Number Employment Permit Valid Date Employment Recognition Employment Start Date End Date End Day End of Term Status English Language Proficiency Progress/Attainment English Proficiency English Proficiency Level Entry Date Entry Type Entry/Grade Level Established IDEA Condition Evaluated for Special Education but Not Receiving Services Evaluation Date Evaluation Extension Date Evaluation Location Evaluation Parental Consent Date Evaluation Sequence Exit/Withdrawal Date Exit/Withdrawal Status Exit/Withdrawal Type Experience Type Expulsion Cause Expulsion Return Date Extension Description Family Income Range Family Perceptions of the Impact of Early Intervention Services on the Child Family Public Assistance Status Federal Program Participant Status Fee Amount Fee Payment Type Financial Assistance Amount Financial Assistance Descriptive Title Financial Assistance Qualifier Financial Assistance Source Financial Assistance Type First Entry Date into a US School First Entry Date into State First Entry Date into the United States First Name Former Legal Name Full Academic Year Status Full-time Equivalent (FTE) Status Full-time/Part-time Status Future Entry Date Generation Code/Suffix Gifted and Talented Status Gifted Eligibility Criteria

GPA Weighted Grade Earned Grade Point Average (GPA): Cumulative (High School) Graduation Testing Status Head of Household Health Care History Episode Date Health Care Plan Health Condition Progress Report Highest Level of Education Completed Hispanic or Latino Ethnicity Homeless Primary Nighttime Residence Homeless Unaccompanied Youth Status Homelessness Status Honors Description Hospital Preference IDEA Status Identification Code Identification Procedure Identification Results Identification System IEP Transition Plan IFSP Goals Met Illness Type Immigrant Status Immunization Date Immunization Status Immunization Type Immunizations Mandated by State Law for Participation Impact of Early Intervention Services on the Family In-school/Post-school Employment Status Individualized Program Date Individualized Program Date Type Individualized Program Type Information Source Initial Language Assessment Status Injury Circumstances Injury Description Insurance Coverage International Code Number IP Address Language Code Language Type Languages Other Than English Last/Surname Last/Surname at Birth Length of Placement in Neglected or Delinquent Program Length of Time Transported Life Status Limitation Beginning Date Limitation Cause Limitation Description Limitation Ending Date Limited English Proficiency Status Marital Status Marking Period Maternal Last Name Meal Payment Method (Reimbursable/Non-reimbursable) Meal Purchase Price (Reimbursable) Meal Service Meal Service Transaction Date Meal Service Transaction Type Meal Type Medical Laboratory Procedure Results Medical Treatment Medical Waiver Middle Initial Middle Name Migrant Certificate of Eligibility (COE) Status Migrant Classification Subgroup Migrant Continuation of Services Migrant Last Qualifying Arrival Date (QAD) Migrant Last Qualifying Move (LQM) Date Migrant Priority for Services Migrant QAD from City Migrant QAD from Country Migrant QAD from State Migrant QAD to City Migrant QAD to State Migrant Qualifying Work Type Migrant Residency Date Migrant Service Type Migrant Status Migrant to Join Date Migratory Status Military Service Experience Minor/Adult Status Multiple Birth Status Name of Country Name of Country of Birth Name of Country of Citizenship Name of County Name of Institution Name of Language Name of State Name of State of Birth National/Ethnic Origin Subgroup Native Hawaiian or Other Pacific Islander NCLB Title 1 School Choice Eligible NCLB Title 1 School Choice Offered NCLB Title 1 School Choice Transfer Neglected or Delinquent Below Grade Level Status Neglected or Delinquent Pre-test and Post-test Status Neglected or Delinquent Program Placement Duration Status Neglected or Delinquent Program Type Neglected or Delinquent Progress Level Neglected or

Delinquent Status Nickname Non-course Graduation Requirement Date Met Non-course Graduation Requirement Scores/Results Non-course Graduation Requirement Type Non-resident Attendance Rationale Non-school Activity Beginning Date Non-school Activity Description Non-school Activity Ending Date Non-school Activity Sponsor Non-school Activity Type Nonpromotion Reason Notice of Recommended Educational Placement Date Number of Days Absent Number of Days in Attendance Number of Days of Membership Number of Dependents Number of Hours Worked per Weekend Number of Hours Worked per Work Week Number of Minutes per Week Included Number of Minutes per Week Non-Inclusion Number of Tardies Other Name Overall Diagnosis/Interpretation of Hearing Overall Diagnosis/Interpretation of Speech and Language Overall Diagnosis/Interpretation of Vision Overall Health Status Participant Role Participation in School Food Service Programs Payment Source(s) Percentage Ranking Personal Information Verification Personal Title/Prefix Placement Parental Consent Date Planned Assessment Participation Points/Mark Assistance Points/Mark Value Points/Mark Value Description Post-school Recognition Post-school Training or Education Subject Matter Postal Code Preparing for Nontraditional Fields Status Present Attendance Categories Primary Disability Type Primary Telephone Number Status Program Eligibility Date Program Eligibility Expiration Date Program Eligibility Status Program Exit Reason Program of Study Relevance Program Participation Reason Program Placement Date Program Plan Date Program Plan Effective Date Progress Toward IFSP Goals and Objectives Promotion Testing Status Promotion Type Public School Residence Status Qualified Individual with Disabilities Status Race Reason for Non-entrance in School Recognition for Participation or Performance in an Activity Reevaluation Date Referral Cause Referral Completion Date Referral Completion Report Referral Date Referral Purpose Related Emergency Needs Released Time Religious Affiliation Religious Consideration Residence after Exiting/Withdrawing from School Residence Block Number Resident Resource Check Out Date Resource Due Date Resource Title Checked Out Responsible District Responsible District Type Responsible School Routine Health Care Procedure Required at School Safety Education Status School Choice Applied Status School Choice Eligible Status School Choice Transfer Status School District Code of Residence School Food Services Eligibility Status Beginning Date School Food Services Eligibility Status Determination School Food Services Eligibility Status Ending Date School Food Services Participation Basis School Health Emergency Action School ID from which Transferred Score Interpretation Information Score Results Screening

Administration Date Screening Instrument Description/Title Screening Location Section 504 Status Service Alternatives Service Category Service Plan Date Service Plan Meeting Location Service Plan Meeting Outcome Service Plan Meeting Participants Service Plan Signature Date Service Plan Signatures Sex Social Security Number Social Security Number (SSN) Special Accommodation Requirements Special Diet Considerations Special Education FTE Start Date Start Day State Abbreviation State FIPS (Federal Information Processing Standards) Code State of Birth Abbreviation State Transportation Aid Qualification State-assigned Code for Institution State-assigned County Code Street Number/Name Student Program Status Substance Abuse Description Technology Literacy Status in 8th Grade Telephone Number Telephone Number Type Telephone Status Title I Instructional Services Received Title I Status Title I Supplemental Services: Applied Title I Supplemental Services: Eligible Title I Supplemental Services: Services Received Title I Support Services: Services Received Title III Immigrant Participant Status Title III LEP Participation Total Cost of Education to Student Total Distance Transported Total Number in Class Transition Meeting Date Transition Meeting Location Transition Meeting Outcome Transition Meeting Participants Transition Plan Signature Transition Plan Signature Date Transition Service Description Transportation at Public Expense Eligibility Transportation Status Tribal or Clan Name Tuberculosis Test Type Tuition Payment Amount Tuition Status Uniform Resource Identifier Unsafe School Choice Offered Status Unsafe School Choice Status User/Screen Name Voting Status Ward of the State White Work Experience Paid Work Experience Required Work Type Zip Code Zone Number (Institute of Education Sciences, 2014).

Although these data points are theoretically customizable by individual jurisdictions, would they be? Or would students be tracked from preschool to doctorate and into their careers, for life, with personally identifying information embedded within their records? Of course, the leaks from Edward Snowdon showed that the National Security Agency (NSA) can already do this. In fact, they already have done so for selected targets like the Obama family and staff, Justice Alito, General Petraeus, and others, as NSA whistleblower Russell Tice has said from first hand knowledge (Martin and Tice, 2013).

Since the 1925 U.S. Supreme Court case of Pierce vs. the Society of Sisters, mass compulsory schooling from ages 5–8 to 16–18 is the law of the land, with a few limited exceptions (Bush, 2010, para. 6). During the

Bush administration, convicted Iran-Contra felon Admiral Poindexter ran the blue sky research arm of the Pentagon for several years, the Defense Advanced Research Projects Agency (DARPA). While Poindexter was head, DARPA came up with the "Total Information Awareness" program in 2002, which was designed to track everybody's every digital trace. It caused a bit of a stir. Clearly, according to the Snowden documents the National Security Agency and their civilian contractors can do it now—and largely do (Bamford, 2009).

With data collection provisions an integral part of NCLB, Race to the Top, and Common Core, we are talking about the possible arrival of an extremely thorough longitudinal dossier on people of K–12 age now, moving forward. It could easily be hacked by federal government agencies like the NSA or other parties like identity thieves. Or the federal government could simply present the governmental, for-profit, or non-profit entities holding this data with warrantless "national security letters" to secure access to the data, and the entities would then be gagged from disclosing anything to the injured party—or anybody else. Or, worse yet, we know from numerous NSA whistleblowers that the NSA already has unfettered access to the traffic of all of the major telecoms, "80 major global corporations" (like "ATT, EDS, Hewlett-Packard, Cisco, Qualcomm, Oracle, IBM, Microsoft, Verizon, Motorola, Qwest, and Intel") and major online service providers (like "Microsoft, Yahoo, Google, Facebook, Paltalk, YouTube, Skype, AOL and Apple") (Democracy Now, May 13, 2014, 16:00–17:00; Greenwald and MacAskill, 2013, para. 15). Is it realistic to count on the good faith of our leaders to not continue doing what they have already been doing for years? This has the potential to be an Orwellian nightmare; the panopticon arrived. There are barely any laws to mitigate against the abuse of this data by a surveillance state gone mad. Any laws that are in place are weak, easily ignored and circumvented, as the testimony of numerous major NSA whistleblowers over the last decade (like Snowdon, Tice, Drake, Binney, Wiebe, Klein, and others, and decades of Foreign Intelligence Surveillance Act Court orders, prove.

In light of all of these many contentious issues, Common Core supporters like Mike Huckabee, "former Republican Arkansas governor and Fox News host… while speaking at a CCSSO conference last fall" acknowledged that Common Core had become so "toxic," that he encouraged the chief "state school officers attending the conference to 'rebrand it, refocus it, but don't retreat'" (Berry, March 20, 2014, para. 30). Arizona, Florida, and Iowa did so, renaming their standards as "Arizona's College and Career Ready Standards, the Next Generation Sunshine State Standards and the Iowa Core" (Bidwell, January 31, 2014, para. 15). In spite of such cosmetic changes, Kentucky (Bidwell, January 31, 2014, para. 4, 6), Louisiana, Massachusetts, New Hampshire, New York, Rhode Island, Wisconsin, Texas (Bidwell, 2014a, para. 1–3; Bidwell, 2014b), Florida, Michigan, Ohio, and Pennsylvania (Exit strategy, 2014) are considering dropping out of Common Core. Indiana, South Carolina, and Oklahoma have dropped out (Rice, 2014). Legislative measures to do so failed to pass in "Alabama, Georgia, Missouri, South Dakota, Indiana [and] Kansas" (Exit strategy, 2014). Minnesota only adopted the English language arts standards; and Virginia, Nebraska, Texas, and Alaska never formally adopted the standards (Standards Adoption).

In a March 21, 2014 letter, Senator Grassley urged his colleagues to join him in an attempt to defund Common Core by means of a letter he sent to Chairman Harkin, Chairman of the Subcommittee on Labor, Health and Human Services, Education, Senate Appropriations Committee (Strauss, March 23, 2014, para. 1–2). "Despite its state-based origins, opposition to Common Core is rapidly becoming a 'true conservative' litmus test, and a major factor in the 'invisible primary' leading into the 2016 presidential cycle" (Kilgore, 2014, para. 2).

Common Core poses two significant questions to American society: 1) who has the right to decide what children learn? and 2) what are the aims of education?

As an interviewee in the anti-Common Core documentary *Building the Machine* put it: "Whose child is it? Is it the government's right to teach the child what the government thinks the child should know or is it my child and I should have some say in it?" (Wurman cited in Home School Legal Defense Fund, 2014, 28: 50). Some may say that such questions are misleading because Common Core is not a government program. It was coordinated by two private non-profit organizations, funded largely by a single private foundation and its adoption by states was voluntary. Strictly speaking, this is true, although it is disingenuous in that adoption of Common Core was, for all intents and purposes, required for a competitive application to Race to the Top. In this sense, Wurman's question becomes a fair one.

The Southern Poverty Law Center asserts that resistance to Common Core comes from people who see it as a form of government indoctrination, although their report claims that this resistance is astroturf, not grassroots, based on "unfounded and paranoid rhetoric" fostered by well-funded right wing and libertarian think tanks (Elias, Gunter, der Valk, and Costello, 2014, pp. 16–17; Simon and Shah, 2013, para. 4). On the other hand, "education expert Joy Pullmann" asserts that "Common Core opposition is so completely grassroots, and support is so astroturf" (Evansky, 2014, pp. 8–9). This is ironic in that she is an "education research fellow for The Heartland Institute," a global warming–denying, Koch brothers–funded think tank that is one of the leading installers of astroturf on this issue (Evansky, 2014, pp. 8–9). In truth, the picture is more complicated. Opposition and support come from the right. Opposition and support come from the left. Opposition and support is astroturf. Opposition and support is grassroots.

One of the largest camps in opposition to Common Core include those who see it as a new front in the ongoing culture war (Frank, 2004) and rush "once more unto the breach." To them, Common Core is the latest example of godless, liberal, LGBT-friendly, socialist, secular humanists trying to use the government to impose their agenda on wholesome, conservative, god-fearing Christian families. No one can deny that this camp hold their values with fervent passion. This very passion, however, makes them susceptible to appeals to emotion rather than appeals to reason. I would suspect that many in this camp would actually identify Obama as a socialist, even though he gave billions of dollars in bail-out money to the banksters, allows dozens of the leading U.S. corporations to get away with paying no taxes whatsoever (even though they rake in billions of dollars a year in profits) and stood by idly as the differences in income and wealth between the rich and everyone else reached their greatest disparities since 1929. In this sense, Obama *is* a socialist: for the rich, as most politicians at his level are, Democrat or Republican, so perhaps this camp's grasp of empirical reality is not always particularly firm. They see Common Core instructional and assessment materials as a clear and explicit program of government indoctrination are not. In truth, these materials are almost always provided by for-profit vendors (exploiting a reform model that was made possible by the sustained and ongoing engagement of big business). Common Core relies on the coercive power of the state as Race to the Top evolved out of NCLB and on the coercive power of the state's role in education generally. As the U.S. Supreme Court opinion in Pierce v. Society of Sisters states: "no question is raised concerning the power of the State reasonably to regulate all schools, to inspect, supervise and examine them, their teachers and pupils; to require that all children of proper age attend some school" (1925, p. 268). Therefore the question of whether Common Core, as it is experienced in the classroom, is a "government program" or not is somewhat nebulous.

Whether it is tagged as such or not, one thing that is surely not astroturf is the rebellion against Common Core by state and local teacher unions, individual teachers, individual parents, and collective parental groups. These parents demand a dominant say in what their children are learning. Evidence is still largely anecdotal but substantial and growing rapidly. Anti–Common Core parents use social media like Twitter, YouTube, websites, and other means very effectively. They post their thoughts against the paradigm, hold cyber rallies, and post their children's Common Core–aligned homework, worksheets, and tests. Mathematics in particular is drawing the ire of parents, for seemingly abandoning the basics of addition, subtraction, multiplication, and division, making it unnecessarily complicated and convoluted.

The other significant question Common Core poses to American society regards the aims of education. Although I will discuss the aims of education at greater length in the conclusion, as it has been relentlessly portrayed throughout the history of standards-based education, especially since Achieve, Inc.'s American Diploma Project, it is to be "college and career ready." What the supporters of standards-based education mean by this is never defined. This is odd considering how often it is referred to. It isn't on the Common Core State Standards Initiative website, www.corestandards.org. After asking Common Core what they meant by those terms through their website's contact page, I received a document defining them.

"College ready" is defined by the Common Core State Standards Initiative as an individual who is

> prepared for all entry-level, credit-bearing, academic college courses in English, mathematics, the sciences, the social sciences, and the humanities. The objective is for all students to enter these classes ready for success (defined for these purposes as a C or better)" (Common Core State Standards Initiative, 2014c).

Any discussion of "college ready" should begin with a consideration of how the college experience has changed over the last few decades. Since then, America has witnessed the collapse of social science, humanities, and liberal arts education, the collapse of the academic labor market (so that most entry level academicians must struggle at poverty or near poverty wages as lecturers or adjunct professors for years), the rise of instrumental college majors like those related to business, and the alignment of the university with the burgeoning national security state and neoliberal imperatives. According to a study sponsored in part by the Bill and Melinda Gates Foundation, the "top 10 most popular majors" and their percentage of total bachelor's degrees granted is as follows:

> Business Management and Administration 8%, General Business 5%, Accounting 5%, Nursing 4%, Psychology 4%, Elementary Education 4%, Marketing and Marketing Research 3%, General Education 3%, English Language and Literature 3%, Communications 3% (Carnevale, Strohl, and Melton, 2011, p. 13).

That means 21% of bachelor's degrees are earned in business-specific majors, even excluding communications (although this can sometimes be a public relations-oriented degree). The acolytes of standards-based education continually speak about jobs in the 21st century knowledge-based economy. This has some basis in fact. Filtered by the projected number of new jobs requiring a bachelor's degree in descending order, a recent report from the United States Department of Labor, Bureau of Labor Statistics (2014) projected "50,000 or more new jobs" to be created between 2012 and 2022 for

> computer and information systems managers; software developers, systems software; general and operations managers; medical and health services managers; construction managers; computer systems analysts; civil engineers; management analysts; [and] personal financial advisors (United States Department of Labor, Bureau of Labor Statistics, 2014).

These means that four out of ten sectors the U.S. Department of Labor predicts will be creating the most jobs until 2022 are information related. Nevertheless, out of a total number of jobs in America in 2012 (145,355,800), only 2,677,000 were in information, 11,918,900 were in manufacturing and 116,067,000 were in services (United States Department of Labor, Bureau of Labor Statistics, 2013).

> "Career ready" is defined by the Common Core State Standards Initiative as ready to succeed... in workforce training programs [in] careers that 1) offer competitive livable salaries above the poverty line, 2) offer opportunities for career advancement and 3) are in a growing or the sustainable industry (Common Core State Standards Initiative, 2014c, para. 5).

As the college experience is ambiguously defined, so too is career-readiness. What workforce training programs is the Common Core State Standards Initiative referring to? In 2013 "poverty guidelines for the 48 contiguous states and the District of Columbia" for a one person household is $11,490 (United States Health and Human Services Department, 2013).

In this chapter I analyzed how standards-based education transitioned from being state-based to being a quasi-national regime under No Child Left Behind, Race to the Top, and Common Core, and delineated the rapidly increasing resistance to Common Core.

· 7 ·
CONCLUSION

So far, I have attempted to describe and explain why policy makers and other interest groups came to embrace standards-based education as the key to recent educational reform efforts. In chapter 2, I examined how elite business interests made common cause with the leading lights of what has been called the "new right" during the late 1960s and 1970s to create a coalition that, while their interests were sometimes in conflict, was nevertheless instrumental in the eventual creation of standards-based education. During this period, we also saw the beginning of a rightward shift in the Democratic party as well, a faction that would join the business-right coalition on education reform issues to later coalesce into standards-based education, making these concerns more bipartisan than they are portrayed in such influential works as Berliner and Biddle (1996) and Apple (2006). In chapter 3, I analyzed a flurry of reports on educational policy reform issued during the 1980s and early 1990s, as well as some groundbreaking examples of reform in practice initiated during the same period, with a special focus on the incredibly influential *A Nation at Risk* report. I chose to focus on these reports because they established much of the rhetoric, proposals, and institutional linkages that would later become standards-based education. Or, more succinctly, "whoever decides what the game is about also decides who gets into the game" (Schattschneider cited in Callahan, 1999, para. 2). In chapter 4, I provided a detailed history of federal law and policies regarding standards-based education during the George H. W. Bush and Clinton presidencies. Bush's *America 2000* legislation failed to pass. Resurrected largely unchanged by Clinton as *Goals 2000*, it passed in 1994. With passage of *Goals 2000* and the *Improving America's Schools Act* (the Elementary and Secondary Education Act reauthorization) in 1994, standards-based education became a settled and integral part of local, state, and federal educational policy. In chapter 5, I offered a case study of how one state, Hawaii, assimilated standards-based education. I charted this from its beginning as an early adopter nationwide to the present day. In chapter 6, I look at the consolidation of states-based standards-based education to quasi-national standards-based education in No Child Left Behind, Race to the Top, and Common Core.

In this conclusion, I will begin with a brief survey of the evaluation literature of standards-based education in America while it was still state-based, briefly evaluate standards-based education now that it is quasi-national under Common Core, offer a novel perspective on standards-based education, one largely at variance with its many advocates.

The strengths and weaknesses of standards-based education have been debated for nearly two decades in the evaluation literature while the reform model was still state-based. The model was adopted in large part because states are under political and economic pressure to continually chase the slowly increasing federal share of state and local education budgets. In 1990–1991, when standards-based education first started coming into being, the federal share of local education was 5.7%. By 2005, after it had become entrenched in federal law, it was still only 8.3%. Yet that money had become a major driver of educational policy over the last two decades at the state and district levels, rising to 15% of total public K–12 spending according to Peng and Guthrie (2010, para. 33) This is what has been called the revenue theory of costs. According to this model, "each institution raises all the money it can and then it spends all it raises in order to maximize its prestige and quality" (Lewis and Dundar, 2001, p. 138). As the 1990s drew to a close, every state except Iowa had drafted standards. By the time President Bush signed the No Child Left Behind Act into law on January 8, 2002, even Iowa had promulgated standards. Standards-based education had became an even more settled and integral part of local, state, and federal educational policy than it had been under the Clinton administration.

Along with charter schools, school choice, and vouchers, standards-based education has been one of the leading and most enduring educational reform models in America over the last few decades; arguably the preeminent one, in terms of overall impact and persistence over time. As "school delivery" and "opportunity-to-learn" standards regarding resources and equity fell to the wayside, the focus shifted to two elements, "content" and "performance" standards. Content standards came to mean what students should know in each academic topic in each grade, while performance standards came to indicate what constituted adequate mastery of the content standard.

By the mid-1990s people and organizations began formulating important characterizations of what they felt quality standards were. Education scholar and then prominent standards advocate Diane Ravitch saw three salient features: "they are clear and measurable; they focus on cognitive learning, not affective traits; and they are usually based on traditional academic disciplines" (cited in Olson, 1995, para. 13).

In 1995 the National Academy of Education endorsed two guiding principles for standards:

1) Because there is not one best way to organize subject matter in a given field of study, rigorous national standards should not be restricted to one set of standards per subject area.
2) Content standards should embody a coherent, professionally defensible conception of how a field can be framed for purposes of instruction. They should not be an exhaustive, incoherent compendium of every group's desired content (McLaughlin, Shepard, and O'Day, 1995, p. xviii).

The formal body created by statute to address the issue, the National Council on Education Standards and Testing, said that

1) Standards must reflect high expectations, not expectations of minimal competency.
2) Standards must provide focus and direction, not become a national curriculum.
3) Standards must be national, not federal.
4) Standards must be voluntary, not mandated by the federal government.
5) Standards must be dynamic, not static (cited in Ravitch, 1995b, p. 140).

Certainly, the model has never been short of critics. Some saw standards-based education as shortchanging the traditional progressive means and ends of education (Kohn, 1999). Some see more value in a vibrant, resourceful, flexible, and democratic school culture (Meier, 2000). Some lambasted the "one-size-fits-all approach" (Ohanian, 1999). Some conceded it may be seen as an "autocratic, regimented throw-back to factory-model approaches to school, where students are forced to regurgitate expert-prescribed sets of facts or face failure" (S. Thompson, 1999, p. 46).

A perceived lack of concern for gender, race, and class differences worried a number of analysts (Berlak, 1995; Marzano and Kendall, 1996; Purpel, 1995; White House Initiative on Educational Excellence for Hispanic Americans, 1999; Horn, 2004). Others took the opposite tack and worried that the conventional stories and historic figures of America were unduly neglected by standards, echoing Lynn Cheney's critique of the initial history standards in the mid-1990s (Cheney, 1994). Given so many diverging viewpoints, many urged standards developers to focus on common values and learning objectives, foreshadowing Common Core (Darling-Hammond, 1997; Darling-Hammond and Falk, 1997b; Falk and Ort, 1998).

Furthermore, some saw rigid, detailed, highly structured standards as a de-skilling of teachers' intellectual work and professional practice in pursuit of "teacher-proof" learning environments (Rothstein, Jacobsen, and Wilder, 2008). Some argued that standards were part of a long-term big business agenda to de-skill intellectual and physical labor in Fordist and post-Fordist economies. This is especially deleterious in teaching because most great teaching is as much art, improvisation, and guild craft as science, and often relies heavily on improvisation and rapid adaptation to tacit cues given off by students in the moment.

Some authors focused their attention on enhanced expectations of students (Hirsch, 1996), while others focus on enhanced standards-based learning through professional development (Alvarado, 1998), assessment (Darling-Hammond and Falk, 1997a, 1997b; Spalding, 2000), leadership (O'Neil and Tell, 1999; Resnick and Hall, 1998), or curriculum (Resnick and Resnick, 1991).

Although testing and accountability are an integral part of the standards-based education reform model (Tucker and Codding, 2002), several aspects of it came under fire while the model was still largely under the purview of the states. For example, the expense and technical challenges posed by creating valid and reliable tests often intimidated states and districts. Often, states and districts assessed student achievement under standards regimes with previously existing testing instruments, or slightly tweaked versions of previously existing testing instruments, even if those instruments were not entirely appropriate for the new standards. This sometimes undermined public trust in the reform concept, especially when the tests had high stakes consequences, such as grade promotion or graduation (Falk, 2000, pp. 90–91).

Another concern was the potential harm that may have been caused by privileging high stakes testing over multiple, diverse, and robust means of assessment (International Reading Association, 1999; Koretz and Linn, 1996; National Council on Education Standards and Testing, 1993; Darling-Hammond and Falk, 1997b). At one point, approximately half of the large urban school districts that linked testing to grade promotion offered summer remedial classes; "in many of them (Chicago, Houston, Oakland, Denver, Washington, DC, and New York City, to name just a few) attendance" is mandatory (Falk, 2000, p. 92). Students were not alone in feeling the pressure against low test scores. Depending on the performance of their schools, teachers and administrators could and can enjoy bonuses—or face sanctions or even dismissal. In some jurisdictions, schools could and can even be shut down or privatized.

In light of the personal and professional stress and potential disruption to educational systems when standards are linked to high stakes testing, it perhaps not surprising that states with milder consequences for low test scores (like Maryland and Maine) often noted more positive benefits from their standards than did states and districts that took a more punitive approach (Clotfeller and Ladd, 1996; Elmore and Fuhrman, 1996; Elmore, Abelmann, and Fuhrman, 1996; Firestone, Mayrowetz, and Fairman, 1997; Murnane and Levy, 1996).

One of the most common complaints against standards-based education is the potential risk it poses to holistic, individualized, multi-faceted, student-centered learning that can come from pressure to "teach to the test." For example, an analysis of the assessment system in Kentucky (often seen as a leader in standards) found it hard for teachers to resist focusing "on whatever is thought to raise test scores rather than on instruction aimed at addressing individual student needs" (Jones and Whitford, 1997, p. 277).

In the perennially tough battle for resources, administrators are not always able to resist the temptation "to manipulate test results by changing the school's student population or keeping certain students out of the testing pool" (Falk, 2000, p. 93; Clotfeller and Ladd, 1996; Darling-Hammond, 1997;

Smith and Rottenberg, 1991). In some cases, this can even rise to the level of potentially criminal activity (Hoff, 1999, para. 30). President George W. Bush's education secretary Rod Paige came under scrutiny over these types of allegations related to his tenure as the Houston schools chief.

Other oft-cited critiques of high stakes tests include their perceived unfairness to those with limited English proficiency and disabilities, their tendency to commandeer huge chunks of instructional time, and their tendency to foster investment in testing over learning (Falk 2000, pp. 93–99). These critiques led stakeholders in some states (such as Texas, Ohio, and Massachusetts) to try and abolish their high stakes tests (Hoff, 1999).

Some have argued that the participation of business in the development of standards has helped business socialize job training costs for the dominant service-clerical labor sector onto public education (Horn, 2004, p. 28). While many have sought redress in the courts with some success, the record is not always a rosy one. In June 2002 the Appellate Division of the New York State Supreme Court ruled 4-to-1 to overturn a landmark decision from Manhattan Supreme Court Justice Leland De Grasse, which had been a major step forward in equity of funding for New York City schools (Ohanian, 2003, p. 736). In his opinion, Justice Alfred Lerner contradicted much of what business had been trying to say in the name of the standards-based education movement for the previous 20 years. Standards-based education wasn't designed to foster higher order thinking skills to remain competitive in a 21st century economy. Rather, it was merely intended to enable students "function productively as civic participants," so they could secure gainful employment, vote, and serve on juries. The justice saw these as relatively simple skills, ones "imparted between grades 8 and 9." He conceded that so little education might qualify a person for only a low-paying job but added, "society needs workers in all levels of jobs, the majority of which may very well be low-level" (cited in Gonzalez, 2002, para. 9–11).

As Ohanian has concurred, the "global economy needs these dropouts. If schools are successful in turning out swarms of well-educated youngsters, who's going to flip our burgers and clean our toilets at minimum wage?" (Ohanian, 2003, p. 737). By labeling so many children as failures, standards, high-stakes testing, and accountability regimes may have also been a factor in filling the burgeoning school-to-prison pipeline as well, sending America's incarceration rates soaring. While there were definitely other social trends in play during the period that standards-based education came into existence, it is interesting to note that "according to a 2010 report from the Center for Economic and Policy Research... the inmate population... [grew] from about 220 per 100,000 in 1980 to 458 in 1990, 683 in 2000, and 753 in 2008" (deRugy, 2011, para. 4).

Since states' standards had (and now Common Core has) a grade or grade span progression, they also assumed that all children develop at the same pace. This is contradicted by much of the literature in child psychology (Klein, 1984, 2002; Matthews, 1980; Piaget and Enhelder, 2000). While there may arguably be general developmental phrases, it seems doubtful that all children pass through them at exactly the same age. Even the conventional educational ideal of moving "from the simple to the complex" in relatively graduated steps, so central to standards-based education, may not be in accordance with how every student learns either.

Since standards emerged, a cottage industry of think tanks, service providers, non-profits, and the like have emerged to serve the model. There is even a sizable coterie of what one might call policy entrepreneurs who have spent much of their careers as technocrats or publicists in favor of standards-based education and other closely related ideas in education policy reform. These include people like Marc Tucker, Denis Doyle, Marsha Levine, Robert Marzano, Lauren Resnick, Paul Peterson, Terry Moe, John Chubb, Chester Finn, Jr., and William Bennett, to name just a few of the more prominent ones.

It also includes the early Diane Ravitch but not the later one. Ravitch is an especially interesting example. In the early portion of her career she was "present at creation," a major proponent who helped to consolidate standards-based education as a settled part of local, state, and federal education policy. According to her, however, "I began to re-evaluate my views as early as 2004, as I watched the implementation of mayoral control in New York City, with its heavy emphasis on accountability and choice" (Ravitch, 2010a, para. 3). She posits her book *The Death and Life of the Great American School System: How Testing and Choice are Undermining Education* (2010b) as a description of how she came to repudiate her "support for choice and accountability, though not for curriculum reform," which she does not see as a "u-turn" but rather as a reversion to the time before she "jumped on the bandwagon of organizational change and accountability, the time [she] knew that the only changes that matter are in the classroom and in children's lives" (Ravitch, 2010a, para. 3).

Whether it is a 180 degree turn, or a 360 degree turn back to her origin, the historical trajectory of Ravitch's career is one of the most interesting in all of standards-based education. To the "left" it seems like one of standards-based education's foremost and most instrumental proponents "saw the light." To the "right," it seems like she become a traitor to the cause and ran to the warm ensconce of the entrenched liberal interests of "the blob" ("Big Learning Organization Bureaucracies") or the "Educational Industrial Complex": "more than 200 groups, associations, federations, alliances, departments, offices, administrations, councils, boards, commissions, panels, organizations, herds, flocks and coveys" (Allen, 2012, para. 1, 3). In either case, it took a tremendous act of conscience and humility for such a prominent person to make such a dramatic change in such a prominent way.

Major defections like that of Ravitch excepted, an institutional inertia can be detected when all of these developments are considered collectively. It is one that is in favor of what already exists and letting the policy elite fine tune it with technocratic tweaks—but never a wholesale rejection of the idea.

An extended discussion of these assumptions, hidden within the policy debate and rarely discussed, is vitally important because it can help explicate clear, distinct, and important characterizations of 1) the disparity between the ideology of weakening nation-states so often professed by neoliberal ideologues and the practical reality of strong nation-states that their technocrats are creating and utilizing, 2) the future, and 3) the ends of education. These ideas have profound geopolitical, environmental, and economic implications. At this point, it is hard to deny that standards-based education has become the most widely implemented of the numerous education policy reform ideas that have circulated in the United States over the last several decades. In spite of all this, neither the numerous supporters nor the detractors have satisfactorily answered these most salient of all implications.

Shuttling back and forth between the public and macrostructural, and the personal and microstructural, we could consider using Gabbard's conception of a market-driven conscience predicated on education successively conceived of as a requirement, an opportunity, and then a right (2003, p. 66) as an organizing principle to examine many of the ideas mentioned above. In the United States, totems of these notions of requirement, opportunity, and right might respectively include 1) the Supreme Court case Pierce v. Society of Sisters of the Holy Names of Jesus and Mary of 1925, 2) the Servicemen's Readjustment Act of 1944 (more commonly referred to as the G.I. Bill), and 3) the Supreme Court case Brown v. Board of Education of 1954. The ever-increasing federal role in American education inherent in each totem enable us to see the contours of the de facto strong nation-state being created by the regime of neoliberal globalization as it has evolved over time.

The archetypical expression of the weakening of the nation-state under globalization can be found in Friedman's *The World Is Flat* (2005). In that volume, Friedman opined that advances in computing and telecommunications, lower cost international travel, the proliferation of international brands, and other related trends have combined to create a global culture and global market where traditional historical, geographical, and cultural divisions have become increasingly irrelevant.

One of the most overt ways in which neoliberals utilize a strong state instead of a weak one is in the very imposition of neoliberal economic policies themselves. As Klein demonstrated in *The Shock Doctrine* (2007) through numerous case studies, the mavens of international neoliberal economics and politics often use their control over the levers of their nation-state to impose neoliberalism on their countries. Or, often, international multilateral organizations (such as the International Monetary Fund) controlled by a select number of strong states dictate the terms of this imposition. In both cases, according to Klein's notion of "disaster capitalism," the consolidation of wealth and power often takes place during or shortly after disasters, with the nation-state sometimes creating these disasters.

One important neoliberal use of the strong state was in the recent reconception of anti-trust law by American government officials and jurists at the beginning of the decades-long rise of standards-based education. These individuals, notably Robert Bork (1978), redefined the potential injury of monopoly as that of higher prices for consumers rather than the concentrated ownership of the means of production. This not only led to significant outsourcing abroad but also inaugurated a powerful re-monopolization of important sectors of the economy by American business. This re-monopolization, however, was of a peculiar sort one with profound implications for the structure of the American economy and employment, particularly in how it hollowed out of the manufacturing base (Lynn, 2010, p. 15).

Manufacturing as a share of the United States' gross domestic product has been declining steadily from its peak shortly after World War II; then from "24.3% in 1970 to 12.8% in 2010" (Perry, 2012, para. 4). During the same period, manufacturing jobs hovered steadily at just under 20 million per year, while service jobs began at just over 20 million at the close of World War II, rising to nearly 120 million at the end of the first decade of the 20th century, an increase of approximately 2.5% annually since 1947 (Strauss, 2008, p. 10).

According to the U.S. Commerce Department, "U.S. multinational corporations, the big brand-name companies that employ a fifth of all American workers" added 4.4 million jobs in the United States during the 1990s, but also increased overseas employment by 2.7 million (Wessel, 2011, para. 1–2). In the first decade of the 21st century, this trend got even worse (from the perspective of the American worker). During that time, domestic employment was cut by 2.9 million jobs, while employment abroad by these corporations increased by 2.4 million (Wessel, 2011, para. 1–2).

Ironically, this outsourcing has been used to lambaste the American educational system again and again for not producing workers competitive enough in the global economy, even though economic competitiveness is not caused primarily by the schools, but rather by governmental policies and corporate decision-making. This is "at worst a crass effort to direct attention away from those truly responsible for doing something about competitiveness and to lay the burden instead on the schools" (Cremin, 1990, p. 103).

For example, when Toyota, BMW, and other high-quality automotive manufacturers choose to establish operations in the United States, they often locate in states with low labor costs, low educational achievement levels, and weak unions, yet they are still able to manufacture competitive, world-class products. Conversely, when American corporate executives relocate American manufacturing abroad, they do not typically send these operations to countries whose educational systems routinely rank near the top of major international benchmarks, but rather to low-wage countries where employees often do not even have a high school diploma.

At this point, it is difficult to argue that America has not become a corporatized plutocracy, arguably a kleptocracy, certainly a prime example of corporate socialism that uses a strong nation-state to socialize the costs and privatize the benefits. Indeed, many increasingly take this as a given, people like Nobel prize-winning economist Joseph Stieglitz (2011), "democratic" national security insider Zbigniew Brzezinski (2007), Citigroup analysts (Kapur, Macleod, and Singh, 2005), and National Academy member Niall Ferguson (2004). Among the most striking characteristics of this transition has been the rollback of the social contract and the concentration of wealth among the elite to levels not seen since before the Progressive Era in the United States in the early part of the 20th century, perhaps even as far back as the Robber Baron era of the late 19th century.

Different people had different indicators and made different analyses of different data to arrive at similar conclusions. Some of these include that:

- "The top 1% of wealth-owning households owned 34.6% of all net worth... while the bottom 90% of households in terms of wealth controlled just 27% of all net worth" (Allegretto, 2011, p. 4);
- "400 people have as much wealth as *half* of our population" (Johnson, 2011, para. 33);
- "In 2007, it was reported that the Walton family wealth was as large as the bottom... 30.5 percent of all American families" (Bivens, 2012, para. 4);
- In "the years 2009–2012... the net worth of the top 7% gained 28% while the bottom 93% dropped 4%" (An investment manager's 2014 update, 2013, para. 2);
- "The 400 wealthiest Americans are worth just over $2 trillion, roughly equivalent to the GDP of Russia. That is a gain of $300 billion from a year ago, and more than double a decade ago" (Kroll, 2013, para. 2); and
- "The bottom 90% of workers have seen a decline in their income of 10.7% from 2002 through 2012; meanwhile, the top 1.0% to 0.5% have seen a gain of 11.3%" (An investment manager's 2014 update, 2013, para. 5).

This was not achieved by the powers of moral suasion alone. More importantly, it required significant influence over the policy-making apparatus of the core states of global "capitalism" in monetary, economic, foreign and educational affairs over time. In the United States, this decimation of the manufacturing base is "virtually assured" to lead to a "decline in living standards in the future" (Joel Popkin and Company, 2003, p. 3).

So, ironically, the captains of industry engineer dramatic changes in the American economy to enhance their corporate profits (even when they are often not taxed in America) and then blame these changes on an "uncompetitive" American education system. As Parenti (2001) has noted, when the mouthpieces of the American government and corporations talk "about 'our global leadership,' 'national security,' 'free markets' and 'globalization,' what they mean is 'all power to the transnationals'" (Parenti, 2001, para. 21). Or, as Wallerstein puts it, "the ideological celebration of so-called globalization is in reality the swan song of our historical system" (1998, pp. 32–33).

In considering what the lasting impact of standards-based education has been, we must concede that it has helped to consolidate the corporation at the center of American life and culture, socialized job training costs, and helped big business' mania for quantification colonize much of K–12 education. Its biggest impact, however, may have been in locking America into a role as "the model and gatekeeper" of neoliberal economics (Chomsky, 2001, track one, 1:00).

Neoliberalism is usually characterized as the dismantling of the Keynesian accommodation between big business and big labor that was in effect in the core states of global capitalism since the Great Depression, typically associated with a strong governmental presence in the economy and extensive social welfare policies.

I would argue that, paradoxically, it is precisely because of these developments that the power elite has been able to strengthen their grip on the levers of state power, enhance their ability to socialize costs and privatize benefits, and increase and consolidate their share of global wealth and power. In this sense, this makes a strong nation-state more important than ever to the super class.

Dator has developed a typology of four potential futures: 1) continuation, 2) collapse, 3) disciplined society, and 4) transformational society (2006, para. 8–11). The first one, continuation, is essentially the official ideology espoused by much of the media, government, academia, and other key agenda setters. It posits that society and the economy can, should, and will continue to operate indefinitely into the future just as it has in the past. The collapse scenario says "that continued economic growth is inherently destructive— whether from a social, cultural, environmental, or economic standpoint" and that "collapse today, unlike in the past, may be global instead of simply local" (Dator, 2006, para. 9). The disciplined society sees a type of continuation, albeit one that focuses beyond a "static and passive notion of sustainability" (Dator, 2006, para. 10). Transformational society anticipates technological and/or spiritual breakthroughs, from as yet largely unknown sources, which will significantly alter the condition of society (Dator, 2006, para. 11).

By stressing the importance of the educational system for training "us vocationally for our allotted positions" (Hedges, 2012, para. 16), global economic competitiveness ideology takes Dator's continuation typology as its bedrock assumption: the resource devouring, technologically dependent and highly urbanized global economy can, should and will continue forever.

Unconditional fealty to this position can be seen in two documents at the center of standards-based education efforts. If students "do not graduate from high school ready for college or a career, America will jeopardize the ability of future generations to enjoy a high quality of life" (Engler and Weingarten,

2013, para. 4). "If the United States raised students' math and science skills to globally competitive levels over the next two decades, its GDP would be an additional 36 percent higher 75 years from now" (National Governors Association, Council of Chief State School Officers, and Achieve, Inc., 2008. p. 5).

Such projections are not grounded in empirical reality. They take for granted that an ever-increasing population using an ever-increasing amount of finite natural resources a rapidly degenerating planetary ecosystem can somehow continue indefinitely (Koetke, 2007, p. 94). Barring some miraculous technological breakthrough, this is mathematically impossible—and yet we continue to structure society, our economy, and personal lives as though it were true.

Scientists critical of the continuation concept often draw attention to what they see as the earth's sustainable human carrying capacity. Some think we began "overshooting" when we left the Neolithic age and entered into urban sedentary civilization approximately 5,000–10,000 years ago (Catton, 1982). This long historical process was rapidly accelerated by the industrial revolution and its utilization of hydrocarbon fuels, a use of energy far in excess of that previously available to us by our finite annual solar energy budget.

Other analysts have put forward the concept of "Hubbert's peak" or "peak oil," building on the work of petroleum geologist M. King Hubbert (Deffeyes, 2008). Hubbert predicted that each major oil-production field in the world would eventually reach a point when half of the oil present will have been extracted. This is the "peak" in peak oil. After that, oil will become more expensive to extract until it finally reached requires more energy to extract a barrel of oil from the ground than is present within it, making it unfeasible to continue.

Others have extrapolated from this to note that many other resources so vital to our "modern standard of living" (so often discussed in the rhetoric of global competitiveness ideology and standards-based education). This has led other skeptics to the similar but even more daunting concept of "peak everything" (Heinberg, 2010).

Peak everything is an important part of the collapse literature, a literature that is substantial, growing, and steadily gaining in mainstream intellectual credibility with each passing year. If the ideas it puts forward are even partially correct, then the continuation typology (the absolute, non-negotiable assumption of the global competiveness ideology underpinning standards-based education) is likely to lead to an increasingly traumatic series of interrelated and convulsive environmental, economic, and geopolitical shocks that may gradually bring much of modern industrial civilization as we know it to a grinding halt. Indeed, we are living on "the bubble economy of the earth's rape" (Barry, 2005, para. 22). Yet the vast majority do not seem to notice or care, certainly none among the bloviating punditocracy of the so-called first world.

Books have drawn similar conclusions (Tainter, 1988; Diamond, 2005). Many more recent reports consider collapse from a variety of perspectives. One looks at "the stretching of resources due to the strain placed on the ecological carrying capacity and the economic stratification of society into Elites and Masses (or Commoners)" (Motesharrei, Rivas, and Kalnay, 2014, p. 91). Another set of analysts express concern over the "new operating reality" being created by "global megatrends," including "demographics, rise of the individual, enabling technology, economic interconnectedness, public debt, economic power shift, climate change, resource stress and urbanization," and stresses that these megatrends could confound governments' ability to "deliver on core responsibilities within the current business model" (KPMG international, 2014, pp. 2–3, 52). Still another report states that "in the last generation, the entire human species, along with virtually all other species and indeed the entire planet, has been thrown into a series of crises, which many of which threaten to converge in global catastrophe" (Ahmed, 2010, para. 2). All would be the result of the continuation typology of the future that is implicit within global competitiveness ideology.

The ends of education have been debated for millennia and it does not appear the question will be settled anytime in the near future. Many observers would probably say that this is a good thing. A vibrant debate on such a topic is a crucial part of constantly reimagining what constitutes a good society, a well-lived life, and the proper stewardship of the earth. Answers to these types of questions must be constantly reevaluated as we adapt to the ever-changing conditions of society as well.

In America, the ends of education are often considered in a continuum of ideas established by the *Committee of Ten* and the *Cardinal Principles* reports (National Education Association, 1893; 1918). The Committee of Ten was a group of university presidents and schoolmasters headed by Harvard president Charles Eliot and convened by the National Education Association to make recommendations regarding the nation's primary and secondary school systems (Rothstein, Jacobsen, and Wilder, 2008, p. 19). During this period, immigration, urbanization, and compulsory mass schooling brought many new people into the rapidly expanding American K–12 education system. Combined with the rise of American research universities modeled after the German example, this also started making the articulation of subject matter preparedness between the nascent K–12 system and colleges and universities more important. To address these changes, the Committee of Ten recommended an academically rigorous college prep-type curriculum for all students. For many, this remains a valuable ideal to aspire to. It can be an important means of achieving a holistic education that combines the integrated cultivation of intellect, affect, and moral sensibilities.

Twenty-three years after the Committee of Ten report, the National Education Association released another brief in 1918 that took a more utilitarian and instrumental approach to education. Instead of demanding high academic standards for all, the emphasis shifted to using the schools to teach job skills, "Americanize" new immigrants from southern and eastern Europe, and codify a two-tiered system of elite curriculum for the few and vocational training and general education for the many. At worst, this approach can solidify a system of tracking, sorting, and selecting that reproduces many essential aspects of the pre-existing class structure. Then again, we must also acknowledge that many learners thrive in the more hands-on conditions of project-based education.

Beyond academic preparation and vocational training, there are many more ends of education that should be considered. Rothstein, Jacobsen, and Wilder have done an admirable job of capturing this diversity (2008, p. 43). Their content analysis of leading 20th century education policy documents and contemporary "survey findings and recommendations of policy makers," led them to develop a typology of "eight broad goal areas for public education" in America that enjoy general consensus (Rothstein, Jacobsen, and Wilder, 2008, p. 43). In descending order of importance, these are: basic academic skills, critical thinking, socials skills and work ethic, citizenship, the arts and literature, preparation for skilled work, physical health and emotional health (Rothstein, Jacobsen, and Wilder, 2008, p. 43).

Whatever pedagogy or goal for education one may prefer, it is hard to deny that global competitiveness ideology presupposes wage-based participation in the globalized economy is the main socially legitimated avenue to personal happiness, fulfillment, and development, as the three following quotes from different phases of globalization attest. The first is a quote from the seminal *A Nation at Risk* report at the beginning of modern globalization.

> Knowledge, learning, information, and skilled intelligence are the new raw materials of international commerce and are today spreading throughout the world as

vigorously as miracle drugs, synthetic fertilizers, and blue jeans did earlier. If only to keep and improve on the slim competitive edge we still retain in world markets, we must dedicate ourselves to the reform of our educational system for the benefit of all—old and young alike, affluent and poor, majority and minority. Learning is the indispensable investment required for success in the "information age" we are entering (National Commission on Excellence in Education, 1983, para. 6–7).

The second quote is from *The Jeffersonian Compact*, a joint statement issued by President Bush and the National Governors Association after the Charlottesville Education Summit, with significant input from a sitting president (Bush) and his immediate successor (Clinton), as well as the nations' governors. This was issued in 1989, just as modern globalization was getting underway in earnest.

The President and the nation's Governors agree that a better educated citizenry is the key to the continued growth and prosperity of the United States…As a nation we must have an educated work force, second to none, in order to succeed in an increasingly competitive world economy. Education has always been important, but never this important because the stakes have changed: Our competitors for opportunity are also working to educate their people. As they continue to improve, they make the future a moving target. We believe that the time has come, for the first time in U.S. history, to establish clear, national performance goals, goals that will make us internationally competitive (Bush and the National Governors Association, 1989, para. 2)

The third quote is from the education section of the Obama administration website in its early years.

Our nation's economic competitiveness and the path to the American Dream depend on providing every child with an education that will enable them to succeed in a global economy that is predicated on knowledge and innovation (Obama, 2010, para. 3).

While these quotes come from governmental or quasi-governmental sources, their sentiments can be easily replicated from other sectors. Critics of the model, however, have different ideas.

As Gabbard says, "across its history, compulsory schooling has provided the state with an increasingly vital ritual for enforcing the market as the only permissible pattern of social organization" (2003, p. 61). Lynn's work (2010) on the evolution of American monopoly law under neoliberalism valorizes the "free market," an ideological leitmotif created several decades ago by "a highly sophisticated political movement" designed to rolling back the New Deal and all subsequent social welfare programs that impinged on the bottom line of corporations, enabling "the few, once again, to consolidate power entirely in their own hands" (Lynn, 2010, p. xvi).

How did the "rich and powerful" accomplish this? By conflating the "free market" with a kind of "divinity," to mask the brutal reality of their concrete and empirically discernable actions through what is arguably "the single most brilliant bit of linguistic legerdemain ever perpetuated in our nation," one that transformed "the scrim behind which they disguise their predations into the religion of the American people" (Lynn, 2010, p. 141). This "linguistic legerdemain" reified compulsory mass schooling as "a ritual" that incorporates

> individuals into a market society, providing them with the means for cultivating their use-value in order that they might be able to find their own individual salvation in the market while contributing to the broader salvation that the market bestows upon the society as a whole (Gabbard, 2003, p. 65).

This "ritual" is predicated around credentials and the supposed use-value they certify, a perquisite for salaried employment in the globalized economy (Gabbard, 2003, pp. 65–66). As education gradually transmogrified from a requirement, to an opportunity, to a right (Gabbard, 2003, p. 66), this fostered the creation of a "market-driven conscience" that led people to judge their self-worth based on "the degree to which they meet [the] demands [of the market], abide by its laws, and conform to its norms by their patterns of consumption" (Gabbard, 2003, p. 67). This conception of the ends of education teaches that "the most essential lessons for learning to 'thrive' within a market society is to eschew the search for meaning" (Gabbard, 2003, p. 73). Extrinsically motivated attainment of credentials provided by education is the primary means of advancement within the globalized economy.

Critical pedagogists note that 30 years of neoliberal education policy "have ensured that students who are marginalized by race and class attend dropout factories, while their affluent counterparts attend schools that prepare them for power in the business and social world" (Carr and Porfilio, 2011, p. xxxv). Dropout factories or school-to-prison pipelines, this is in spite of the fact that many civil right groups and educational liberals have actively campaigned for, been influential in supporting, and framed standards-based education in terms of revising long-standing equity arguments, especially by use of data-driven solutions to help close the achievement gap between high- and low-achieving students. Some scholars have labeled critical pedagogists as "authoritarians...seeking to foist their beliefs on the children of others" (Maranto and McShane, 2012, p. 119–120), while purporting to offer up their own analyses as neutral, data-driven and free of "faith-based social science" (Maranto and McShane, 2012, p. 4).

One of education's primary functions to imagine, design, and create the future world we want to live in. How could this not involve "value judgments" or feelings of moral urgency? In an academic and scientific world that regards positivism and the correspondence theory of the truth with skepticism and acknowledges quantum physics as a given, why are we in the human sciences still so wedded to such concepts as "empiricism," "materialism," and "objectivity" as though they were entirely without any ambiguity whatsoever? As though any departure from them is to be regarded as heresy? After a century of assaults on these concepts, it seems hard to believe and yet there it is and there it remains.

If truth is not something we "find" but something we "make," the more we reveal our biases in its making, the closer we approach "truth." This reminder is all the more vital as America faces the onslaught of Common Core, where "truth" on a huge number of incredibly vital issues is poised to become ossified and highly centralized, in a way that it hasn't been in the 400-year-old tradition of local control over education in America.

In the colonial era, "America" was largely composed of white European Protestants doing their best to wrest a continent from its original inhabitants. Now that America has become far more racially heterogeneous, now that America has seen the equity regimes of the Great Society and the New Deal rolled back to a post-industrial version of the Robber Baron era (with the income and asset disparities to match), now that transnational global kleptocracy has assumed control of education, electoral politics, and the media—which is to say, every center for the manufacture of consent, consciousness and "voluntary servitude" of the masses—it is all the more important than ever to demand, sustain, and celebrate diversity in pedagogical aims (de la Boetie, 1942). Especially those that inspire curiosity, empathy, and moral courage. This is not an "ideal," a "goal," an "objective," or a "utopian hope." It is a demand made of those who would be leaders.

> Leadership has got to have [responsibility] above all. They've got to have vision. They've got to have compassion for the future. They've got to make that decision for seven generations. That's not just a casual term. That's a real instruction for survival (Indigenous Native American Prophecy, 2:40).

CONCLUSION

In the "texts illustrating the complexity, quality, and range of student reading" for grades 6–12 in Common Core, *Politics and the English Language* by George Orwell (1946) is listed as an appropriate text for 11th graders. This essay asks the rhetorical question that

> since you don't know what Fascism is, how can you struggle against Fascism? One need not swallow such absurdities as this, but one ought to recognize that the present political chaos is connected with the decay of language, and that one can probably bring about some improvement by starting at the verbal end (Orwell, 1946, para. 13).

True education (as distinct from compulsory mass schooling) might create curious, powerful thinkers in self-possession of their own minds. Those minds would be able to understand Mussolini's definition of fascism: "the merger of state and corporate power" (cited in Mills, 2004, para. 1).

As Nietzsche has written:

> our own existence now must encourage us most strongly to live according to our own laws and standards: it is an inexplicable fact that we live precisely today, and had an infinite time to develop—nevertheless, we possess only a short-lived today to show why and to what end we evolved. We have only ourselves to answer for our existence; consequently we want to be the real helmsman of this existence and not permit our existence to be a thoughtless accident (Nietzsche, 1876, para. 3).

When standards were still largely under the purview of the states, they were typically imbued with narrow, utilitarian, and instrumental notions of the knowledge, skills, and dispositions required of each student in each subject in each grade. These notions were so narrow that the self-possessed and self-actualized person sketched in the Nietzsche quote above (and also often found in anarchist educational theory and practice) had little room to develop and come to fruition. Now that standards are quasi-national under Common Core, these notions are even more narrow.

During the state regime, there were typically content standards (what a student should know) and performance standards (what constituted adequate mastery of what should be known). There were also opportunity-to-learn standards, which were basically about ensuring adequate funding. Today the Common Core standards seem to be neither about content nor performance but rather about process. Instead of knowledge, skills, and dispositions required of each student in each subject in each grade, the Common Core standards themselves are largely about skills alone (although "Common Core-aligned" curriculum and assessments are certainly about content). Dismembered from content, these "skills" float alone at a very high level of abstraction.

Some traditional images of the educated person give wide latitude for self-creation and self-possession according to Nietzsche's conception of one's own "laws and standards." These have gone largely "absent without leave" in government educational policy. Among the many images of the educated person in the western world is that a well-rounded liberal arts education. This might be difficult to achieve by means of standards-based education as currently envisioned.

If it could be allowed to develop, then perhaps the educational system might help cultivate people ready, willing, and able to use autonomous critical rationality, creativity, and empathetic spiritual intuition. This might also help enable us to see through the manifold hypocrisies and deleterious conventions of modern society, to create a just and sane social world, and take seriously our sacred roles as custodians of posterity and our one and only spaceship.

Instead, in the corporation, we have let an immortal psychopath structure almost every significant aspect of economic, political, and cultural life on the planet. This characterization is not meant as hyperbole in any way but rather as an attempt at a clinical diagnosis right out of the DSM IV, via Bakan's outstanding book *The Corporation* (2004) and, especially, the documentary of the same name (Achbar and Abbott, 2003). The DSM IV lists these symptoms for a diagnosis of psychopathology.

> 1) Callous unconcern for the feelings of others. 2) Incapacity to maintain enduring relationships. 3) Reckless disregard for the safety of others. 4) Deceitfulness; repeated lying and conning others for profit. 5) Incapacity to experience guilt. 6) Failure to conform to social norms with respect to lawful behaviors (cited in Achbar and Abbott, 2003).

This describes the "immortal person" of the corporation very accurately. We are receptive to this assault because the profound emptiness of mainstream secular, scientific, and materialist conceptions of the universe have enabled the extraordinary psychological sophistication of consumerist ontologies to define us and our desires, infantilizing us in the process.

The "enduring contradiction" of liberal democracy is between its "theoretical universalism" and "historical viciousness" (Singh, 2006, p. 81), a viciousness predicated on the ongoing use of the state's alleged "monopoly on legitimate violence" (Weber, 1958, pp. 77–128) against the working and middle classes at home and broad swathes of humanity abroad, particularly in the global south. Technology, according to Max Frisch in his 1957 novel *Homo Faber*, "is the knack of arranging the world so that we need not experience it" (p. 178). What we have never experienced, we are unlikely to love. What we do not love, we are unlikely to defend.

This trend has been a long time coming. As many commentators have noted, the word "civilization" comes from the root Latin word "civitas," city or town. As participants in civilization, inhabiting socio-economic roles that rely on incredibly minute subdivisions of labor, few of us comprehend what we are doing to the planet in the normal course of our everyday lives. Unable to see beyond the social system to the natural system that makes the social system possible, we have brought our species and the planet to a moment of grave crisis.

Ironically, the most vaunted ideals of western civilization may in fact be the very lies that keep us in chains. As the aphorism commonly attributed to Goethe goes: "none are more hopelessly enslaved than those who falsely believe they are free." Yet the dialectic of the enlightenment contains the cure as well as the disease. We can only hope this former impulse will succeed. As Jefferson puts it

> I know no safe depository of the ultimate powers of the society but the people themselves; and if we think them not enlightened enough to exercise their control with a wholesome discretion, the remedy is not to take it from them, but to inform their discretion by education (1820, para. 1).

This was the goal set for us by the Enlightenment. Some interpretations of globalization promise us the hope of moving beyond the realm of necessity into the realm of freedom, with the ability to choose meaningful goals based on autonomous rationality, informed leisure, and notions of the perfectibility of "man" and "society." Yet what goals do we typically pursue in practice after we have achieved or been given a modicum of affluence? All too often, we pursue those goals that satisfy our most primordial urges, often carefully triggered by an omnipresent, finely-tuned, and scientifically-honed marketing establishment developed over the last century, now available to the highest bidders in business, government, and the military.

Instead of using "man's emergence from his self-imposed immaturity," we wallow in our "inability to use understanding without guidance from another" (Kant, 1784, para. 1–2). This immaturity is self-imposed when it lies not in a lack of understanding, but in a lack of resolve to use it. "Sapere Aude! [dare to know] Have the courage to use your own understanding!—that is the motto of enlightenment" (Kant, 1784, para. 1–2).

Certainly, the Enlightenment was not perfect and oceans of ink have been spilt criticizing, for example, the instrumental rationality that was such an important part of it. Nevertheless, the notion of enlightened self-interest is certainly one aspect of the era that remains valuable today. It also accords with the notion of wise human stewardship and co-participation with the earth so often found among the world's indigenous peoples. As, for example, in the tradition of thinking and acting for the good of seven generations ahead, as some native American traditions would have it. This is an appropriately humble sense of place for human beings in the broader scheme of things, and a practical means of survival as well.

Education must be a part of our means of survival. It will not be, however, as long as we continue to allow our mainstream educational establishment world-wide to be predominately led by the ideological driver of global competitiveness ideology and the empirical drivers of the Fortune Global 500 corporations instead of by the interests of the people and the planet.

To regain our natural propensity to love, be creative, use tools and symbols, and live in harmonious connection with the earth will require a major shift in character and a widespread healing of perception. As Edward Dowling has said, "the two greatest obstacles to democracy in the United States are, first the widespread delusion among the poor that we have it, and second, the chronic terror among the rich, lest we get it" (cited in Pilger, 2008, para. 1).

Until that cherished delusion is shattered, the people, like little children idolizing their infallible parents, will continue to live in ignorance: an ignorance that is arguably willful. They will ignore the fact that their leaders lie, murder, steal, harass, beat, imprison, and monitor in their name on a truly epic scale while cynically manipulating religious, political and commercial symbols in an attempt to sell them a bill of goods in the service of a select group of commercial dynasties, their lackeys and trans-national corporations. This is especially true of an even more select group who comprise the "deep state," those who sit at the intersection of politics, law, high finance, big oil, intelligence, diplomacy, paramilitary operations, narco-trafficking, organized crime, the media, religion, and the police state. This is a nexus where state power is used when it can be, but none of whose actors are subject or beholden to the nation-state at all.

Ultimately, this transition away from willful ignorance towards sanity may prove too difficult for many people to endure. Nevertheless, it must be attempted, not merely for its potential social and environmental utility, but because those given the unique ability to see and do what must be done have to respect the responsibility entrusted to their care, especially in this dark hour.

In addition to the policy entrepreneurs mentioned above, there have been several business leaders whose sustained and ongoing participation in standards-based education has been crucial to its success. Among the many candidates for the most influential business leaders in the realm of standards-based education was Edward Rust (Chairman and CEO of State Farm Insurance). On March 30, 2013 Rust issued a letter entitled *Want to Save the American Dream? Start Here*. In it, he wrote that "education has always been—and can still be—the key to fulfilling the American Dream" (Rust, 2013 para. 10). Some did not agree. "In the next decade, something must give. Either America must accept that the American Dream of widespread economic mobility is dead, or new policies must emerge that will begin to restore broadly shared prosperity" (Sommeiller and Rice, 2014, p. 18).

Standards-based education and Common Core, in stultifying our minds towards a narrowly prescribed vision in accord with governmental and corporate interests, not "our own laws and standards," makes our existence "a thoughtless accident" with no nobler purpose than getting a job on the treadmill to death in futile pursuit of the American dream. But, as comedian and social commentator George Carlin (2005) said: "the owners of this country know the truth. It's called the American dream, because you have to be asleep to believe it."

REFERENCES

A Goals 2000 time line. (1998, January 21). *Education Week*. Retrieved from http://www.edweek.org/ew/articles/1998/01/21/19goals1.h17.html?r=817581612

About Us. (2010). New York: The Conference Board. Retrieved from http://www.conference-board.org/about/index.cfm?id=1980

Achbar, M., & Abbott, J. [Directors]. (2004). *The corporation*. [Digital videodisc]. Vancouver: Big Picture Media Corporation.

Achieve, Inc., (2005, January 25). *Bill Gates to join nation's governors, education and business leaders*. Retrieved from http://www.achieve.org/bill-gates-join-nations-governors-education-and-business-leaders. Washington, DC: Author.

Achieve, Inc. (2006). *How does Hawaii high school assessment measure up? A comparison of the 2005 grade 10 Hawaii State Assessment in Reading and Mathematics with high school graduation exams from other states*. Washington, DC: Author. (ERIC Document Reproduction Service No. ED499895).

Achieve, Inc. (2007). *Closing the expectations gap 2007, An annual 50-state progress report on the alignment of high school policies with the demands of college and work*. Washington, DC: Author. Retrieved from http://www.achieve.org/files/50-state-07-Final.pdf

ACT. (2011). *Affirming the goal, Is college and career readiness an internationally competitive standard?* Iowa City, IA: Author. Retrieved from http://www.act.org/research/policymakers/pdf/AffirmingtheGoal.pdf

Ahmed, N. M. (2010, September 20). The end of the world as we know it? The rise of the post-carbon era. *Ceasefire*. Retrieved from http://ceasefiremagazine.co.uk/the-end-of-the-world-as-we-know-it-the-rise-of-the-post-carbon-era/

Albert Shanker Institute. (2011, Spring). A call for common content. *American Educator*. Washington, DC: Author.

Albrecht, J. E. (1984, June). A nation at risk: Another view. *Phi Delta Kappan*, 65(10), 684–685.

Alexander, L. (1986). Time for results: An overview. *Phi Delta Kappan*, 68(3), 202–204.

Allegretto, S. A. (2011, March 23). *The state of working America's wealth, 2011, Through volatility and turmoil, the gap widens*. Washington, DC: Economic Policy Institute.

Allen, J. (2014). What is the blob? Washington, DC: The Center for Education Reform. Retrieved from http://www.edreform.com/2012/09/what-it-is/

Allen, J., & McLaughlin, M. (1990). *A businessman's guide to the education reform debate*. Washington, DC: Heritage Foundation.

Altman, A. (2014, April 10). Common Core sparks parent revolt. *Time*. Retrieved from http://time.com/57166/common-core-sparks-parent-revolt/

Alvarado, A. (1998). Professional development is the job. *American Educator*, 22(4), 18–23.

American Federation of Teachers. (1996). *Making standards matter, 1996: An annual fifty-state report on efforts to raise academic standards*. Washington, DC: Author. (ERIC Document Reproduction Service No. ED410660).

American Federation of Teachers. (1997). *Making Standards Matter, 1997: An annual fifty-state report on efforts to raise academic standards*. Washington, DC: Author. (ERIC Document Reproduction Service No. ED410661).

American Federation of Teachers. (1998). *Making standards matter 1998: An annual fifty-state report on efforts to raise academic standards*. Washington, DC: Author. (ERIC Document Reproduction Service No. ED429979).

American Federation of Teachers. (1999). *Making standards matter 1999: An update on state activity, Educational issues policy brief number 11*. Washington, DC: Author. (ERIC Document Reproduction Service No. ED436607).

American Federation of Teachers. (2001). *Developing a standards-based system in Hawaii*. Washington, DC: Author. Retrieved from http://www.aft.org/pubs-reports/downloads/teachers/msm2001.pdf

American Federation of Teachers. (2006). *American Federation of Teachers report: Hawaii's lack of documentation puts alignment of content standards and tests in doubt*. Washington, DC: Author. Retrieved from http://www.aft.org/presscenter/releases/2006/smarttesting/Hawaii.pdf

Anderson, J. (1972a, September 28). Powell's lessons to business aired. *Washington Post*, p. C27.

Anderson, J. (1972b, September 29). FBI missed blueprint by Powell. *Washington Post*, p. C27.

Anderson, R., & Saxon, D. (1983). *America's competitive challenge, The need for a national response, A report to the President of the United States from the Business-Higher Education Forum*. Washington, DC: Business-Higher Education Forum.

An investment manager's 2014 update on the top 1% (December 2013). *Who rules America?* Retrieved from http://www2.ucsc.edu/whorulesamerica/power/investment_manager_2014.html

Ansary, T. (2007, May). Education at risk: Fallout from a flawed report. *Edutopia.* Retrieved from http://www.edutopia.org/landmark-education-report-nation-risk

Apple, M. (2006). *Educating the "right" way, Markets, standards, God, and inequality.* New York: Routledge.

Archer, J., & Walsh, M. (1996, April 3). Summit garners mixed reviews from pundits, practitioners. *Education Week.* Retrieved from http://web.ebscohost.com.eres.library.Mānoa.Hawaii.edu/ehost/detail?vid=4&hid=107&sid=8fee3418-a928-46ba-a0a5-2ecd0f2e4068%40sessionmgr104&bdata=JnNpdGU9ZWhvc3QtbGl2ZQ%3d%3d#db=aph&AN=9604162915

Arnesen, E. (Ed.). (2007). *Encyclopedia of U.S. labor and working-class history, Volume 1.* Boca Raton, FL: CRC Press.

Aronowitz, S., & Giroux, H. A. (1993). *Education: Still under siege,* (2nd ed.). Westport, CN: Bergin & Garvey.

ASCD. (2010, March 5). *ASCD works with CCSSO and NGA on Common Core State Standards Initiative* [Press Release]. Alexandria, VA: Author.

ASCD. (2012). *Fulfilling the promise of the Common Core State Standards: Moving from adoption to implementation to sustainability.* Alexandria, VA: Author.

Ashwell, A., & Caropreso, F. (Eds.). (1989). *Business leadership: The third wave of education reform.* New York: The Conference Board.

Associated Press. (2010, January 9). States change policies with eye to winning federal grants. *Education Week.* Retrieved from http://www.edweek.org/ew/articles/2010/01/06/16states-2.h29.html

As the school-reform debate heats up, Where's business? (2001, April 29). *Business Week.* Retrieved from http://www.businessweek.com/stories/2001-04-29/as-the-school-reform-debate-heats-up-wheres-business

Atwater, D. M. et al. (1991). *Building local labor market dynamics into workforce 2000: Research report 53.* Washington, DC: Office of the Chief of Naval Operations.

Bacevich, A. (2010). *Washington Rules, America's path to permanent war.* New York: Henry Holt and Company.

Bakan, J. (2004). *The corporation.* New York: Metropolitan Books.

Baker, A. (2014, February 16). Common Core curriculum now has critics on the left. *New York Times.* Retrieved from http://www.nytimes.com/2014/02/17/nyregion/new-york-early-champion-of-common-core-standards-joins-critics.html?src=un&feedurl=http%3A%2F%2Fjson8.nytimes.com%2Fpages%2Fnyregion%2Findex.jsonp

Baker, P. (2007, November 5). An unlikely partnership left behind. *Washington Post.* Retrieved from http://www.washingtonpost.com/wp-dyn/content/article/2007/11/04/AR2007110401450_pf.html

Bamford, J. (2009). *The shadow factory: The NSA from 9/11 to the eavesdropping on America*. New York: Anchor.

Barnhardt, K. A. (2000). Crisis. In D. A. Gabbard (Ed.), *Knowledge and power in the global economy, Politics and the rhetoric of school reform* (pp. 17–24). Mahwah, NJ: Lawrence Erlbaum Associates, Publishers.

Barrett, C., & Rust, E. (2008, July 31). This recess is really from accountability. *Wall Street Journal*. Retrieved from http://online.wsj.com/news/articles/SB121746669458299283

Barry, G. (2005, April 11). The earth is dying: world ruination is at hand. Retrieved from http://omega.twoday.net/stories/623237/.

Barth, P. (2003, Winter). A common core curriculum for the new century. *Thinking K-16*, (7)1, 3–25.

Barton, P. (1990). *From school to work, Policy information report*. Princeton, NJ: Educational Testing Service.

Beck, G. (2014). *Conform: Exposing the truth about Common Core and public education*. New York: Threshold Editions.

Bell, T. H. (1993, April). One decade after "A Nation at Risk." *Phi Delta Kappan*, (74)8, 592–597.

Bennett, W. (1994). *De-valuing of America: The fight for our culture and our children*. New York: Simon & Schuster.

Berenbeim, B. R. (1991). *Corporate support of national education goals, report no. 978*. New York: The Conference Board.

Berlak, H. (1995). Culture, imperialism, and goals 2000. In R. L. Miller (Ed.), *Educational freedom in a democratic society, A critique of national standards, goals and curriculum* (pp. 132–153). Brandon, VT: Holistic Education Press.

Berliner, D. C., & Biddle, B. J. (1996). *The manufactured crisis: Myths, fraud, and the attack on America's public schools*. New York: Basic Books.

Berman, P. (1983). *Improving student performance in California: Analysis of first year's education legislation*. Berkeley: California Business Roundtable.

Berman, P. (1988a). *Restructuring California education: A design for public education in the twenty-first century*. Berkeley: California Business Roundtable.

Berman, P. (1988b). *The Hawaii plan: Educational excellence for the pacific era. Recommendations to the Hawaii Business Roundtable*. Honolulu: Hawaii Business Roundtable.

Berman, P., & Clugston, R. (1988). A tale of two states: The business community and educational reform in California and Minnesota. In M. Levine & R. Trachtman (Eds.), *American business and public schools: Case studies of corporate involvement in public education* (pp. 121–149). New York: Teachers College Press.

Berry, S. (2014, January 15). Panelist defends Common Core. *Breitbart*. Retrieved from http://www.breitbart.com/Big-Government/2014/02/03/Center-For-American-Progress-Panelist-On-Common-Core-The-Children-Belong-To-All-Of-Us

Berry, S. (2014, March 20). Invited media only at Tennessee Common Core even event featuring Jeb Bush and Sen. Lamar Alexander. *Breitbart*. Retrieved from http://www.breitbart.com/Big-Government/2014/03/19/Invited-Media-Only-At-Tennessee-Common-Core-Event-Featuring-Jeb-Bush-and-Sen-Lamar-Alexander

Bidwell, A. (2013, December 31). Common Core, college cost and quality among education issues to watch in 2014. *U.S. News & World Report.* Retrieved from http://www.usnews.com/news/articles/2013/12/31/common-core-college-cost-and-quality-among-education-issues-to-watch-in-2014

Bidwell, A. (2014a, January 31). More states seek to repeal Common Core. *U.S. News & World Report.* Retrieved from http://www.usnews.com/news/articles/2014/01/31/more-states-seek-to-repeal-common-core

Bidwell, A. (2014b, February 13). Critics say growth in Common Core delay hurts students, teachers. *U.S. News & World Report.* Retrieved from http://www.usnews.com/news/special-reports/a-guide-to-common-core/articles/2014/02/13/critics-say-growth-in-common-core-delays-hurts-students-teachers

Bidwell, A. (2014, February 20). Wisconsin schools chief begs public to stop anti-Common Core vote. *U.S. News & World Report.* Retrieved from http://www.usnews.com/news/articles/2014/02/20/wisconsin-schools-chief-begs-public-to-stop-anti-common-core-vote

Bivens, J. (2012, July 17). Inequality, exhibit A: Walmart and the wealth of American families. *Working Economics, Economic Policy Institute blog.* Retrieved from http://www.epi.org/blog/inequality-exhibit-wal-mart-wealth-american/

Blair, J. (2002, November 6). Union' positions unheeded on ESEA. *Education Week.* Retrieved from http://www.edweek.org/ew/articles/2002/11/06/10esea.h22.html

Blum, W. (2008). *Killing hope: U. S. Military and C.I.A. interventions since world war II.* Monroe, ME: Common Courage Press.

Bork, R. (1978). *The antitrust paradox.* New York: Basic Books.

Borman, K., Castanell, L., & Gallagher. (1994). Business involvement in school reform: The rise of the Business Roundtable. In C. Marshall (Ed.), *The new politics of race and gender: The 1992 yearbook of the Politics of Education Association* (pp. 69–84). Washington, DC: Falmer.

Bouie, J. (2014, April 22). Conservative tribalism. Mass transit. Common Core. Light bulbs. *Slate.* Conservatives hate these things for no better reason than that liberals like them. Retrieved from http://www.slate.com/articles/news_and_politics/politics/2014/04/conservative_tribalism_conservatives_hate_anything_barack_obama_and_liberals.single.html

Bowman, S. R. (1996). *The modern corporation and American political thought, law, power, and ideology.* University Park, PA: Penn State Press.

Bracey, G. (2000). The 10th Bracey report on the condition of public education. *Phi Delta Kappan,* (82)2, 133–144.

Bracey, G. (2004). *Setting the record straight: Responses to misconceptions about public education in the U.S.,* 2nd ed. Portsmouth, NH: Heinemann.

Bracey, G. (2007a, December 3). Righting wrongs. *The Huffington Post.* Retrieved from http://www.huffintonpost.com/gerald-bracey/righting-wrongs_b_75189.html

Bracey, G. (2007b, December 6). Diane does Rush. *The Huffington Post.* Retrieved from http://www.huffintonpost.com/gerald-bracey/diane-does-rush_b_75696.html

Brock, D. (2004). *The Republican noise machine, Right-wing media and how it corrupts democracy.* New York: Crown Publishers.

Brookings Institution. (2011). *Distributed presses, The Century Foundation, (formerly the Twentieth Century Fund)*. Retrieved from http://www.brookings.edu/press/DistributedPress.aspx

Brooks, D. (2014, April 17). When the circus descends. *New York Times*. Retrieved from http://www.nytimes.com/2014/04/18/opinion/brooks-when-the-circus-descends.html?_r=0

Brown, B. (2009a). *Standards-based education reform in the United States since A Nation at Risk*. Honolulu, HI: Curriculum Research and Development Group. Retrieved from http://www.hawaii.edu/hepc/pdf/Reports/FINAL-History_of_Standards-Based_Education_Reform.pdf

Brown, B. (2009b). *A policy history of standards-based education reform in Hawaii*. Honolulu, HI: Curriculum Research and Development Group. Retrieved from http://www.hawaii.edu/hepc/pdf/Reports/FINAL-History_of_Standards-Based_Education_in_Hawaii.pdf.

Bryant, J. (2014, April 24). It's not just wing-nuts! Slate gets liberal opposition to the Common Core, all wrong, Slate oversimplifies Common Core debate as Obama vs. the Tea Party, and misses serious, sophisticated left critique. *Salon*. Retrieved from http://www.salon.com/2014/04/24/its_not_just_wing_nuts_slate_gets_liberal_opposition_to_the_common_core_all_wrong/

Brzezinski, Z. (2007). *Second chance: Three presidents and the crisis of American superpower*. New York: Basic Books.

Bush, G. H. W. (1990). *State of the Union address*. Retrieved from http://www.presidency.ucsb.edu/ws/index.php?pid=18095

Bush, G. H. W. (1991, June 3). *Remarks to the National Education Goals Panel*. Retrieved from http://bulk.resource.org/gpo.gov/papers/1991/1991_vol1_599.pdf

Bush, G. H. W., & the National Governors Association. (1989, October 1). Ideas & trends: 'A Jeffersonian compact'; The statement by the President and Governors. *New York Times*. Retrieved from http://www.nytimes.com/1989/10/01/weekinreview/ideas-trends-a-jeffersonian-compact-the-statement-by-the-president-and-governors.html?scp=1&sq=a%20jeffersonian%20compact%20October%201,%201989&st=cse&pagewanted=all

Bush, M. (2010, June). *State notes, Attendance, Compulsory school age requirements*. Washington, DC: Education Commission of the States. Retrieved from http://www.ncsl.org/documents/educ/ECSCompulsoryAge.pdf

Business Coalition for Student Achievement. (2007, September 11). *BCSA statement on reauthorization of the Elementary and Secondary Education Act of 1965*. Washington, DC: Business Roundtable. Retrieved from http://businessroundtable.org/media/news-releases/bcsa-statement-on-reauthorization-of-the-elementary-and-secondary-education

Business Roundtable. (1988). *The role of business in education reform: Blueprint for action. Report of the Business Roundtable Ad Hoc Committee on Education*. Washington, DC: Author. (Eric Document Reproduction Service No. ED302602).

Business Roundtable. (1989a). *Essential components of a successful education system: The Business Roundtable education public policy agenda*. Washington, DC: Author.

Business Roundtable. (1989b). *Business means business about education. A synopsis of the Business Roundtable companies' education partnerships*. Washington, DC: Author. (Eric Document Reproduction Service No. ED310180).

Business Roundtable. (1992a). *Essential components of a successful education system: Putting policy into practice.* Washington, DC: Author.

Business Roundtable. (1992b). *Agents of change.* Washington, DC: Author.

Business Roundtable. (1993). *Workforce training and development for economic competitiveness.* Washington, DC: Author.

Business Roundtable. (1995). *Continuing the commitment: Essential components of a successful education system.* Washington, DC: Author.

Business Roundtable. (1996). *A business leader's guide to setting academic standards.* Washington, DC: Author.

Business Roundtable. (1998). *Building support for tests that count: A business leader's guide.* Washington, DC: Author.

Business Roundtable. (1999). *Transforming educational policy: Assessing ten years of progress in the states.* Washington, DC: Author.

Business Roundtable. (2000a). *What parents, teachers, and students think about standards, tests, and accountability…And more.* Washington, DC: Author.

Business Roundtable. (2000b). *On the same page: Building local support for higher standards and local schools.* Washington, DC: Author.

Business Roundtable. (2000c). *Essential components of a successful education system.* Washington, DC: Author.

Business Roundtable. (2001). *Assessing and addressing the "testing backlash": Practical advice and current public opinion research for business coalitions and standards advocates.* Washington, DC: Author.

Business Roundtable. (2001, March 20). *Business Roundtable brings employers to Capitol Hill to make the case for education reform* [Press Release]. Retrieved from http:www.web.archive.org/web/20011225092617/http://www.brtable.org/press.cfm/518

Callahan, D. (1999, February 28). *$1 billion for ideas: Conservative think tanks in the 1990s.* National Committee for Responsive Philanthropy. Retrieved from http://www.commonwealinstitute.org/archive/1-billion-for-ideas-conservative-think-tanks-in-the-1990s

Campbell, J. (2014, February 11). *Regents approve Common Core changes.* Retrieved from http://www.wgrz.com/story/news/education/2014/02/11/regents-approve-common-core-changes/5398673/

Campbell, J. B. (1983). *The role of the business community in improving the American education system.* Washington, DC: United States Chamber of Commerce.

Carlin, G. (2005). The American dream, an excerpt from life is worth losing [Online Video]. Retrieved from http://www.youtube.com/watch?v=acLW1vFO-2Q

Carnegie Forum on Education and the Economy. (1986). *A nation prepared: Teachers for the 21st century.* Washington, DC: Author.

Carnegie Foundation for the Advancement of Teaching. (1988). *The condition of teaching: A state analysis.* Princeton, NJ: Author.

Carnevale, A. P., Strohl, J., & Melton, M. (2011, May 24). *What's it worth? The economic value of college majors.* Washington, DC: Georgetown University Center on Education and the Workforce. Retrieved from cew.georgetown.edu/whatsitworth

Carr, P. R., & Porfilio, B. J. (2011). Introduction: Audaciously espousing hope within a torrent of hegemonic neoliberalism: The Obama educational agenda and the potential for change. In P. R. Carr & B. J. Porfilio (Ed.), *The phenomenon of Obama and the agenda for education: Can hope audaciously trump neoliberalism?* Charlotte, NC: Information Age Publishing, Inc.

Carter, J. (1978, January 19). *State of the union address.* Retrieved from http://www.usa-presidents.info/union/carter-1.html

Catton, Jr., W. R. (1982). *Overshoot: The ecological basis of revolutionary change.* Champaign, IL: University of Illinois Press.

Cavanagh, S. (2004, May 19). Bush takes on critics of No Child Left Behind. *Education Week.*

CBS News New York. (2014, March 27). *Some NYC, L.I. parents say their kids are opting out of Common Core tests.* New York: Author. Retrieved from http://newyork.cbslocal.com/2014/03/27/some-nyc-parents-say-their-kids-are-opting-out-of-common-core-tests/

Chambers, W. (1952). *Witness.* New York: Random House.

Cheney, L. (1994, October 20). The end of history. *Wall Street Journal,* p. A22.

Chira, S. (1992, January 29). Prominent educators oppose national tests. *New York Times.* Retrieved from http://www.nytimes.com/1992/01/29/education/prominent-educators-oppose-national-tests.html

Chomsky, N. [Writer, Performer]. (2001). *Prospects for democracy.* [compact disc]. Oakland, CA: AK Press.

Chubb, J. (2008). *Learning from No Child Left Behind.* Palo Alto, CA: Stanford University/Hoover Institution Press.

Clinton, W. J. (1993, April 21). *Message to the Congress transmitting the "Goals 2000: Educate America Act."* Retrieved from http://www.presidency.ucsb.edu/ws/index.php?pid=46465

Clinton, W. J. (1994). *State of the Union address.* Retrieved from http://www.presidency.ucsb.edu/ws/index.php?pid=50409

Clotfeller C., & Ladd, H. (1996). Recognizing and rewarding success in public schools. In H. Ladd (Ed.), *Holding schools accountable: Performance-based reform in education* (pp. 23–64). Washington, DC: Brookings Institution.

Coleman, J. S. (1966). *Equality of educational opportunity.* Washington, DC: United States Department of Health, Education, and Welfare.

College Board. (1983). *Academic preparation for college: What students need to know and be able to do.* New York: College Entrance Examination Board.

College Board. (2014). *Our leadership, David Coleman, president and chief executive officer.* New York: Author. Retrieved from https://www.collegeboard.org/about/leadership

Committee for Economic Development, Research and Policy Committee. (1985). *Investing in our children: Business and the public schools.* New York: Author.

Common Core State Standards Initiative. (2014a). *Development process, See the timeline, April 2009.* Washington, DC: Author. Retrieved from http://www.corestandards.org/about-the-standards/development-process/

Common Core State Standards Initiative. (2014b). *Public license.* Washington, DC: Author. Retrieved from http://www.corestandards.org/public-license/

Common Core State Standards Initiative. (2014c). *Standards Setting Criteria*. Washington, DC: Author.

Conference Board. (1989). *Business leadership: The third wave*. New York: Author.

Council of Chief State School Officers. (2014a). *Corporate partners*. Washington, DC: Author. Retrieved from http://www.ccsso.org/Who_We_Are/Business_and_Industry_Partnerships/Corporate_Partners.html

Council of Chief State School Officers. (2014). *Leadership team, CCSSO executive director Chris Minnich*. Washington, DC: Author. Retrieved from http://www.ccsso.org/Who_We_Are/Leadership_Team.html

Cremin, L. A. (1990). *Popular education and its discontents*. New York: Harper & Row.

Cuban, L. (2004). *The blackboard and the bottom line: Why schools can't be businesses*. Cambridge, MA: Harvard University Press.

Darling-Hammond, L. (1997). *The right to learn: A blueprint for school reform*. New York: Jossey-Bass.

Darling-Hammond, L. (2010, June 14). Restoring our schools. *The Nation*, pp. 14–20. Retrieved from http://www.thenation.com/article/restoring-our-schools

Darling-Hammond, L., & Falk, B. (1997a). Supporting teaching and learning for all students, Policies for authentic assessment systems. In A. L. Goodwin (Ed.), *Assessment for equity and inclusion* (pp. 51–76). London: Routledge.

Darling-Hammond, L., & Falk, B. (1997b). Using standards and assessments to support student learning. *Phi Delta Kappan, 79*(3), 190–199.

Dator, J. (2006, April-June). Campus futures. *Planning for Higher Education, (34)*3, 45–48. Retrieved from http://www.futures.Hawaii.edu/CampusFutures.htm

DeBray-Pelot, E. (2007). Dismantling educations "iron triangle," Institutional relationships in the formation of federal education policy between 1998 and 2001. In C. F. Kaestle and A. E. Lodewick (Eds.), *To educate a nation, Federal and national strategies of school reform*. Lawrence: University of Kansas.

Deffeyes, K. S. (2008). *Hubbert's peak: The impending world oil shortage*. Princeton: Princeton University Press.

de la Boetie, E. (1942). *Discourse on voluntary servitude*. New York: Columbia University Press. Retrieved from http://www.constitution.org/la_boetie/serv_vol.htm

Democracy Now. (2014, May 13). *"Collect it all": Glenn Greenwald on NSA bugging tech hardware, economic espionage & spying on U.N*. [Online video]. Retrieved from http://www.democracynow.org/2014/5/13/collect_it_all_glenn_greenwald_on

DeParle, J. (2005, May 29). Goals reached, donor on right closes up shop. *New York Times*. Retrieved from http://query.nytimes.com/gst/fullpage.html?res=9901EEDD1E39F93AA15756C0A9639C8B63&sec=&spon=&scp=22&sq=&pagewanted=print

Dertouzos, M. (Ed.). (1990). *Made in America: Regaining the productivity edge*. New York: HarperCollins.

deRugy, V. (2011, June 24). The facts about American prisons, Separating economic myths from economic truths. *Reason*. Retrieved from http://reason.com/archives/2011/06/24/the-facts-about-americas-priso

Dewey, J. (1966). *Democracy and education*. New York: Free Press.

Diamond, J. M. *Collapse: How societies choose to fail or succeed*. NewYork: Viking Press, 2005.

Diegenmueller, K. (1995, April 12). Standards: Running Out of Steam. *Education Week*. Retrieved from http://www.edweek.org/ew/articles/1995/04/12/29steam.h14.html?qs=Standards:%20Run ning%20Out%20of%20Steam

Dillon, S. (2009, August 17). Dangling money, Obama pushes states to shift on education. *New York Times*. Retrieved from http://www.nytimes.com/2009/08/17/education/17educ.html?pagewanted=all&_r=0

Dodge v. Ford Motor Company, 204 Mich. 459, 170 N.W. 668. (Mich. 1919).

Donohue, T. (2007, December 5). *Education reform: A moral imperative* [Address]. Washington, DC: U.S. Chamber of Commerce. Retrieved from https://www.uschamber.com/speech/education-reform-moral-imperative-remarks

Doyle, D. P. (1991, October 2). Promising children, An endangered species. *Business Week*.

Doyle, D. P. (1993, April). American schools: Good, bad, or indifferent? *Phi Delta Kappan*, 74(8), pp. 626–631.

Doyle, D. P., & Levine, M. (1985, October). Business and the public schools: observations on the policy statement of the Committee for Economic Development. *Phi Delta Kappan*, (67)2, 113–118.

Duncan, A. (2010, September 2). *Beyond the bubble tests: The next generation of assessments—Secretary Arne Duncan's remarks to state leaders at Achieve's American Diploma Project leadership team meeting* [Speech]. Washington, DC: Author. Retrieved from http://www.ed.gov/news/speeches/beyond-bubble-tests-next-generation-assessments-secretary-arne-duncans-remarks-state-1

Duncan, A. (2011, September 23). *Elementary & secondary education, Letters from the Education Secretary or Deputy Secretary, September 23, 2011* [Letter]. Washington, DC: U.S. Department of Education.

Duncan, A., & Abercrombie, N. (2014, April 16). Hawaii emerges as a rising star in education reform. Honolulu Star Advertiser. Retrieved from http://www.staradvertiser.com/s?action=login&f=y&id=255451021&id=255451021

Education Testing Service. (2004). *Equity and adequacy: Americans speak on public school funding*. Lawrence Township, NJ: Author.

Education Trust. (2007, August 29). Statement from The Education Trust on House No Child Left Behind reauthorization draft [Press Release]. Retrieved from http://www.edtrust.org/dc/press-room/press-release/education-trust-statement-on-house-no-child-left-behind-reauthorization-0

Education Week. (1999). *Quality Counts '99 Hawaii report card*. Washington, DC: Author. Retrieved from http://rc- archive.edweek.org/sreports/qc99/states/grades/hi-rc.htm

Edwards, L. (1998). *The power of ideas, The Heritage Foundation at 25 years*. Ottawa, IL: Jameson Books, Inc. Retrieved from http://www.nytimes.com/books/first/e/edwards-ideas.html

Eidelson, J. (2014, March 12). Say goodbye to public schools: Diane Ravitch warns Salon some cities will soon have none. *Salon*. Retrieved from http://www.salon.com/2014/03/12/public_schools_under_siege_diane_ravitch_warns_salon_some_cities_soon_will_have_none/

Eitel, R. S., Talbert, K. D., & Evers, W. M. (2012, February). *The road to a national curriculum, the legal aspects of the Common Core standards, Race to the Top, and conditional waivers*. Boston: Pioneer Institute.
Elementary & Secondary Education Part I—General Provisions § 1905. (2002). Retrieved from http://www2.ed.gov/policy/elsec/leg/esea02/pg18.html
Elias M., Gunter, B., van der Valk, A, & Costello, M. (2014, May). *Public schools in the crosshairs, Far-right propaganda and the Common Core State Standards*. Montgomery, AL: Southern Poverty Law Center.
Elmore, R. F., Abelmann, C. H., & Fuhrman, S. (1996). The new accountability in state education reform: From process to performance. In H. Ladd (Ed.), *Holding schools accountable: performance-based reform in education* (pp. 65–98). Washington, DC: Brookings Institution.
Elmore, R., & Fuhrman, S. (1996). Getting to scale with good educational practice. *Harvard Educational Review*, 66(1), 1–26.
Emery, K. (2002). *The Business Roundtable and systemic reform: How corporate-engineered high-stakes testing has eliminated community participation in developing educational goals and policies*. PhD dissertation, University of California at Davis. Retrieved from http://www.educationanddemocracy.org/Emery/Emery_Dissertation_all.pdf
Emery, K., & Ohanian, S. (2004). *Why is corporate America bashing our public schools?* Portsmouth, NH: Heinemann.
Engler, J., & Weingarten, R. (2013, November 26). *Letter to governors from BRT, AFT on the Common Core State Standards* [Press Release]. Washington, DC: Business Roundtable. Retrieved from http://businessroundtable.org/resources/letter-governors-brt-aft-common-core-state-standards
Erbes, K. M. (2003). School/community-based management, Discursive politics in action. [Dissertation]. Honolulu: University of Hawaii at Mānoa.
Ericson, D. (2011, March 3). Professor of Educational Foundations, University of Hawaii at Mānoa. [Personal communication].
Essoyan, S. (2005, May 13). Isles sixth in school standards, Hawaii's tests for proficiency in reading and math are among the toughest in the nation, an educational journal says. *Honolulu Star-Bulletin*. Retrieved from http://archives.starbulletin.com/2005/05/13/news/story1.html
Evansky, B. (2014, March 29). Common Core emerges as potent election issue for fed-up parents. *Fox News*. Retrieved from http://www.foxnews.com/us/2014/03/29/common-core-emerges-as-potent-election-issue-for-fed-up-parents/
Exit strategy: State lawmakers consider dropping Common Core. (2014, April 1). *Education Week*. Retrieved from http://www.edweek.org/ew/section/multimedia/anti-cc-bill.html
Falk, B. (2000). *The heart of the matter, Using standards and assessment to learn*. Portsmouth, NH: Heinemann.
Falk, B., & Ort, S. (1998). Sitting down to score: Teacher learning through assessment. *Phi Delta Kappan*, 80(1), 59–64.
Farbman, D. A., Goldberg, D. J., & Miller, T. D. (2014, January). *Redesigning and expanding school time to support Common Core implementation*. Washington, DC: Center for American Progress, National Center on Time and Learning.

Feingold, R. D., Leahy, P. J., Cantwell, M. E., Nelson, E. B. Levin, C., Stabenow, D., Salazar, K., Klobuchar, A., McCaskill, C., & Durbin, R. J. (2007, February 15). Feingold, Senators Call For NCLB Law Overhaul. Wisconsin Education Association Council. Retrieved from http://www.weac.org/news_and_publications/at_the_capitol/archives/2006–2007/feingold_nclb.aspx

Ferguson, N. (2004). *Colossus: the price of America's empire*. New York: Penguin.

Ferrar, E. & Cippollone, A. (1988). *The business community and school reform: The Boston Compact at five years*. Madison, WI: National Center on Effective Secondary Schools.

Fine, L. (2001, May 30). ESEA, minus vouchers, easily passes house. *Education Week*. Retrieved from http://www.edweek.org/ew/articles/2001/05/30/38esea.h20.html

Finn Jr., C. E. (1993). *We must take charge, Our schools and our future*. New York: Free Press.

Finn Jr., C. E., Davis Jr., M. A., & Mead, W. R. (2006). The state of state world history standards. Washington, DC: Thomas Fordham Foundation. Retrieved from http://edexcellence.net/publications/soswhs2006.html

Finn Jr., C. E., & Pertrilli, M. J. (Eds.). (2000). *The state of state standards 2000*. Washington, DC: Thomas Fordham Foundation. Retrieved from http://www.edexcellence.net/detail/news.cfm?news_id=24&id=

Finn Jr., C. E., Pertrilli, M. J., & Julian, L. (2006). *The state of state standards 2006*. Washington, DC: Thomas B. Fordham Foundation. Retrieved from http://www.edexcellence.net/detail/news.cfm?news_id=358&id=

Finn Jr., C.E., Pertrilli, M. J., & Vanourek, G. (1998). *The state of state standards 1998*. Washington, DC: Thomas Fordham Foundation. Retrieved from http://www.edexcellence.net/detail/news.cfm?news_id=25&id=

Firestone, W. A. (1997, October 8). Standards reform run amok. *Education Week*. Retrieved from http://www.edweek.org/ew/articles/1997/10/08/06fire.h17.html?r=1082760888

Firestone, W., Mayrowetz, D., & Fairman, H. (1997). *Rethinking high stakes: External obligation in assessment policy*. Chicago: American Educational Research Association.

Fortune. (1990, May 28). *Saving our schools, A special issue*.

Fosler, R. S. (1990). *The business role in state education reform*. Washington, DC: Business Roundtable.

Frank, T. (2004). *What's the matter with Kansas, How conservatives won the heart of America*. New York: Henry Holt and Company.

Friedman, M. (1962). *Capitalism and freedom*. Chicago: University of Chicago Press.

Friedman, M. (1982). *Capitalism and freedom, Revised edition*. Chicago: University of Chicago Press.

Friedman, T. (2005). *The world is flat*. New York: Farrar, Straus & Giroux.

Frisch, M. (1957). *Homo faber*. Boston: Houghton Mifflin Harcourt.

Gabbard, D. A. (2003). Education is enforcement! The centrality of compulsory schooling in market societies. In K. J. Saltman & D. A. Gabbard (Eds.), *Education as enforcement, The militarization and corporatization of schools*. New York: RoutledgeFalmer.

Gardner, H. E. (2006). *Multiple intelligences: New horizons in theory and practice*. New York: Basic Books.

Gerson, M. (2013, May 20). GOP fear of Common Core education standards unfounded. *Washington Post*. Retrieved from http://www.washingtonpost.com/opinions/michael-gerson-gop-fear-of-common-core-education-standards-unfounded/2013/05/20/9db19a94-c177-11e2-8bd8-2788030e6b44_story.html

Gerstner, L. (1994, May 27). Our schools are failing: Do we care? *New York Times*. Retrieved from http://www.mathcs.duq.edu/~packer/WR/WRimages/fail.jpg

Gerstner, L., Semerad, R. D., & Doyle, D. P. (1995). *Reinventing education: Entrepreneurship in America's public schools*. New York: Plume.

Gewertz, C. (2011, May 9). Critics post 'manifesto' opposing shared curriculum. *Education Week*, 30(31), p. 9. Retrieved from http://www.edweek.org/ew/articles/2011/05/09/31curriculum.h30.html

Giroux, H. (2009, October 1). The Powell memo and the teaching machines of right-wing extremists. *Truthout*. Retrieved from http://www.truth-out.org/100109A?print

Gonzalez, J. (2002, July 27). School ruling defies logic. *New York Daily News*. Retrieved from http://www.nydailynews.com/archives/news/2002/06/27/2002-06-27_schools_ruling_defies_logic.html

Gordon, R. (2005, June 6). Class struggle. *The New Republic*. Retrieved from http://www.newrepublic.com/article/class-struggle

Gorman, S. (2001, July 14). Education: Behind bipartisan. *National Journal*, 33(28), pp. 2228–2233. Retrieved from http://web.a.ebscohost.com.ezproxy.librarieshawaii.org:2048/eh...N1c3RpZD1zNDgwMDI0NCZzaXRlPWVob3N0LWxpdmU%3d#db=aph&AN=4904058

Govtrack. *H.R. 1 (107th): No Child Left Behind Act of 2001*. Retrieved from https://www.govtrack.us/congress/bills/107/hr1

Graham, F. P. (1972, September 29). Powell proposed business defense. *New York Times*, p. 31.

Grann, D. (1997, October 27). Robespierre of the right, What I ate at the revolution. *New Republic*. Retrieved from http://web.archive.org/web/19991011170703/http://magazines.enews.com/magazines/tnr/archive/10/102797/grann102797.html

Grassley, C. (2013, April 26). *Dear Chairman Harkin and Ranking Member Moran* [Letter]. Retrieved from http://caffeinatedthoughts.com/2013/04/grassley-launches-effort-to-prohibit-common-core-funding/

Greenberg, D. (1998, May 10). Right thinking, An authorized history of a foundation that has set the conservative agenda for 25 years. *New York Times*. Retrieved from http://www.nytimes.com/books/98/05/10/reviews/980510.10greenbt.html?_r=5

Greene, J., Stotsky, S. Evers, B. Forster, G., & Wurman. (2011, May). Closing the door on innovation, Why one national curriculum is bad for America. (2011, May). Retrieved from http://www.edweek.org/media/closingthedoor-blog.pdf

Greenwald, G., & MacAskill, E. (2013, June 6). NSA Prism program taps in to user data of Apple, Google and others. *The Guardian*. Retrieved from http://www.theguardian.com/world/2013/jun/06/us-tech-giants-nsa-data.

Gross, P., Goodenough, U., Lerner, L. S., Haack, S., Schwartz, M., Schwartz, R., & Finn Jr., C. E. (2005). *The state of state science standards 2005*. Washington, DC: Thomas B.

Fordham Institute. Retrieved from http://www.edexcellence.net/detail/news.cfm?news_id=352&id=

Grossman, R. L. (1993, Fall). Review and commentary of "Justice for sale: Shortchanging the public interest for private gain." *The Workbook, 18*(3), Retrieved from http://www.ratical.org/corporations/Justice4sale.html

Hamilton, L. S., Stecher, B. M., Marsh, J. A., McCombs, J. S., Robyn, A., Russell, J. L. Naftel, S., & Barney, H. (2007). *Standards-based accountability under No Child Left Behind: Experiences of teachers and administrators in three states.* Santa Monica, CA: RAND Corporation.

Hamilton, L. S., Stecher, B. M., & Yuan, K. (2008). *Standards-based reform in the United States: History, research, and future directions.* Santa Monica, CA: RAND Corporation. Retrieved from http://www.rand.org/pubs/reprints/2009/RAND_RP1384.pdf

Hammonds, K. (1999, March 22). The mission: David Kearns's crusade to fix America's schools. *Business Week.* Retrieved from http://www.businessweek.com/1999/99_12/b3621153.htm

Harnischfeger, A. (1995). Fad or reform? The standards movement in the United States. In W. Bos & R. H. Lehmann (Eds.), *Reflections on educational achievement, Papers in honour of T. Neville Postlethwaite* (pp. 107–118). Münster, Germany: Waxman Verlag.

Harvey, D. (2007). *A brief history of neoliberalism.* Oxford: Oxford University Press.

Hawaii Board of Education (2014). *Race to the Top.* Retrieved from http://www.hawaiiboe.net/Pages/RacetotheTop.aspx.

Hawaii Department of Education. Hawaii Common Core Standards. Retrieved from http://www.hawaiipublicschools.org/TeachingAndLearning/StudentLearning/CommonCoreStateStandards/Pages/home.aspx

Hawaii Department of Education. *Leadership profiles and staff.* Honolulu, HI: Author. Retrieved from http://www.hawaiipublicschools.org/ConnectWithUs/Organization/LeadershipProfilesAndStaff/Pages/home.aspx

Hawaii Department of Education. (1991a, February 21). *Update,* (5), 4. Honolulu, HI: Author.

Hawaii Department of Education. (1991b, August 1). *Update.* (5), 15. Honolulu, HI: Author.

Hawaii Department of Education. (1999a). *Strategic plan for standard-based reform.* Honolulu, HI: Author.

Hawaii Department of Education, Office of Accountability and School Instructional Support/School Renewal Group. (1999b). *Making sense of standards, Moving from the blue book to HCPS II.* Honolulu, HI: Author. Retrieved from http://www.hcps.k12.hi.us/PUBLIC/contst1.nsf/2be12f699cdba2840a2567830069239d/fbc32f9bf7fcc6bd0a2567e000146fc7/$FILE/Making%20Sense%20of%20Standards.pdf

Hawaii Department of Education. (2003). *Strategic implementation plan.* Honolulu, HI: Author.

Hawaii Department of Education. (2005a). *Hawaii Department of Education's response to Fordham Foundation's "The state of state math standards 2005."* Retrieved from http://www.Hawaiireporter.com/file.aspx?Guid=5e5ff82d-969e-4459-a7ab- 922474acab52

Hawaii Department of Education, Office of Curriculum, Instruction & Student Services [OCISS]. (2006). OCISS presentation to the Performance Standards Review Commission. Honolulu: Author.

Hawaii Department of Education. (2010). *Race to the Top, Application for initial funding* [Grant Application]. Honolulu, HI: Author.

Hawaii Department of Education. (2013, September 5). *Superintendent Matayoshi rated 'exceptional' by Board of Education.* Honolulu, HI: Author. Retrieved from http://www.hawaiipublicschools.org/ConnectWithUs/MediaRoom/PressReleases/Pages/Superintendent-Matayoshi-rated-'Exceptional'-by-Board-of-Education.aspx

Hawaii Department of Education. (2014, March 31). Arne Duncan praises Hawaii's education leadership. Honolulu, HI: Author. Retrieved from http://www.hawaiipublicschools.org/ConnectWithUs/MediaRoom/PressReleases/Pages/Secretary-Duncan-visit.aspx

Hawaii School University Partnership, Department of Education, Kamehameha Schools, & University of Hawaii. (1994, January). *Hawaii state framework for student assessment and accountability.* Honolulu, HI: Author.

Hawaii State Auditor. (2001). *A review and assessment of the Department of Education's development of educational standards.* Honolulu: Author. Retrieved from http://www.state.hi.us/auditor/Reports/2001/01-15.pdf

Hawaii State Commission on Performance Standards. (1993). *Hawaii State Commission on Performance Standards preliminary final report.* Honolulu: Author.

Hawaii State Commission on Performance Standards. (1994). *Hawaii State Commission on Performance Standards final report.* Honolulu: Author.

Hawaii State Legislature. (1989). Act 366, Session Laws of Hawaii, 1989. Honolulu: Author.

Hawaii State Legislature. (1991). *A bill for an act relating to the creation of a commission for performance standards.* Act 334, Session Laws of Hawaii, 1991. Honolulu: Author.

Hawaii State Legislature. (1994). *Hawaii Revised Statutes 302A-201.* Honolulu: Author.

Hawaii State Legislature. (2000). *Senate concurrent resolution 57 requesting the Auditor to review and assess the Department of Education's development of educational standards for public schools statewide.* Retrieved from http://www.capitol.hawaii.gov/session2000/bills/scr57_.htm

Hawaii State Legislature. (2014). Governor's Message 706, Submitting for consideration and confirmation to the Board of Education, Gubernatorial Nominee, Donald Horner, for a term to expire 6-30-2017 [Legislative Measure Status]. Honolulu, HI: Author. Retrieved from http://www.capitol.hawaii.gov/measure_indiv.aspx?billtype=GM&billnumber=706&year=2014

Hawaii State Performance Standards Review Commission. (1999). *Hawaii State Performance Standards Review Commission final report.* Honolulu: Author.

Hawaii State Performance Standards Review Commission. (2003). *Hawaii State Performance Standards Review Commission 2002 final report.* Honolulu: Author.

Hawaii State Performance Standards Review Commission. (2006). *Hawaii State Performance Standards Review Commission final report.* Honolulu: Author. Retrieved from http://doe.k12.hi.us/curriculum/2006PSRCBookFinal.pdf

Haycock, K. (2003, Winter). A new core curriculum for all: Aiming high for other people's children. *Thinking K-16 (7)*1, 1–2.

Hayek, F. V. (1944). *The road to serfdom.* Chicago: University of Chicago Press.

Hazen, D. (2005, February 7). The right-wing express. *Alternet*. Retrieved from http://www.alternet.org/media/21192?page=entire

Hedges, C. (2012, November 5). The S & M Election. *Truthdig*. Retrieved from http://www.truthdig.com/report/item/the_sm_election_20121105/

Heinberg, R. (2010). *Peak everything: Waking up to the century of declines*. Gabriola Island, BC, Canada: New Society Publishers.

Heritage Foundation. (1981). *Mandate for leadership*. Washington, DC: Author.

Heritage Foundation. (1990). *A businessman's guide to the education reform debate*. Washington, DC: Author.

Hess, F. M., & Petrilli, M. J. (2006). *No Child Left Behind primer*. New York: Peter Lang.

Hill, P. T. & Warner, K. E. (1994). *A new architecture for education reform*. Washington, DC: Business Roundtable.

Himmelstein, J. L. (1989). *To the right, The transformation of American conservatism*. Berkeley: University of California Press.

Hirsch, E. D. (1996). *The schools we need and why we don't have them*. New York: Doubleday.

Hoff, D. J. (1999). Standards at crossroads after decade. *Education Week*. Retrieved from http://www.edweek.org/ew/articles/1999/09/22/03stand.h19.html?qs=Standards+at+crossroads+after+decade

Hoff, D. J. (2005, April 7). Education department announces more flexible approach to NCLB law. *Education Week*. Retrieved from http://www.edweek.org/ew/articles/2005/04/07/31spellings_web.h24.html

Hoff, D. (2007, March 13). Conservative plan would shift accountability to the states. *Education Week*. Retrieved from http://www.edweek.org/ew/articles/2007/03/14/27hoekstra.h26.html

Hoff, D. (2008, July 15). Obama sounds as if he wants to get NCLB right. *Education Week*. Retrieved from http://blogs.edweek.org/edweek/NCLB-ActII/2008/07/obama_sounds_as_if_he_wants_to_1.html

Holmes Group. (1986). *Tomorrow's teachers: A report of the Holmes Group*. East Lansing, MI: Author.

Home School Legal Defense Association. (2014). *Building the machine—The Common Core documentary* [Online video]. Purcellville, VA. Retrieved from http://www.youtube.com/watch?v=zjxBClx01jc

Honolulu Civil Beat. *Kathryn Matayoshi*. Retrieved from http://www.civilbeat.com/topics/kathryn-matayoshi/.

Horkheimer, M., & Adorno, T. W. (1976). *The dialectic of enlightenment*. New York: Continuum International Publishing Group.

Horn, R. A. (2004). *Standards primer*. New York: Peter Lang.

Hudson Institute. *History*. (2010). Washington, DC: author. Retrieved from http://www.hudson.org/learn/index.cfm?fuseaction=history

Hudson Institute. (1987). *Workforce 2000: Work and workers for the twenty-first century*. Indianapolis: Author.

Huelskamp, R. M. (1993a, May). Perspectives on Education in America. *Phi Delta Kappan*, (74)9, 718–721. Retrieved from http://www.jstor.org/stable/20404979

Huelskamp, R. M. (1993b, September). The second coming of the Sandia Report. *Education Digest (59)*1, 4–5. Retrieved from http://eres.library.Mānoa.hawaii.edu/login?url=http://search.ebscohost.com/login.aspx?direct=true&db=f5h&AN=9309080046&site=ehost-live

Hunt, J. (1983a). *Action for excellence*. Denver: Education Commission of the States, Task Force on Economic Growth.

Hunt, J. (1983b, September). Action for excellence, Excerpts from the task force report. *Educational Leadership*, 14–18.

Hunt, J. (1984). Task force on education for economic growth. In M. I. Frank (Ed.), *Teachers, economic growth and society* (pp. 11–50). New York: Routledge.

Indigenous Native American Prophecy (Elders Speak Part 2) [Online Video]. Retrieved from http://www.youtube.com/watch?v=tqfvUA2vRAM#aid=P-WpLnvZVHI

Institute for Policy Studies Right Web. (2009, February 22). *John M. Olin Foundation*. Retrieved from http://www.rightweb.irc-online.org/profile/John_M_Olin_Foundation#_edn6

Institute of Education Sciences. (2014). *National education data model, Student elementary secondary*. Retrieved from https://nces.ed.gov/forum/datamodel/eiebrowser/techview.aspx?instance=studentElementarySecondary

International Reading Association. (1999). High-stakes assessments in reading: A position statement of the International Reading Association. *The Reading Teacher*, 53(3), 257–264.

Iowa State Department of Education. (2010, July 29). *State board of education adopts common core state standards*. Des Moines, IA: Author. Retrieved from http://www.iowa.gov/educate/index.php?option=com_content&view=article&id=2025:state-board-of-education-adopts-common-core-state-standards&catid=666:highlights

Jacobson, L. (2000). Hawaii, the Aloha state focuses on teacher standard and certification in push to improve quality. In V. B. Edwards (Ed.), Who should teach? Quality counts 2000 (p. 112). Washington, DC: *Education Week*. Retrieved from http://www.edweek.org/media/ew/qc/archives/QC00full.pdf

Jacobson, L. (2001). State of the states, Hawaii, Quality counts. In V. B. Edwards (Ed.), *A better balance, Standards, tests, and the tools to succeed, Quality Counts 2001* (pp. 130–131). Washington, DC: Education Week. Retrieved from http://www.edweek.org/media/ew/qc/archives/QC01full.pdf

Jacobson, L. (2003). State of the states, Hawaii. In V. B. Edwards (Ed.), *If I can't learn from you, Ensuring a highly qualified teacher for every classroom* (pp. 123–124). Washington, DC: Education Week. Retrieved from http://www.edweek.org/media/ew/qc/archives/QC03full.pdf

Jefferson, T. (1787, November 13). Letter to William S. Smith. In T. Jefferson, *Memoirs, correspondence, and private papers of Thomas Jefferson, volume 2*. Retrieved from http://books.google.com/books?id=imMmIlv1G7MC&pg=PA268&q=&f=false#v=onepage&q=&f=false

Jefferson, T. (1820). *Letter to William Charles Jarvis*. Retrieved from http://rationalnationusa.blogspot.com/2011/05/liberty-then-and-liberty-now.html

Jennings, J. E. (1998). *Why national standards and tests? Politics and the quest for better schools*. Thousand Oaks, CA: Sage Publications.

Jerald, C. D. (2008). *Benchmarking for success: Ensuring U.S. students receive a world-class education*. Washington, DC: National Governors Association, Council of Chief State School Officers and Achieve, Inc.

Joel Popkin and Company. (2003). *Securing America's future: The case for a strong manufacturing base*. Washington, DC: NAM Council of Manufacturing Associations.

Johnson, D. (2003, February 10). Who's behind the attack on liberal professors? *History News Network*. Retrieved from http://hnn.us/articles/printfriendly/1244.html

Johnson, D. (2011, February 14). 9 pictures that expose this country's obscene division of wealth. *Alternet*. Retrieved from http://www.alternet.org/story/149918/9_pictures_that_expose_this_country%27s_obscene_division_of_wealth?paging=off&current_page=1#bookmark

Johnston, R. C., & Diegmueller, K. (1995, January 25). Senate approves resolution denouncing history standards. *Education Week*. Retrieved from http://www.edweek.org/ew/articles/1995/01/25/18stand.h14.html?qs=Senate%20approve s%20resolution%20denouncing%20history%20standards

Jones, K., & Whitford, B. L. (1997). Kentucky's conflicting reform principles: High-stakes school accountability. *Phi Delta Kappan, 79*(4), 276–281.

Jossey-Bass. (2001). *The Jossey-Bass reader on school reform*. San Francisco: Author.

Judis, J. B. (2000). *The paradox of America democracy: Elites, special interests, and the betrayal of public trust*. New York: Pantheon Books.

Kalani, N. (2014, March 19). State's schools praised for progress. Honolulu Star Advertiser, p. B1.

Kant, I. (1784). *An answer to the question: What is enlightenment?* Retrieved from http://www.english.upenn.edu/~mgamer/Etexts/kant.html

Kapur, A., Macleod, N., & Singh, N. (2005, October 16). *Industry note: Equity strategy: Plutonomy: Buying luxury, explaining global imbalances*. Citigroup: New York.

Keller, B. (2003, July 7). NEA takes stand against Bush education law. *Education Week*. Retrieved from http://www.edweek.org/ew/articles/2003/07/07/42nea_web.h22.html

Kendall, J. S., & Marzano, R. J. (1996). *Content knowledge: A compendium of standards and benchmarks for K-12 education*. Alexandria, VA: Association for Supervision and Curriculum Development.

KHON Channel 2. (2010, June 8). *Hawaii adopts Common Core State Standards in education*. Honolulu, HI: Author. Retrieved from http://racetotop.com/2010/06/18/hawaii-adopts-common-core-state-standards-in-education/

Kilgore, E. (2014, April 23). Bush and Christie stand alone amid GOP's slow-motion revolt on Common Core. *Talking Points Memo*. Retrieved from http://talkingpointsmemo.com/cafe/republicans-common-core

Kirk, R. (1953). *The conservative mind: From Burke to Santayana*. Chicago: H. Regnery Co.

Klein, A. (2010, July 29). Obama defends Race to the Top. *Education Week*. Retrieved from http://www.edweek.org/ew/articles/2010/07/29/37obama.h29.html

Klein, D., Braams, B. J., Parker, T., Quirk, W., Schmid, W., Wilson, S., Finn, C., Torres, J., Braden, L., & Raimi, R. A. (2005). *The state of state math standards 2005*. Washington,

DC: Thomas B. Fordham Foundation. Retrieved from http://www.edexcellence.net/detail/news.cfm?news_id=338

Klein, M. (1984). *The psycho-analysis of children, The works of Melanie Klein, volume 2.* New York: Free Press.

Klein, M. (2002). The early development of conscience in the child. In M. Klein, *Love, guilt and reparation and other works 1921–1945; The works of Melanie Klein, volume 1* (pp. 248–257). New York: Simon and Schuster.

Klein, N. (2007). *The shock doctrine: The rise of disaster capitalism.* New York: Metropolitan Books.

Klein, R. (2014, May 1). Louis C. K. Has More To Say About Common Core: 'None Of This Feels Careful To Me.' *Huffington Post.* Retrieved from http://www.huffingtonpost.com/2014/05/01/common-core-louis-ck_n_5249712.html?utm_hp_ref=comedy&ir=Comedy.

Koetke, W. (2007). *The final empire: The collapse of civilization and the seed of the future.* Bloomington, IN: AuthorHouse. Retrieved from http://www.primitivism.com/final-empire.htm

Koga, D. (2011, February 18). Don Horner, The banker brings passion and vision to the Board of Education. *Honolulu Star Bulletin.* Retrieved from http://www.staradvertiser.com/editorials/20110218_Don_Horner.html

Kohn, A. (1999). *The schools our children deserve: Moving beyond traditional classrooms and "tougher standards."* Boston: Houghton Mifflin.

Kolb, C. (1998). *White House daze, The unmaking of domestic policy in the Bush years.* New York: Simon & Schuster.

Koretz, D., & Linn, R. L. (1996). *Summary of findings: Technical advisory group for the New York state new assessments project.* New York: National Center for Restructuring Education, Schools, and Teaching.

Kosar, K. R. (2005). *Failing grades: The federal politics of education standards.* Boulder: Lynne Rienner Publishers.

KPMG International. (2014). *Future state 2030: The global megatrends shaping governments.* Amstelveen, The Netherlands: Author.

Kristol, I. (1978). *Two cheers for capitalism.* New York: Basic Books, Inc.

Kroll, L. (2013, September 16). Inside the 2013 Forbes 400: Facts and figures on America's richest. *Forbes.* Retrieved from http://www.forbes.com/sites/luisakroll/2013/09/16/inside-the-2013-forbes-400-facts-and-figures-on-americas-richest/

Lafer, G. (2002). *The job training charade.* Ithaca, NY: Cornell University Press.

Lai, M. (1998). *Hawaii content and performance standards: Schools' review of standards and instructional module development.* Honolulu: University of Hawaii at Mānoa Curriculum Research & Development Group.

Landay, J. (2002, August 20). *The Powell manifesto, How a prominent lawyer's attack memo changed America.* Retrieved from http://old.mediatransparency.org/story.php?storyID=21

Lapham, L. H. (2004, September). Tentacles of rage, The republican propaganda mill, a brief history. *Harpers Magazine.* Retrieved from http://www.mindfully.org/Reform/2004/Republican-Propaganda1sep04.htm

Lee, J. (2014, January 27). Common Core: The business side of the new modern global education system. *Activist Post*. Retrieved from http://www.activistpost.com/2014/01/common-core-business-side-of-new-modern.html

Lerner, L. S. (1998). *State science standards*. New York: Thomas B. Fordham Foundation. Retrieved from http://www.edexcellence.net/detail/news.cfm?news_id=26&id=

Levitan, S. A., & Cooper, M. A. (1984). *Business lobbies, The public good and the bottom line*. Baltimore: Johns Hopkins University Press.

Lewis, A. C. (1993, February). From education governor to education secretary. *Phi Delta Kappan, (74)*6, 428–429.

Lewis, D., & Dundar, H. (2001). Cost and productivity in higher education: Theory, evidence and policy implications. In M. B. Paulson & J. C. Smart (Eds.), *The Finance of Higher Education: Theory, Research, Policy and Practice* (pp. 133–188). New York: Agathon Press.

Libbey, K. M. (2013, May 22). *A guide to writing right-wing, anti-Common Core articles and blog posts*. Retrieved from http://kenmlibby.com/2013/05/22/guide-to-writing-anti-common-core-blog-posts/

Lips, D. (2007, September 7). *Education notebook: Making No Child Left Behind worse*. Washington, DC: Heritage Foundation. Retrieved from http://www.heritage.org/research/education-notebook/making-no-child-left-behind-worse

Luetkemeyer, B. (2013, April 30). *Dear Secretary Duncan*. Retrieved from http://massie.house.gov/sites/massie.house.gov/files/documents/commoncore.pdf

Lynn, B. (2010). *Cornered, The new monopoly capitalism and the economics of destruction*. Hoboken, NJ: John Wiley and Sons, Inc.

Manzo, K. K. (1998). Partner in paradise, Though the only urban center in Hawaii, Honolulu shares equal partnership in the statewide school system. In V. B. Edwards (Ed.), *Quality counts 1998, The urban challenge, Public education in the fifty states* (pp. 137–140). *Education Week*. Retrieved from http://www.edweek.org/media/ew/qc/archives/QC98full.pdf.

Maranto, R. & McShane, M. Q. (2012). *President Obama and education reform: The personal and the political*. New York: Palgrave Macmillan.

Marshall, R., & Tucker, M. (1992). *Thinking for a living: Education and the wealth of nations*. New York: Basic Books.

Martin, A., & Tice, R. (2013, July 10). *Interview with Russell Tice, NSA Whistleblower, by Abby Martin on RT's Breaking the Set*. Retrieved from http://whowhatwhy.com/2014/01/16/transcript-another-nsa-whistleblower-russell-tice/

Martin, J. (2014, April 19). Republicans See Political Wedge in Common Core. *New York Times*. Retrieved from http://www.nytimes.com/2014/04/20/us/politics/republicans-see-political-wedge-in-common-core.html?_r=0

Marzano, G. F., & Kendall, J. (1996). *Designing standards-based districts, schools, and classrooms*. Aurora, CO: Mid-continent Regional Educational Laboratory.

Matthews, G. B. (1980). *Philosophy and the small child*. Cambridge, MA: Harvard University Press.

Matthews, K. (2014, April 20). The big story, Brand names in NY standardized tests vex parents. *Associated Press*. Retrieved from http://bigstory.ap.org/article/brand-names-ny-standardized-tests-vex-parents

Mattson, K. (2008). *Rebels all! A short history of the conservative mind in postwar America*. New Brunswick, NJ: Rutgers University Press.

McClelland, R. (2007). *Hawaii state assessment: Proficiency scores improve under new test*. Honolulu: Hawaii Department of Education. Retrieved from http://www.hcps.k12. hi.us/STATE/COMM/DOEPRESS.NSF/a1d7af052e94dd120a2561f7000a037c/ab64998 a16e079d50a25731d00823c4c?OpenDocument

McCluskey, N., & Coulson, A. (2007, September 5). End it, don't mend it: What to do with No Child Left Behind. *Cato Institute Policy Analysis No. 599*. New York: Cato Institute.

McGroarty, E., & Robbins, J. (2012, May). *Controlling education from the top, Why Common Core is bad for America*. Boston: Pioneer Institute.

McGrory, K., Bousquet, S., & Leary, A. (2013, September 18). Gov. Rick Scott considering executive action to address Common Core controversy. *Miami Herald*. Retrieved from http://www.miamiherald.com/2013/09/18/3635556/gov-rick-scott-considering-executive. html

McGuinn, P. J. (2006). *No Child Left Behind and the transformation of federal education policy, 1965–2005*. Lawrence: University of Kansas Press.

McKenzie, F. D., & Cromer, J. L. (1984). Schools and businesses, A partnership for children. In M. I. Frank (Ed.), *Teachers, economic growth and society* (pp. 133–145). New York: Routledge.

McLaughlin, M. W., Shepard, L. A., & O'Day, J. A. (1995). *Improving education through standards-based reform, Report by the National Academy of Education panel on standards-based education reform*. Washington, DC: National Academy of Education. Retrieved from http://www.reading.org/Publish.aspx?page=bk889-introduction.html&mode=retrieve&D= 10.1598/0814146767.intro&F=bk889-introduction.html&key=F19C180D-D3D5-4B46-A565-F04117B76F92

McNeill, M. (2014, March 27). Race to the Top reports detail winners' progress, challenges. *Education Week*. Retrieved from http://www.edweek.org/ew/articles/2014/03/19/26rtt.h33. html

McQuaid, K. (1981, May/June). The roundtable: getting results in Washington. *Harvard Business Review*, 111–123.

Mead, R. (2014, May 1). Louis C. K. against the Common Core. *The New Yorker*. Retrieved from http://www.newyorker.com/online/blogs/comment/2014/05/louis-ck-

Mead, W. R., Finn Jr., C. E., & Davis Jr., M. A. (2006). *The state of state world history standards*. Washington, DC: Thomas B. Fordham Institute. Retrieved from http://www.edexcellence.net/detail/news.cfm?news_id=356&id=

Meier, D. (Ed.). (2000). *Will standards save public education?* Boston, MA: Beacon Press.

Meyer, F. (1962). *In defense of freedom, A conservative credo*. Chicago: Henry Regnery Company.

Mickelson, R. A. (1999, Spring). International business machinations: A case study of corporate involvement in local educational reform. *Teachers College Record, (100)*3, pp. 476–512.

Mickelson, R. A. (2000). Corporations and classrooms: A critical examination of the business agenda for urban school reform. In K. A. McClafferty, C. A. Torres, & T. R. Mitchell (Eds.).

Challenges of urban education, Sociological perspectives for the next century (pp. 127–174). Albany: State University of New York Press.

Micklethwait, J., & Wooldridge, A. (2004). *The right nation, Conservative power in America*. New York: Penguin.

Mid-continent Research for Education and Learning. (2009). *Standards improvement-Technical services*. Retrieved from http://mcrel.org/our_work/standardsTechAsstSheet.asp

Miller, G. (2007, July 30). *Chairman Miller's remarks on the future of the No Child Left Behind education law* [Speech]. Washington, DC: National Press Club. Retrieved from http://votesmart.org/public-statement/280043/chairman-miller-remarks-on-the-future-of-the-no-child-left-behind-education-law#.U3BaE8ZX9g0

Miller, J. A. (1989, September 27). Democrats stress party's historic role with set of six key goals for schools. *Education Week*. Retrieved from http://www.edweek.org/ew/articles/1989/09/27/09070016.h09.html?r=1752180853

Miller, J. A. (1991a, May 15). Most of Bush plan would need Congressional nod, Lawmakers say. *Education Week*. Retrieved from http://www.edweek.org/ew/articles/1991/05/15/10280041.h10.html?qs=Most+of+Bush+ plan+would+need+Congressional+nod,+Lawmakers+Say

Miller, J. A. (1991b, June 5). Bush's school plan is 'Lamar's baby,' Participants agree. *Education Week*. Retrieved from http://www.edweek.org/ew/articles/1991/06/05/10310028.h10.html?qs=Bush%27s+scho ol+plan+Is+%27Lamar%27s+baby,%27+Participants+agree

Miller, J. A. (1991c, September 4). Administration says it lacks funds to support goals panel. *Education Week*. Retrieved from http://www.edweek.org/ew/articles/1991/09/04/01admin.h11.html?qs=Administration+sa ys+it+lacks+funds+to+support+goals+panel

Miller, J. A. (1991d, September 11). Administration makes p.r. splash for America 2000. *Education Week*. Retrieved from http://www.edweek.org/ew/articles/1991/09/11/02splash.h11.html

Miller, J. A. (1991e, October 9). Report questioning 'crisis' in education triggers an uproar. *Education Week*. Retrieved from http://perimeterprimate.blogspot.com/2009/07/history-lesson-about-sandia-report.html

Miller, J. A. (1992a, March 4). Buoyed by Senate vote, Ford backs off deal on school choice. *Education Week*. Retrieved from http://www.edweek.org/ew/articles/1992/03/04/24ford.h11.html?qs=Buoyed+by+Senate +vote,+Ford+backs+off+deal+on+school+choice

Miller, J. A. (1992b, March 25). Legislation to create national system of standards, assessments under fire. *Education Week*. Retrieved from http://www.edweek.org/ew/articles/1992/03/25/27debate.h11.html?qs=Legislation+to+create+national+system+of+standards,+assessments+under+fire

Miller, J. A. (1992c, May 27). House's bill would authorize standards, but not assessment. *Education Week*. Retrieved from http://www.nytimes.com/1991/10/01/us/first-report-card-issued-on-us-education- goals.html?pagewanted=2.

Miller, J. A. (1992d, October 7). Reform measure dies-Except as campaign issue? *Education Week*. Retrieved from http://www.edweek.org/ew/articles/1992/10/07/05omni.h12.html?qs=Reform+measure+d ies-Except+as+campaign+issue?

Miller, J. A. (1992e, October 9). Energy Dept. lab's report still on hold. *Education Week.* Retrieved from http://perimeterprimate.blogspot.com/2009/07/history-lesson-about-sandia-report.html.

Miller, V. (2001). *Backgrounder 1427 on education, The new definition of standards in American education.* Washington, DC: Heritage Foundation.

Mills, C. W. (1956). *The power elite.* London: Oxford University Press.

Mills, D. G. (2004, November 10). *It's the corporate state, stupid.* Information Clearing House. Retrieved from http://www.informationclearinghouse.info/article7260.htm

Morrison, A. M. (1990, May 28). Saving our schools, By working together, business leaders, parents, teachers, and communities can revitalize America's most endangered institution. *Fortune.* Retrieved from http://money.cnn.com/magazines/fortune/fortune_archive/1990/05/28/73595/index.htm

Morrison, R. G. (1996, June 5). An exercise in government-approved truth. *Education Week.* Retrieved from http://www.edweek.org/ew/articles/1996/06/05/37morris.h15.html

Motesharrei, S., Rivas, J., & Kalnay, E. (2014, May). Nature dynamics (HANDY): Modeling inequality and use of resources in the collapse or sustainability of societies. Retrieved from http://www.sciencedirect.com/science/article/pii/S0921800914000615

Munroe, S., & Smith, T. (1998). *State geography standards.* New York: Thomas Fordham Institute. Retrieved from http://www.edexcellence.net/detail/news.cfm?news_id=28&id=

Murmane, R., & Levy, F. (1996). Teaching new standards. In S. Fuhrman & J. O'Day, (Eds.), *Rewards and reform: Creating educational incentives that work.* San Francisco: Jossey-Bass.

National Academy of Education. (2008). *Recovering the promise of standards-based education.* Washington, DC: Author. Retrieved May 13, 2009, from http://www.naeducation.org/White_Papers_Project_Standards_Assessments_and_Accountability_Briefing_Sheet.pdf

National Alliance of Business. (1989). *A blueprint for business on restructuring education. Corporate action program.* Washington DC: Author.

National Alliance of Business. (1990). *Education: The next battleground for corporate survival, An urgent message from twenty-one Harvard business school students.* Washington, DC: Author.

National Alliance of Business. (1991). *The Business Roundtable participation guide.* New York: Business Roundtable.

National Center for Education Statistics, Institute of Education Sciences. *National* United States Department of Education *Education Data Model, What is NEDM.* Washington, DC: Author.

National Center on Education and the Economy. (1990). *America's choice, High skills or low wages.* Rochester, NY: author. (ERIC Document Reproduction Service No. 323297).

National Commission on Excellence in Education. (1983). *A nation at risk: The imperative for educational reform.* Washington, DC: National Commission on Excellence in Education. Retrieved from http://www.ed.gov/pubs/NatAtRisk/risk.html

National Council of Teachers of English & International Reading Association. (1996). *Standards for the English language arts.* Urbana, IL: National Council of Teachers of English & International Reading Association. Retrieved from http://www.ncte.org/standards

National Council of Teachers of Mathematics. (1989). Curriculum and evaluation standards for school mathematics. Reston, VA: Author.

National Council on Education Standards and Testing. (1993). *Raising standards for American education*. Washington, DC: National Council on Education, Standards, and Testing. (ERIC Document Reproduction Service No. ED338721).

National Data Campaign. (2013, September). *Fact sheet*. Washington, DC: Author.

National Education Association (1893). *Committee of ten on secondary school studies*. Washington, DC: Bureau of Education.

National Education Association (1918). *Cardinal principles of secondary education*. Washington, DC: Government Printing Office.

National Education Goals Panel. (1993). *Background on the National Education Goals Panel*. Washington, DC: Author.

National Education Goals Panel. (1996). *The National Education Goals report: Building a nation of learners, 1996*. Washington, DC: Author.

National Education Goals Panel. (1997). *The National Education Goals report: Building a nation of learners, 1997*. Washington, DC: Author.

National Education Goals Panel. (1998). *The National Education Goals report: Building a nation of learners, 1998*. Washington, DC: Author.

National Education Goals Panel. (1999a). *The National Education Goals report: Building a nation of learners, 1999*. Washington, DC: U.S. Government Printing Office.

National Education Goals Panel. (1999b). *Tenth anniversary, National Educational Goals Panel, Building on the momentum*. Washington, DC: U.S. Government Printing Office.

National Education Goals Panel. (1999c). *Tenth anniversary program, Building on the momentum*. Washington, DC: U.S. Government Printing Office.

National Governors Association. (1988a). *Making America work: productive people, productive policies*. Washington, DC: Author.

National Governors Association. (1988b). *Getting ready for the National Board for Professional Teaching Standards: What a governor can do*. Washington, DC: Author.

National Governors Association. (2009, June 1). *Forty-Nine States and Territories Join Common Core Standards Initiative, NGA Center, CCSSO convene state-led process to develop common English-language arts and mathematics standards*. Washington, DC: Author. Retrieved from http://www.nga.org/cms/home/news-room/news-releases/page_2009/col2-content/main-content-list/title_forty-nine-states-and-territories-join-common-core-standards-initiative.html

National Governors Association. (2010, June 2). *National Governors Association and state education chiefs launch common state academic standards*. Washington, DC: Author. Retrieved from http://www.nga.org/cms/home/news-room/news-releases/page_2010/col2-content/main-content-list/title_national-governors-association-and-state-education-chiefs-launch-common-state-academic-standards.html

National Governors Association, Council of Chief State School Officers, and Achieve, Inc., (2008). Benchmarking for success: Ensuring U.S. students receive a world-class education. Washington, DC: National Governors Association.

National Research Council. (2008). *Common standards for K-12 education? Considering the evidence*. Washington, DC: Author.

National Science Board, Commission on Precollege Education in Mathematics, Science, and Technology (1983). *Educating Americans for the 21st century*. Washington, DC: Author.

Nazworth, N. (2013, April 29). Eight senators join fight against Common Core. *Christian Post*. Retrieved from http://www.christianpost.com/news/eight-senators-join-fight-against-common-core-94876/

Nietzsche, F. Schopenhauer as educator. (1876). In F. Nietzsche, *Untimely meditations*. Retrieved from http://users.compaqnet.be/cn127103/Nietzsche_untimely_meditations/schopenhauer_as_educator.htm.

Nisbit, R. (1953). *The quest for community, A study in the ethics of order and freedom*. London: Oxford University Press.

Noddings, N. (2005, February 25). Rethinking a bad law. *Education Week*. Retrieved from http://www.edweek.org/ew/articles/2005/02/23/24noddings.h24.html

Obama, B. H. (2008, May 28). Full text of Obama's education speech. *Denver Post*. Retrieved from http://www.denverpost.com/ci_9405199

Obama, B. H. (2010). *Reform and invest in K-12 education*. Retrieved from http://www.whitehouse.gov/issues/education

O'Donoghue, J. (2014, April 14). Bobby Jindal says he will get Louisiana out of Common Core test group, if Legislature won't. *The Times-Picayune*. Retrieved from http://www.nola.com/politics/index.ssf/2014/04/bobby_jindal_will_put_out_of_c.html

Ohanian, S. (1999). *One size fits few: The folly of educational standards*. Portsmouth, NH: Heinemann.

Ohanian, S. (2003, June). Capitalism, calculus, and conscience. *Phi Delta Kappan*, 736–747.

Olson, L. (1995, April 12). Standards: Standards times 50. *Education Week*. Retrieved from http://www.edweek.org/ew/articles/1995/04/12/29st50.h14.html?qs=Standards:+Standards+times+50

O'Neil, J., & Tell, C. (1999). Why students lose when "tougher standards" win. *Educational Leadership, 57*(1), 18–22.

Orwell, G. (1946, April). *Politics and the English language. Horizon*. London. Retrieved from http://www.orwell.ru/library/essays/politics/english/e_polit

Otterbourg, S. D. (1997). *A business guide to support employee and family involvement in education*. New York: The Conference Board.

Parenti, M. (2001). *Monopoly media manipulation*. Retrieved from http://www.michaelparenti.org/MonopolyMedia.html.

Passow, H. W. (1984, June). Tackling the reform reports of the 1980s. *Phi Delta Kappan*, (65)10, 674–683.

Pelto, J. (2014, January 5). *Funding "education reform": The big three foundations*. Retrieved from http://www.publicschoolshakedown.org/funding-education-reform.

Peng, A., & Guthrie, J. (2010, Winter). The phony funding crisis, Even in the worst of times, schools have money to spend. *Education Next*, (10)1. Retrieved from http://educationnext.org/the-phony-funding-crisis/

Perry, M. J. (2012, March). Manufacturing's declining share of GDP is a global phenomenon, and it's something to celebrate. Washington, DC: United States Chamber of Commerce. Retrieved from http://www.uschamberfoundation.org/blog/post/manufacturing-s-declining-share-gdp-global-phenomenon-and-it-s-something-celebrate/34261

Peterson, P. (1983). *Making the grade, Report of the Twentieth Century Fund Task Force on Federal Elementary and Secondary Education Policy [and] background paper.* Washington, DC: Twentieth Century Fund.

Peterson, P. E & Hess, F. M. (2005). Johnny can read... in some states. *Education Next, (5)*3, 52–53. Retrieved from http://media.hoover.org/documents/ednext20053_52.pdf

Phillips-Fein, K. (2009). *Invisible hands: The making of the conservative movement from the new deal to Reagan.* New York: W.W. Norton.

Piaget, J., & Enhelder, B. (2000). *The psychology of the child.* New York: Basic Books.

Pierce v. Society of Sisters, 510 U.S. 268 (1925). Retrieved from http://supreme.justia.com/cases/federal/us/268/510/case.html

Pilger, J. (2008, June 13). Obama is a truly Democratic expansionist. *Antiwar.com.* Retrieved from http://www.antiwar.com/orig/pilger.php?articleid=12983

Popham, J. (2001, April 25). *Interview by Public Broadcasting Service Frontline producer John Tulenko.* Boston: WGBH Educational Foundation, Retrieved from http://www.pbs.org/wgbh/pages/frontline/shows/schools/interviews/popham.html

Popham, W. J. (2003). *Instructionally supportive tests: Why they're needed, How to get them.* Retrieved from http://www.eplc.org/forum_2003speakers_popham.html

Popkewitz, T. S. (1991). *A political sociology of educational reform, Power/knowledge in teaching, teacher education, and research.* New York: Teachers College Press.

Powell, L. (2004). *The Powell memo.* Reclaimdemocracy.org. Retrieved from http://www.reclaimdemocracy.org/corporate_accountability/powell_memo_lewis.html

Presseisen, B. Z. (1985). *Unlearned lessons: Current and past reforms for school improvement.* Philadelphia: Falmer Press.

Project Censored. (1994). Number 3, *The Sandia report on education, A perfect lesson in censorship.* Retrieved from http://www.projectcensored.org/static/1994/1994-story3.htm

Public Broadcasting Service Frontline. (2002). *Are we there yet? Business, politics, and the long (unfinished) road to national standards.* Retrieved from http://www.pbs.org/wgbh/pages/frontline/shows/schools/standards/bp.html

Pullman, J. (2013, January). *The Common Core: A poor choice for states.* Chicago: Heartland Institute.

Purpel, D. (1995). Goals 2000: The triumph of vulgarity and the legitimization of social injustice. In R. Miller (Ed.), *Educational freedom in a democratic society.* Brandon, VT: Holistic Education Press.

Quality Counts 2005, No small change, targeting money towards student achievement, Report card, Hawaii, Standards and accountability. (2005, January 6). *Education Week.* Retrieved from http://www.edweek.org/ew/articles/2005/01/06/17sos- hi.h24.html

Raimi, R. A., & Braden, L. S. (1998). *State mathematic standards, An appraisal of math standards in 46 states, the District of Columbia, and Japan.* New York: Thomas Fordham Institute.

Ravitch, D. (Ed.). (1995a). *Debating the future of American education: Do we need national standards and assessments?* Washington, DC: The Brookings Institution.

Ravitch, D. (1995b). *National standards in American education: A citizen's guide.* Washington, DC: Brookings Institution. Retrieved from http://books.google.com/books?id=8fk2yE1a0PEC&printsec=frontcover#PPA14,M

Ravitch, D. (2000). *Left back: A century of failed school reforms.* New York: Simon & Schuster.

Ravitch, D. (2007, December 5). Is U.S. education better than ever? *Huffington Post.* Retrieved from http://www.huffintonpost.com/diane-ravitch/is-us-education-better-th_b_75441.html

Ravitch, D. (2010a, May 27). Why I changed my mind. *The Nation.* Retrieved from http://www.thenation.com/article/why-i-changed-my-mind

Ravitch, D. (2010b). *The death and life of the great American school system: How testing and choice are undermining education.* New York: Basic Books.

Ravitch, D. (2014, May 2). Louis C. K. takes aim at Common Core—And we're all smarter for it. *Huffington Post.* Retrieved from http://www.huffingtonpost.com/diane-ravitch/louis-ck-common-core_b_5250982.html

Reich, R. B. (1991). *The work of nations.* New York: Alfred A. Knopf.

Reid, K. S. (2004, July 28). Paige blasts NAACP leaders' 'hateful' rhetoric on Bush. *Education Week.* Retrieved from http://www.edweek.org/ew/articles/2004/07/28/43paige.h23.html

Republican National Committee (2013, April 12). *Resolution concerning Common Core educational standards.* Washington, DC: Author. Retrieved from http://www.gop.com/wp-content/uploads/2013/07/Resolution_Concerning_Common_Core_Education_Standards.pdf

Resnick, L. B., & Hall, M. W. (1998). Learning organizations for sustainable educational reform. *Daedalus, 127*(4), 89–118.

Resnick, L. B., & Nolan, K. J. (1995). Standards for education. In D. Ravitch (Ed.), *Debating the future of American education: Do we need national standards and assessments?* Washington, DC: The Brookings Institution.

Resnick, L. B., & Resnick, D. P. (1991). Assessing the thinking curriculum: New tools for educational reform. In B. G. Gifford & M. C. O'Conner (Eds.), *Changing assessments: Alternative views of aptitude, achievement, and instruction* (pp. 37–75). Boston: Kluver Academic Publishers.

Rhodes, J. H. (2012). *An education in politics, The origin and evolution of No Child Left Behind.* Ithaca, NY: Cornell University Press.

Rice, B. (2014, June 8). Three states are now ditching the Common Core. *State Impact.* Retrieved from http://stateimpact.npr.org/ohio/2014/06/08/three-states-are-now-ditching-the-common-core/

Rich, J. M., & Devitis, J. L. (1992). *Competition in education.* Springfield, IL: Charles C. Thomas.

Riley, R. W. (1986, February) Can the school reform effort be sustained? *Educational Leadership,* 40–41.

Robelen, E. W. (2004, September 20). Kerry softens rhetoric on 'No Child Left Behind.' *Education Week.* Retrieved from http://www.edweek.org/ew/articles/2004/08/02/43kerryagenda_web.h23.html

Rogalsky, J. (2007, October 1). Edwin Feulner: The Heritage Foundation's president revolutionized the Washington think tank scene. *Washington Examiner*. Retrieved from http://www.washingtonexaminer.com/local/edwin_feulner_the_heritage_foundations_president_revolutionized_the_washington_think_tank_scene2007-10-01T07_00_00.html

Rose, L. C., & Gallup, A. M. (2007, September 27). The 39th annual Phi Delta Kappa/Gallup poll of the public's attitudes toward the public schools. Phi Delta Kappa. Retrieved from http://www.stateinnovation.org/Research/Education/Adequacy-Based-School-Funding/pdkpoll39_2007.aspx

Rotherham, A. (2001, February 7). The new three R's of education. *Democratic Leadership Council Blueprint Magazine*. Retrieved from http://www.dlc.org/ndol_ci40ea.html?kaid=110&subid=900023&contentid=2990

Rothkopf, A. (2007, March 13). *Statement before the Senate on Health, Education, Labor, and Pensions and the House Committee on Education and Labor* [Statement]. Washington, DC: U.S. Chamber of Commerce. Retrieved from http://www.help.senate.gov/imo/media/doc/Rothkopf.pdf

Rothstein, R. (2004). Class and Schools: Using Social, Economic, and Educational Reform to Close the Black-White Achievement Gap. Washington, DC: Economic Policy Institute and Teachers College.

Rothstein, R., Jacobsen, R., & Wilder, T. (2008). *Grading education: Getting accountability right*. Washington, DC: Economic Policy Institute.

Rust, E. B. (2013, March 30). *Want to save the American dream? Start here*. Yahoo. Retrieved from http://finance.yahoo.com/news/want-save-american-dream-start-205059249.html

Saxe, D. W. (1998). *State history standards, An appraisal of history standards in 37 states and the District of Columbia*. New York: Thomas Fordham Institute. Retrieved from http://www.edexcellence.net/detail/news.cfm?news_id=29&id=

Schlafly, P. (1964). *A choice not an echo*. Alton, IL: Pere Marquette Publishers.

Schmidt, W. H., Houang, R., & Shakrani. (2009). *International lessons about national standards*. Washington, DC: Thomas B. Fordham Institute.

Schmitt, M. (2005, April 27). The legend of the Powell memo. *The American Prospect*. Retrieved from http://www.prospect.org/cs/articles?articleId=9606

Schneider, J., & Houston, P. D. (1993). *Exploding the myths: Another round in the education debate*. Arlington, VA: American Association of School Administrators.

Schrag, P. (2000, February 16). Education and the election. *The Nation*. Retrieved from http://www.thenation.com/doc/20000306/schrag

Scott, C. (2008). *A call to restructure restructuring: Lessons from No Child Left Behind in five states*. Washington, DC: Center on Education Policy.

Scott, R. (2013, September). *A republic of republics, How Common Core undermines state and local autonomy over K-12 education*. Boston: Pioneer Institute.

Shulman, L., & Sykes, G. (1986). *A national board for teaching? In search of a bold standard*. New York: Carnegie Forum on Education and the Economy.

Simon, S. (2013, March 3). K-12 student database jazzes tech startups, spooks parents. *Reuters*. Retrieved from http://www.reuters.com/article/2013/03/03/us-education-database-idUSBRE92204W20130303

Simon, S. (2013, November 18). 'White moms' remark fuels Common Core clash. *Politico*. Retrieved from http://www.politico.com/story/2013/11/arne-duncan-common-core-comment-99987.html

Simon, S., & Shah, N. (2013, September 18). The Common Core money war. *Politico*. http://www.politico.com/story/2013/09/education-common-core-standards-schools-96964.html

Simon, W. E. (1978). *A time for truth*. New York: Reader's Digest Press.

Singh, N. (2006). The afterlife of fascism. *South Atlantic Quarterly, 105*(1), 71–92.

Slaughter, S. (1985, April). The pedagogy of profit. *Higher Education, (14)*2, 217–222.

Smith, J. A. (1991). *The idea brokers, Think tanks and the rise of the new policy elite*. New York: Free Press.

Smith, M. L., & Rottenberg, C. (1991). Unintended consequences of external testing in elementary schools. *Educational Measurement, Issues and Practices, 10*(4), 7–11.

Smith, M. L., Miller-Kahn, L., Heinecke, W., & Jarvis, P. F. (2004). *Political spectacle and the fate of American schools*. New York: RoutledgeFalmer.

Smith Richardson Foundation. *History*. Retrieved from http://www.srf.org/mission/history.php

Sole, E. (2014, March 25). Read parent's Facebook response to 'ridiculous' Common Core math homework. *Yahoo Shine*. Retrieved from https://shine.yahoo.com/healthy-living/common-core-parent-facebook-post-indiana-school-181841158.html

Sommeiller, E., & Rice, M. (2014, February 19). *The increasingly unequal states of America, Income inequality by state, 1917 to 2011*. Washington, DC: Economic Policy Institute. Retrieved from http://www.epi.org/publication/unequal-states/

Sorin, H. (2010, July 22). Today in Texas history: GW Bush delivers first presidential campaign speech. *Texas on the Potomac*. Retrieved from http://blog.chron.com/txpotomac/2010/07/today-in-texas-history-gw-bush-delivers-first-presidential-campaign-speech/

Spalding, E. (2000). Performance assessment and the new standards project: A story of serendipitous success. *Phi Delta Kappa International, 81*, 758–764.

Spellings, M. (2005, April 5). Our high schools need help. *Washington Post*. Retrieved from http://www.washingtonpost.com/wp-dyn/articles/A20064-2005Apr1.html

Spellings, M. (2008, January 10). *Secretary of Education Margaret Spellings delivers remarks at the National Press Club on the No Child Left Behind Act*. Washington, DC: National Press Club.

Spelling, M. (2009, June 13). *Remark by Margaret Spellings in White House domestic policy making symposium, Session 3: Selling domestic policy from the White House*. Charlottesville, VA: Oral History Program, Miller Center of Public Affairs, University of Virginia. Retrieved from http:www.millercenter.org/scripps/archive/conference/detail/5471

Spring, J. (1988). *Sorting machine revisited: National educational policy since 1945*. White Plains, NY: Longman Inc.

Spring, J. (1998). *Education and the rise of the global economy*. Mahwah, NJ: Lawrence Erlbaum Associates, Inc.

Standards Adoption. (2014, April 18). *Education Week*. Retrieved from http://www.edweek.org/media/2014/04/18/29srcc-adoptionmapc1.jpg

Standards: Setting the standards from state to state. (1995, April 12). *Education Week*. Retrieved from http://www.edweek.org/ew/articles/1995/04/12/29stcht.h14.html?r=201434128

Standards: Struggling for standards. (1995, April 12). *Education Week*. Retrieved from http://www.edweek.org/ew/articles/1995/04/12/29intro.h14.html?qs=Standards:+Standards+times+50

Starr, L. (1998, January 12). Setting standards in our schools: What can we expect? *Education World*. Retrieved from http://www.education-world.com/a_admin/admin/admin042.shtml

Stedman, J. B. (1991). *America 2000: The President's education strategy, CRS report for Congress*. Washington, DC: Library of Congress. (ERIC Document Reproduction Service No. 359635).

Stedman, J. B., & Riddle W. C. (1992). *National education goals and federal policy issues: Action by the 102nd Congress*. Washington, DC: Library of Congress. (ERIC Document Reproduction Service No. 355626).

Stedman, L. C. (1994, January-February). The Sandia report and U.S. achievement: An assessment. *Journal of Educational Research, (87)*3, 133–146.

Stern, S. M., Chesson, M., Klee, M. B., & Spoehr, L. (2003). *Effective state standards for U.S. History: A 2003 report card*. Washington, DC: Thomas B. Fordham Institute. Retrieved from http://www.edexcellence.net/detail/news.cfm?news_id=320&id=

Stieglitz, J. E. (2011, May). Of the 1%, by the 1%, for the 1%. *Vanity Fair*. Retrieved from http://www.vanityfair.com/society/features/2011/05/top-one-percent-201105

Stoskopf, A. (2000). Clio's lament. *Education Week*. Retrieved from http://www.edweek.org/ew/articles/2000/02/02/21stoskopf.h19.html?qs=Clio%27s+lament

Stotsky, S. (1997). *The state of state English standards, Hawaii*. Washington, DC: Thomas B. Fordham Foundation. Retrieved from http://edexcellence.net/detail/news.cfm?news_id=30&pubsubid=523#523

Stotsky, S. & Finn Jr., C.E. (2005). *The state of state English standards, Hawaii*. Washington, DC: Thomas B. Fordham Foundation. Retrieved from http://www.edexcellence.net/doc/En05Hawaii.pdf

Strauss, V. (2013, February 26). Why I oppose Common Core standards: Ravitch. *Washington Post*. Retrieved from http://www.washingtonpost.com/blogs/answer-sheet/wp/2013/02/26/why-i-oppose-common-core-standards-ravitch/

Strauss, V. (2013, August 26). Common Core tests widen achievement gap in New York. *Washington Post*. Retrieved from http://www.washingtonpost.com/blogs/answer-sheet/wp/2013/08/26/common-core-tests-widen-achievement-gap-in-new-york/

Strauss, V. (2014, January 27). Why support for Common Core is sinking. *Washington Post*. Retrieved from http://www.washingtonpost.com/blogs/answer-sheet/wp/2014/01/27/why-support-for-common-core-is-sinking/

Strauss, V. (2014, March 23). Sen. Grassley seeking to defund Common Core in Congress. *Washington Post*. Retrieved from http://www.washingtonpost.com/blogs/answer-sheet/wp/2014/03/23/sen-grassley-seeking-to-defund-common-core-in-congress/

Strauss, V. (2014, April 4). Student privacy activists win a big one. *Washington Post*. Retrieved from http://www.washingtonpost.com/blogs/answer-sheet/wp/2014/04/04/student-privacy-activists-win-a-big-one/

Strauss, V. (2014, April 21). $100 million Gates-funded student data project ends in failure. *Washington Post*. Retrieved from http://www.washingtonpost.com/blogs/answer-sheet/wp/2014/04/21/100-million-gates-funded-student-data-project-ends-in-failure/

Strauss, W. (2008). *Is the U.S. losing its manufacturing base?* [Presentation]. Chicago, IL: Economic Development Council.

Supreme Court Historical Society. *Lewis F. Powell, Jr., 1972–1987*. Retrieved from http://www.supremecourthistory.org/history/supremecourthistory_history_assoc_084powell.htm

Tainter, J. A. *The collapse of complex societies*. Cambridge: Cambridge University Press, 1988.

Text of policy statement issued at national summit. (1996). *Education Week*. Retrieved from http://web.ebscohost.com.eres.library.Mānoa.Hawaii.edu/ehost/detail?vid=4&hid=107&sid=8fee3418-a928-46ba-a0a5-2ecd0f2e4068%40sessionmgr104&bdata=JnNpdGU9Whvc3QtbGl2ZQ%3d%3d#db=aph&AN=9604162916

Thompson, E. P. (1999). *The making of the English working class*. Gloucester, MA: Peter Smith Publisher, Inc.

Thompson, S. (1999, October 6). Confessions of a "standardisto," A "standardisto" confronts his critics. *Education Week*. Retrieved from http://www.edweek.org/ew/articles/1999/10/06/06thomps.h19.html?qs=Confessions%20 of%20a%20%27standardisto%27

Thurow, L. (1992). *Head to head: The coming economic battle among Japan, Europe, and America*. New York: Morrow.

Tirozzi, G. N. (1991). Must we reinvent the schools? In William T. Grant Foundation Commission on Work, Family, and Citizenship and the Institute for Educational Leadership (Ed.). *Voices from the field: Thirty expert opinions on "America 2000," the Bush administration strategy to "reinvent" America's schools* (pp. 9–10). Washington, DC: Author.

Trilling, L. (1950). *The liberal imagination: Essays on literature and society*. New York: New York Review of Books.

Trotter, A. (1997). Paradise foundering, A centralized system and low levels of funding hamper Hawaii's reform efforts. In R. A. Wolk, *Quality Counts, A report card on the condition of public education in the fifty states*. Washington, DC: Education Week. Retrieved from http://www.edweek.org/media/ew/qc/archives/QC97full.pdf

Tucker, M. S., & Codding, J. (1998). *Standards for our schools: How to set them, measure them, and reach them*. San Francisco: Jossey-Bass.

Ujifusa, A. (2014, March 18). State chiefs spar with AFT and NEA presidents over Common Core. *Education Week*. Retrieved from http://blogs.edweek.org/edweek/state_edwatch/2014/03/state_chiefs_spar_with_aft_and_nea_presidents_over_common_core.html

United States Chamber of Commerce. (1982). *American education, An economic issue*. Washington, DC: Author.

United States Chamber of Commerce and the Center for American Progress. (2007). *A joint platform for education reform*. Washington, DC: Author.

United States Congress. (1991a). *National Council on Education Standards and Testing Act. Report by Mr. Ford of Michigan, Committee on Education and Labor, House of Representatives, 102nd Congress, 1st session, June 10, 1991. Report to accompany H.R. 2435, the National Council on Education Standards and Testing Act*. Washington, DC: United States Government Printing Office. (ERIC Document Reproduction Service No. ED335403).

United States Congress. (1991b, July 18). *Testimony of Robert M. Huelskamp on the Sandia report*. Subcommittee on Elementary, Secondary, and Vocational Education of the Committee on Education and Labor of the United States House of Representatives. Washington, DC: Author.

United States Congress. (1994a). *Goals 2000: Educate America act, H.R. 1804 conference report*. Washington, DC: United States Government Printing Office.

United States Congress. (1994b). *Goals 2000: Educate America act. Public law 103–227*. Washington, DC: United States Government Printing Office. Retrieved from http://www.ed.gov/legislation/GOALS2000/TheAct/sec203.html

United States Congress. (1996). *The Omnibus Consolidated Rescissions and Appropriations Act of 1996*. Washington, DC: United States Government Printing Office. Retrieved from http://frwebgate.access.gpo.gov/cgi-bin/getdoc.cgi?dbname=104_cong_public_laws&docid=f:publ134.104.pdf

United States Congress, Senate, Committee on Labor and Human Resources. (1993). *Hearing on examining the need to improve national education standards and job training opportunities*. Washington, DC: Author. (ERIC Document Reproduction Service No. ED358333).

United States Department of Education. *Elementary & secondary education, ESEA flexibility*. Washington, DC: Author. Retrieved from http://www2.ed.gov/policy/elsec/guid/esea-flexibility/index.html.

United States Department of Education. (1986). *What works: Research about teaching and learning*. Washington, DC: Author.

United States Department of Education. (1987). *What works: Schools that work, educating disadvantaged children*. Washington, DC: Author.

United States Department of Education. (1991). *America 2000, An education strategy, revised*. Washington, DC: Author. (ERIC Document Reproduction No. ED332380).

United States Department of Education. (2005). *Archived information, Goals 2000 legislation and related archived information, Goals 2000 legislation and related items*. Washington, DC: Author. Retrieved from http://www.ed.gov/G2K/index.html

United States Department of Education. (2009, July 24). *President Obama, U.S. Secretary of Education Duncan announce national competition to advance school reform, Obama Administration starts $4.35 billion "Race to the Top" Competition, Pledges a total of $10 billion for reforms* [Press Release]. Washington, DC: Author. Retrieved from http://www2.ed.gov/news/pressreleases/2009/07/07242009.html

United States Department of Education. (2009, November). *Race to the Top program, Executive summary*. Washington, DC: Author.

United States Department of Education. (2010a, February 15). *States' applications, Scores and comments for phase 1.* Washington, DC: Author. Retrieved from http://www2.ed.gov/programs/racetothetop/phase1-applications/index.html

United States Department of Education. (2010b, February 15). *States' applications for phase 2.* Washington, DC: Author. Retrieved from http://www2.ed.gov/programs/racetothetop/phase2-applications/index.html

United States Department of Education. (2010, March 18). *Awards, Scopes of work decision letters.* Washington, DC: Author. Retrieved from http://www2.ed.gov/programs/racetothetop/awards.html

United States Department of Education. (2010, March 29). *Delaware and Tennessee win first Race to the Top grants* [Press Release]. Washington, DC: Author. Retrieved from http://www.ed.gov/news/press-releases/delaware-and-tennessee-win-first-race-top-grants

United States Department of Education. (2010, June 2). *Statement on National Governors Association and state education chiefs Common Core standards* [Press Release]. Washington, DC: Author. Retrieved from http://www.ed.gov/news/press-releases/statement-national-governors-association-and-state-education-chiefs-common-core-

United States Department of Education. (2010, August 24). *Nine states and the District of Columbia win second round race to the top grants* [Press Release]. Washington, DC: Author. Retrieved from http://www.ed.gov/news/press-releases/nine-states-and-district-columbia-win-second-round-race-top-grants

United States Department of Education. (2010, September 2). *U.S. Secretary of Education Duncan announces winners of competition to improve student assessments.* Washington, DC: Author. Retrieved from https://www.ed.gov/news/press-releases/us-secretary-education-duncan-announces-winners-competition-improve-student-asse

United States Department of Education. (2011, September 28). *ESEA flexibility, September 28, 2011 (MSWord)*, [MSWord Doc Download]. Washington, DC: Author. Retrieved from www.ed.gov/sites/default/files/esea-flexibility.doc

United States Department of Education. (2011, December 23). *Department of Education awards $200 million to seven states to advance K-12 reform* [Press Release]. Washington, DC: Author. Retrieved from http://www.ed.gov/news/press-releases/department-education-awards-200-million-seven-states-advance-k-12-reform

United States Department of Education. (2012, January 10). *Race to the Top, Hawaii report, School year 2010–11.* Washington, DC: Author.

United States Department of Education. (2012, June 7). *ESEA flexibility.* Washington, DC: Author.

United States Department of Education. (2013b, March 18). *Awards, Scopes of work decision letters* [Press Release]. Washington, DC: Author. Retrieved from http://www2.ed.gov/programs/racetothetop/awards.html

United States Department of Education, National Center for Education Statistics. (2013). *The condition of education 2013 (NCES 2013–037), Public school expenditures.* Washington, DC: Author. Retrieved from https://nces.ed.gov/programs/coe/indicator_cmb.asp

United States Department of Health and Human Services. (2013, January 24). *Annual update of the HHS poverty guidelines*. Washington, DC: Federal Register. Retrieved from https://www.federalregister.gov/articles/2013/01/24/2013-01422/annual-update-of-the-hhs-poverty-guidelines

United States Department of Labor. (1989). *Investing in people: A strategy to address America's workforce crisis*. Washington, DC: Author.

United States Department of Labor, Bureau of Labor Statistics. (2013, December 19). *Employment by major industry sector*. Washington, DC: Author. Retrieved from http://www.bls.gov/emp/ep_table_201.htm.

United States Department of Labor, Bureau of Labor Statistics. (2014, January 8). *Occupational outlook handbook, occupation finder*. Washington, DC: Author. Retrieved from http://www.bls.gov/ooh/occupation-finder.htm?pay=&education=Bachelor%26rsquo%3Bs+degree&training=&newjobs=&growth=&submit=GO

United States Department of Labor, Secretary's Commission on Achieving Necessary Skills (SCANS). (1991). *What work requires of schools*. Washington, DC: Department of Labor.

University of Hawaii. (2011, December 19). *Hawaii selected for Common Core Standards grant*. Honolulu, HI: Author. Retrieved from http://www.hawaii.edu/news/2011/12/19/common-core-grant/

Upadhyaya, P. (2013, November 25). *How Apple, Google, Cisco are competing for the $5 billion K-12 ed-tech market*. Retrieved from http://www.bizjournals.com/sanjose/news/2013/11/25/heres-how-silicon-valley-will-make.html?s=print

Viadero, D. (2008, December 3). Researchers pitch policy ideas as power shifts in capital. *Education Week*, 11.

Vierick, P. (1940, April). But—I'm a conservative. *Atlantic Magazine*. Retrieved from http://www.theatlantic.com/magazine/archive/1969/12/but-i-apos-m-a-conservative/4434/

Vinovskis, M. (1999a). *The road to Charlottesville: The 1989 education summit*. Washington, DC: National Education Goals Panel.

Vinovskis, M. (1999b). *History and educational policymaking*. New Haven: Yale University Press.

Vinovskis, M. A. (2009). *From a nation at risk to no child left behind, national educational goals and the creation of federal education policy*. New York: Teachers College Press.

Von Mises, L. (1944). *Planned chaos*. Chicago: University of Chicago Press.

Walker, R. (1990, February 28). Governors set to adopt national educational goals. *Education Week*. Retrieved from http://www.edweek.org/ew/articles/1990/02/28/09280037.h09.html?tkn=SYLFC3jRkRUS8m1IzkB%2BoJ%2FEu%2Brg7pBGZiJc&print=1

Wallerstein, I. M. (1998). *Utopistics: Or historical choices of the twenty-first century*. New York: New Press.

Watt, M. G. (2000). *Applications of information technology for standards-based reform in the United States of America: Their implications for the discovering democracy program in Australia*. Conference of the New Zealand Association for Research in Education. Hamilton, New Zealand. (ERIC Document Reproduction No. ED449072).

Weaver, R. (1948). *Ideas have consequences*. Chicago: University of Chicago Press.

Weber, M. (1958). Politics as a vocation. In M. Weber, *From Max Weber: Essays in sociology* (pp. 77–128). Oxford: Oxford University Press.

Wessel, D. (2011, April 19). Big U.S. firms shift hiring abroad, Work forces shrink at home, Sharpening debate on economic impact of globalization. *Wall Street Journal*. Retrieved from http://online.wsj.com/article/SB10001424052748704821704576270783611823972.htm

Westervelt, E. (2014, January 28). *Political rivals find common ground over Common Core*. Washington, DC: National Public Radio. Retrieved from http://www.npr.org/2014/01/28/267488648/backlash-grows-against-common-core-education-standards

White House Initiative on Educational Excellence for Hispanic Americans. (1999). *A report to the nation: Policies and issues on testing Hispanic students in the United States*. Washington, DC: Author.

Will, G. (2014, January 15). Doubts over Common Core. *Washington Post*. Retrieved from http://www.washingtonpost.com/opinions/george-will-doubts-over-common-core-wont-be-easily-dismissed/2014/01/15/68cecb88-7df3-11e3-93c1-0e888170b723_story.html

Williams, J. P. (2014, February 27). Who Is Fighting Against Common Core? The push against Common Core is coming from both sides of the political aisle. U.S. *New and World Reports*. Retrieved from http://www.usnews.com/news/special-reports/a-guide-to-common-core/articles/2014/02/27/who-is-fighting-against-common-core

Wilson, L. (2005). Controlling the power over knowledge: Selling the crisis for self-serving gains. In D. R. Boyles (Ed.), *Schools or markets? Commercialism, privatization, and school-business partnerships?* (pp. 195–216). Mahwah, NJ: Lawrence Erlbaum Associates, Publishers.

Winfield, U., & Woodward, M. D. (1992, January 29). Where are equity and diversity in America 2000? *Education Week*. Retrieved from http://www.edweek.org/ew/articles/1992/01/29/19woodar.h11.html?r=35715159

Wodiska, J. (2007, September 10). *Testimony before the House Education and Labor Committee on reauthorization of the No Child Left Behind act*. Retrieved from http://www.nga.org/cms/home/federal-relations/nga-testimony/page_2007/col2-content/main-content-list/september-10-2007-testimony--nc.html

THIS SERIES EXPLORES THE HISTORY OF SCHOOLS AND SCHOOLING in the United States and other countries. Books in this series examine the historical development of schools and educational processes, with special emphasis on issues of educational policy, curriculum and pedagogy, as well as issues relating to race, class, gender, and ethnicity. Special emphasis will be placed on the lessons to be learned from the past for contemporary educational reform and policy. Although the series will publish books related to education in the broadest societal and cultural context, it especially seeks books on the history of specific schools and on the lives of educational leaders and school founders.

For additional information about this series or for the submission of manuscripts, please contact the general editors:

>   Alan R. Sadovnik
>   Rutgers University-Newark
>   Education Dept.
>   155 Conklin Hall
>   175 University Avenue
>   Newark, NJ 07102
>
>   Susan F. Semel
>   The City College of New York, CUNY
>   138th Street and Convent Avenue
>   NAC 5/208
>   New York, NY 10031

To order other books in this series, please contact our Customer Service Department:

>   800-770-LANG (within the U.S.)
>   212-647-7706 (outside the U.S.)
>   212-647-7707 FAX

Or browse online by series at:

>   www.peterlang.com

www.ingramcontent.com/pod-product-compliance
Ingram Content Group UK Ltd.
Pitfield, Milton Keynes, MK11 3LW, UK
UKHW022239230426
12048UKWH00018BA/1345